284

A THIRST FOR GLORY

Tom Pocock has been described as the foremost current authority on Lord Nelson, and has written six books about Nelson and his time. His *Horatio Nelson* was runner-up for the Whitbread Biography Award of 1987, and has subsequently been published twice in paperback. His other ten books include biographies of the writers Alan Moorehead and Sir Rider Haggard, and the artist Walter Greaves, studies of Venice and Norfolk and two volumes of his memoirs as a newspaper war correspondent. *Norfolk*, *Horatio Nelson* and *Alan Moorehead* are all available in Pimlico. Tom Pocock is married with two daughters and lives in London.

A THIRST FOR GLORY

The Life of Admiral
Sir Sidney Smith

───────

TOM POCOCK

PIMLICO

Published by Pimlico 1998

2 4 6 8 10 9 7 5 3 1

First published by
Aurum Press in 1996

Pimlico
Random House, 20 Vauxhall Bridge Road,
London SW1V 2SA

Random House Australia (Pty) Limited
20 Alfred Street, Milsons Point, Sydney,
New South Wales 2061, Australia

Random House New Zealand Limited
18 Poland Road, Glenfield,
Auckland 10, New Zealand

Random House South Africa (Pty) Limited
Endulini, 5A Jubilee Road, Parktown 2193, South Africa

Random House UK Limited Reg. No. 954009

A CIP catalogue record for this book
is available from the British Library

ISBN 0-7126-7341-5

Papers used by Random House UK Limited are natural,
recyclable products made from wood grown in sustainable forests.
The manufacturing processes conform to the environmental
regulations of the country of origin.

Printed and bound in Great Britain by
Mackays of Chatham PLC, Chatham, Kent

Contents

Illustrations

a drawing by F.B. Spilsbury, surgeon in the *Tigre*. (National Maritime Museum)

5A.   In an Ottoman tent: Captain Sir Sidney Smith confers with Djezzar Pasha at Acre, while similarly moustached British naval officers smoke. Another engraving by Surgeon Spilsbury. (Parker Gallery)

5B.   On the ramparts: Captain Sir Sidney Smith striking an heroic attitude during the siege. (Grosvenor Gallery)

6A.   The national hero: Lord Nelson at the height of his fame, painted by James Northcote. (Private collection)

6B.   The aspiring hero: Sir Sidney Smith sketched by Thomas Stothard. (British Museum)

6C.   Naval officer and secret agent: Captain John Wright in an illustration from the *Naval Chronicle*.

6D.   Smuggler, spy and inventor: Captain Tom Johnson drawn by Harry Hunter. (Author's collection)

7A.   *Death of the CORSICAN FOX*: a caricature from 1803 showing a Napoleonic fox being thrown to hounds whose collars bear the names of British admirals, including Nelson, St Vincent and Smith. (British Museum)

7B.   *The Passage of the Dardanelles*: a glorified version of Admiral Duckworth's fleet entering the narrows on 19th February 1807, painted by Thomas Whitcombe. (National Maritime Museum)

8A.   *THE BOMBARDMENT OF ALGIERS*: the final reckoning in 1816, inspired by Sir Sidney Smith and carried out by Lord Exmouth; painted by P.H. Rogers. (National Maritime Museum)

8B.   Remembered in London: the statue of Sir Sidney Smith by Thomas Kirk outside the National Maritime Museum, Greenwich.

8C.   Remembered in Paris: the tomb of Admiral Sir Sidney and Lady Smith in the cemetery of Père Lachaise.

'The defence of Acre had left him [Sir Sidney Smith]
with ... an unbridled thirst for glory.'

– Piers Mackesy

For Richard Hough

Preface to the Pimlico Edition

WHEN LORD CARRINGTON read this book, he remarked of Sir Sidney Smith, 'I don't think I would have liked him.' His sentiment was an exact echo of the Duke of Wellington and those other gentlemen of action and intellect, such as Lord St Vincent and Sir John Moore, who found their contemporary too flash for their liking.

That off-hand remark brought the subject of my book into sudden, sharp focus. Smith might be beyond the range of living memory but he could still produce a reaction from somebody he would certainly have known had the span of their lives coincided.

During and since his own lifetime, Sidney Smith, the naval officer, has often been confused with Sydney Smith the witty, literary clergyman. So it was with delight that I read a letter to the *Sunday Times* from Mr Norman Taylor of the Sydney Smith Association, recalling that, in 1825, the two Smiths had met in Paris. 'Parisian society was confused by their simultaneous presence,' he wrote, 'and the clergyman suggested to the admiral that they might happily increase the confusion by accepting invitations in common: "You shall go as the Clergyman when it suits your convenience, and I will go as the hero. The Physiognomists and Craniologists will discover in you a love of Tithes – and of conformity to the Thirty-Nine Articles – and in me a contempt of death and a Love of Glory".'

Then it was with the air of a slightly malicious gossip that an historian friend asked whether I knew that Smith had had an affair with an American woman, Elizabeth Patterson, who had been married to Napoleon's brother, Jérôme Bonaparte. Another led me to a scarce print showing Smith and his officers seated on cushions in Djezzar Pasha's tent at Acre, all the British wearing extraordinary, curled moustaches in the fashion that Smith himself had set. This can now be seen on page 5 of the illustrations.

Other echoes bounced across two centuries. Eric Newby described how the British constructed a fortress near Tripoli on the Syrian coast in 1941 to halt a possible German offensive through the Levant. It was sited to the north of Acre and designed for exactly the same purpose.

Speculating on the mysterious death of Captain John Wright, Alan Schom, the American historian, was certain that it was murder and had been ordered by Napoleon himself. In his own book *Trafalgar* he had stated that Admiral Villeneuve, the defeated French commander of the combined fleets, had not committed suicide on his return to France, as has always been assumed, and he produced evidence strongly suggesting murder. Napoleon had a record of hinting that some dangerous or embarrassing person would be better out of the way and, so Schom believes, his chief of police, Fouché, understood his meaning and acted upon it.

One of the most dramatic characters in Smith's story, Captain Louis Boisgirard, the royalist agent whose cover was dancing at the Paris Opéra, stepped from the shadows when Ivor Guest told me of his research into the history of French ballet. He discovered that Boisgirard, too, was finally arrested, but after eighteen months was released and was able to resume dancing before finally making his way to England, where he was given a secret pension for his services.

A new edition offers an opportunity to right wrongs. In this one, a mistake in the first, originating in a computer, is corrected and rightly names Nelson – and not Smith – as the suitor of Elizabeth Andrews in St Omer, she being fully named here for the first time.

Reflection on the telling of a story may lead to intriguing speculations. Since writing this one I have come across letters to Captain Sir Sidney Smith from the captain of the sloop *Peterel*, cruising off Alexandria in 1800. The young captain was involved in the negotiations with Marshal Kléber over the possible evacuation of the French from Egypt under the Convention of El Arish. His name was Captain Francis William Austen and he was also writing letters home to his sister Jane. Had Jane Austen

met Sir Sidney Smith, might he have appeared, lightly dis-
guised, in one of her novels? She surely must have heard Frank
Austen talk about Sir Sidney but perhaps he was too strong
meat for her, as for so many?

Tom Pocock
Chelsea, 1998

Introduction

OUTSIDE THE ENTRANCE to the National Maritime Museum at Greenwich stands a marble statue of a British naval officer, sword in hand. He seems to be fighting on land, for a cannon-ball has smashed into the stonework at his feet. His name, carved on the plinth, is Sir Sidney Smith, and most of those crowding into the museum for the exhibition marking the ten years of Nelson bicentennaries, have never heard of him.

Yet Admiral Sir Sidney Smith shadowed the great Nelson and together they shared one of the great naval and military achievements of the wars with Revolutionary and Napoleonic France; together they did change the course of history. Yet Nelson is the British national hero and Smith is almost forgotten. This is not only unjust to him but unfair to his present compatriots because his is a strange and entertaining story. Repeatedly, the parallels, personal and professional, between him and Nelson become apparent, and yet only one of them gathered the laurels.

This neglect has been reflected in the small number of his biographies, compared with Nelson's scores. The first was written by Edward Howard, a former naval officer, who served with Captain Marryat and adopted his style for his own nautical novel *Rattlin the Reefer*. His biography of Smith was published a year before his subject's death in 1840, and that he was helped in his researches by the elderly Smith himself is admitted and apparent in the fulsomeness of the prose. The second, written by John Barrow, son of Sir John Barrow, the former Secretary to the Admiralty, who had known Sir Sidney well, was published eight years later; this made good use of Smith's surviving friends, particularly his son-in-law, Captain

Septimus Arabin. Since then there have been two further biographies: Lord Russell of Liverpool's *Knight of the Sword*, published in 1964, and, in 1975, Peter Shankland's *Beware of Heroes*.

There is only a small archive of Smith's papers at the National Maritime Museum; otherwise he must be sought in the collected manuscripts of his contemporaries – officers of the Royal Navy and the Army and politicians – at Greenwich and in the British Library and Public Record Office. I was fortunate to be loaned two unpublished manuscripts: the diary kept by Sir Sidney's brother, Spencer Smith, when young, and the memoirs of Lieutenant Robert James, R.N., and I am grateful for this to John Munday and Alex Wills respectively. In Norfolk, Diana Mansell helped with the background to their family's connections at Burnham Market; in Berkshire, Mrs Dorothy Collier of Midgham, and Victor Pocock helped explain the family's stay there; and, in Paris, Commander Mark Ruddle, R.N., of the British Embassy, went beyond the call of duty to help me find Sir Sidney's tomb in the cemetery of Père Lachaise; Michael Tapper, Clive Richards, Michael Nash, Louis Roeder and Michael Charlton produced fascinating naval material.

The Librarian and staff of the London Library, the National Maritime Museum and the National Army Museum have been as helpful as usual, and I am grateful to the staff of the Public Record Office and the British Library. Richard Ollard kindly read and commented upon the typescript. I am grateful to Andrew Lownie for literary advice and to my wife, Penny, for compiling the index.

Tom Pocock
Chelsea, 1996.

Prologue

GUNFIRE NO LONGER echoed from the limestone ribs of the Alps and the plains below lay quiet under the hot sun. But, on 13th September 1796, the straight roads across the hot plains of Venezia Giulia were busy with horses and riders. Couriers in uniforms of red, white, blue and green, rode with the flash and jingle of steel and the swing of fur-trimmed pelisse, east and west from the Villa Manin. The Palladian palace that had been the summer residence of the Doges of Venice since the seventeenth century, and which was named after the last of them, faced sweeps of lawn and gravel drive, embraced by curving, arcaded wings, giving on to the roads across the green levels beyond. Behind that haughty facade, the vast halls housed the headquarters of *l'Armée d'Italie*, which had fought its way from France, across the northern plains of Italy and the mountains that barred the way to Vienna. A courier riding eastward would be heading for the nearby town of Udine, where the emissaries of their enemies, the Austrians, waited. Westward, a courier would be making for Milan or, perhaps, France.

On this day, the courier riding west was carrying a letter to Paris from the army-commander, General Napoleon Bonaparte. Aged only twenty-six, he was remarkable not only for his youth but his presence and appearance, which were in contrast to the architectural splendour of his headquarters, which gave the gorgeously uniformed officers such high theatricality. He was a stocky young man of sallow complexion, dressed in a plain uniform, his lank hair hanging to his shoulders. Yet he carried himself with total confidence, an air of purpose and of ruthlessness relieved, only occasionally, by an attractive curl of the lip in what was sometimes described as a seductive smile.

A man of contrasts, one who knew him at this time described, 'a charming personality, a handsome eye, a pale complexion, a hint of fatigue',[1] while another thought him, 'courteous, cold and inscrutable'.[2] Yet another was also struck by his 'strikingly fascinating smile', but added, 'His expression becomes terrible when angry; his manner is that of a man who nourishes vast projects. His features seem to betray a violent and murderous ambition; something in them reveals sombre and turbulent passions.'[3]

This particular letter was to Charles de Talleyrand, the unfrocked bishop – clever, dissolute and a natural survivor of crises – who had recently been appointed foreign minister of the French Republic. But it was not about the eighteen-month campaign in Italy, which had defeated the Piedmontese, captured the northern Papal States, taken the French into Austria and subjugated the ancient republic of Venice, and which had now reached a climax. Instead, at a time when he himself was unwell, and hankering after his wife, the beguiling Josephine, to whom he had been married for a year, his imagination was bounding into reaches of ambition bordering on the fantastic.

Perhaps the inspiration was Venice itself – the aquatic city that Goethe, who had been there a few months earlier, had called 'this beaver republic'[4] – he had yet to see its islands beyond the great, green plain of the Veneto. The Serene Republic, as it described itself, had been founded upon trade with the East and it was now the East that called to Napoleon Bonaparte. One of his senior officers, Desaix, scribbled notes of his musings: 'Ideas about Egypt, its resources ... Embark at Venice with 10,000 men ... for Egypt. Seize it. Advantages ...'[5]

The letter Bonaparte wrote to Secretary Talleyrand on 13th September was specific:

Why should we not occupy the island of Malta? ... We shall be masters of the whole Mediterranean ... We must occupy Egypt. That country has never belonged to a European nation. The Venetians alone had a certain, but very precarious, preponderance there several centuries ago. We could leave here with 25,000 men, escorted by eight or ten ships of the line or Venetian frigates and take it.[6]

The idea was not new. More than a century before, King

Louis XIV had been urged to invade Egypt to damage Dutch trade rather than invade Holland itself: 'It is in Egypt, the road to India, that you must deliver your blow', he was urged, 'and ruin Dutch commerce.'[7] Louis XV had considered annexing Egypt after he had lost Canada to the British. Then, in the first weeks of 1797, the French consul in Cairo, Charles Magallon, sent a memorandum to the ruling Directory repeating the suggestion because, he maintained, both the Egyptians them- selves and the Turkish rulers of the Ottoman Empire, of which the country was ostensibly part, would welcome the overthrow of the Mamelukes, the strange warrior-caste of Caucasian descent who dominated the country. The idea was considered by Talleyrand's predecessor, Delacroix, but rejected on the grounds that France could not afford to alienate the Turks. When Talleyrand came to power he favoured bold moves and Bonaparte's letter matched his mood.

Long afterwards, Napoleon Bonaparte was to muse upon his hankering after the East. Such an adventure would have three aims: 'To establish on the Nile a French colony, which would prosper without slaves and serve France in place of the repub- lic of Santo Domingo [a rich West Indian island taken by the British] and all the sugar islands; to open a market for our manufactures in Africa, Arabia and Syria and supply our commerce with all the production of those vast countries.'[8]

It would also be a means of attacking Revolutionary France's most implacable enemy, Great Britain. At the end of the year, having made peace with Austria and with the agreement signed at Campo Formio, under which the Venetian republic was given to the Austrians, Bonaparte returned to Paris and was appointed to the command of the Army of England with orders to prepare for the invasion of the British Isles. It had been a bad year for the British with revolution coming to the boil in Ireland and major mutinies in the Royal Navy at Spithead and at the Nore.

The Army of England would be composed of the best troops from the campaigns in Italy and on the Rhine, and its divisional commanders would include such brilliant officers as Kléber, Junot, Joubert and Bernadotte, with Desaix as chief of staff. Taking them on a reconnaissance of the Channel coast, Bonaparte realized that invasion was an impossibility: the French Navy was too inexperienced in seagoing and too scattered around the coasts of France to be able to face the British, who, despite the mutinies, had demonstrated their abilities during 1797 by defeating the Spanish at the Battle of Cape St Vincent and the Dutch at Camperdown. 'I will not remain,' Bonaparte decided. 'There is nothing to be done here. My glory is almost forgotten: this Europe is too small to give me scope.'[9]

Again he looked to the East, the road to India, that great source of British wealth. His imagination was to conjure up fantasies of conquest and colonization in Egypt:

> What could be made of that beautiful country in fifty years of prosperity and good government? One's imagination delights in the enchanting vistas. A thousand irrigation sluices would tame and distribute the overflow of the Nile over every part of the territory ... Numerous immigrants from deepest Africa, from Arabia, from Syria, from Greece, from France, from Italy, from Poland, from Germany, would quadruple the population. Trade with India would again flow through its ancient route ... France, being mistress of Egypt, would also regain mastery over Hindustan.[10]

He concluded, 'The day is not far off when we shall appreciate the necessity, in order really to destroy England, to seize Egypt.'[11]

But while the British victors of the naval battles, Jervis and Duncan, could prevent him from invading England, there seemed nobody, or almost nobody, who could prevent him from invading Egypt. Bonaparte told the Directory:

> To go to Egypt, to establish myself there and found a French colony will require some months, but as soon as I have made England tremble for the safety of India, I shall return to Paris and give the enemy its death-blow. There is nothing to fear in the interval. Europe is calm. Austria cannot move, England is occupied with preparing her defence against invasion and Turkey will welcome the expulsion of the Mameluke.[12]

But his political masters in Paris protested that if their fleet could not command the English Channel long enough for an army to cross, how could they hope to escort another army down the length of the Mediterranean? Bonaparte had explained that there was not a single British warship east of Gibraltar. The Royal Navy might, of course, return but its senior admirals were so preoccupied with the security of the

British Isles and of the West Indian islands that only a commander of originality, imagination and dash would be any threat.

There were, in September 1797, only two British naval
officers – one a rear-admiral, the other, a captain – who fitted
that description, and who were known to him, for he had
suffered at the hands of both. The two men were highly original but strangely alike: imaginative, brave, ambitious, volatile
and vain but with vision and a flair for leadership. They were
Rear-Admiral Sir Horatio Nelson and Captain Sir Sidney
Smith. Fortunately for the prospects of his ambition, both were
now out of action and unlikely to return to sea.

Admiral Nelson had, as a captain and a commodore, done
much damage to the French cause. Now aged thirty-eight – a
slightly-built man with a deeply lined face and a firm but
sensual mouth – he had, since returning to sea in 1793 after five
years of enforced unemployment on half-pay, made his presence felt. He had been instrumental in bringing Neapolitan
reinforcements to the defence of royalist Toulon – although that
had not saved the city from the republicans – and had taken the
magnificent warship, *Ça Ira*, with his smaller *Agamemnon*. He
had played a decisive part in the capture of the fortress-cities of
Bastia and Calvi in Bonaparte's native Corsica, and he had
brought about the defeat of the Spanish fleet by Admiral Jervis
by hauling out of the British line without orders and hurling
himself between the Spanish divisions, so preventing them
from joining forces. But, as all Europe had now heard, he had
met with disaster at Tenerife. Leading in person the assault
landing at the port of Santa Cruz, he had been wounded and
lost his right arm; the attack had been bloodily repulsed.

Indeed, Nelson himself believed his career was finished. 'A
left-handed admiral will never again be considered useful,' he
wrote to Admiral Jervis, 'therefore the sooner I get to a very
humble cottage the better... '[13] Convalescent in London, he was
passing his time giving sittings to the painter Lemuel Abbott
for a sad, thoughtful portrait, and wearing a wry, resigned
smile, for the sculptor Lawrence Gahagan's marble bust.

The other potential threat, Captain Smith, was aged thirty-
two, dashing, quick-witted with dark, vivid looks and a
glittering eye. But, in September 1797, he was imprisoned in
Paris and there seemed every chance that he would be sent to
the guillotine as a spy and an arsonist, despite being a British

naval officer. Certainly, Bonaparte did not expect to meet him again in war, any more than he could have expected to meet Admiral Nelson. But with Captain Smith, that extraordinary officer with the most ordinary name – as with Admiral Nelson – the unexpected was always to be expected.

CHAPTER ONE

'If that zeal carries me too far'

WILLIAM SIDNEY SMITH was born on 21st June 1764, into a family on the fringes of fashionable society and political power. The Smiths, then staying in Park Lane, a smart residential address on the western edge of London, overlooking Hyde Park, liked to stress their connections with families with the more genteel name of Smythe and, more importantly, with the political aristocracy, notably the Pitts.

The Smiths themselves were a military and naval family. A Captain Cornelius Smith was born in Kent at the end of the seventeenth century and one of his sons, Edward, became a naval officer and was mortally wounded in action in the West Indies. Another Edward became a soldier, rising to command an infantry regiment, becoming Governor of Fort Charles at Kingston, Jamaica, and fighting as one of Wolfe's subordinate commanders at Quebec. His eldest son, John, was to be commissioned in the Guards and appointed aide-de-camp to Lord George Germaine at the beginning of the Seven Years' War in 1756. He had resigned, however, apparently over a supposed injustice to his general; he was subsequently appointed a gentleman-usher to Queen Charlotte, the wife of King George III, to whom his youngest son, Spencer, was to become a page.

This Captain Smith earned himself a reputation as a rake through extravagance and fast-living. At Bath, he sighted an heiress, a woman past thirty but the daughter of Pinkney Wilkinson, an extremely rich merchant in the City of London, who was married to a Norfolk heiress, Mary Thurlow, and, in 1760, he eloped with her. Wilkinson, regarding his son-in-law as an adventurer, disinherited his daughter and severed all connection with her and the three sons who were to be born to her: Charles Douglas, William Sidney and John Spencer, both younger boys being known by their second names.

Wilkinson's younger daughter, Ann, had married into the aristocracy. Not only was her husband Thomas Pitt, the first Baron Camelford, but his great-grandfather, after whom he had been named, had been Governor of Madras, from whence he returned an immensely rich nabob. More importantly, his great-uncle had been the elder William Pitt, the Earl of Chatham, the great statesman of the mid-century. William Pitt, who was also to lead the nation, was his cousin.

The Pitts interceded on the Smiths' behalf and Wilkinson relented enough to pay for his grandsons' education at Tonbridge School. Then, Captain Smith and his wife quarrelled. Threatened with violence, she fled to Bath. Her father insisted her boys be moved to a boarding school there to be near her. However, Captain Smith did not give up hope and his father-in-law eventually paid him an annuity of £200, conditional upon his behaviour.

The boys were allowed to spend some time with their father at Midgham, a pretty village in low, wooded hills to the north of the Bath Road, a few miles to the east of Newbury, in Berkshire, where he had rented a cottage. Although Sidney might later refer airily to a mansion, Captain Smith rented Midgham Cottage in the grounds of Midgham Hall, the seat of the Poyntz family, kinsmen of the Earls Spencer. It was there that the character of Sidney first came into focus as, according to a description by one of his contemporaries, 'a most vivacious specimen of juvenility – quick, daring and mercurial and not far removed from a little Pickle'.[1]

There was a story, reminiscent of those to be told of his contemporary, Horatio Nelson, about an escapade that would foreshadow future feats of daring; suitably, it was aquatic. Apparently, one summer evening, the eleven-year-old Sidney was missing at the assembly for evening prayers, which were presided over daily by his father. A search was begun in the grounds of Midgham Hall, where the boys were allowed to play. Finally, the boy was found on the lake, sitting with a little girl in a washtub, in which he had taken her for an expedition, only to drop and lose the punt-pole. Since they were in deep water and there was no boat available for rescue, none of the adults could think of means to bring them ashore. Then little

Sidney piped up with instructions: they should take the string from his kite and tie it to his favourite dog, which he would then call. So a towing line was passed to the wash-tub, which was hauled ashore, the two children being snatched simultaneously by the adults to prevent the tub capsizing. Before his father could begin scolding him, the boy calmly suggested, 'Now, father, we will go to prayers.' 'We had better', came the exasperated reply.[2]

Captain Smith now began to make further demands on his aged father-in-law, sending not only begging letters but despatching his youngest son, Spencer, to call with such a message at his house in north-west Norfolk, Westgate Hall, in the village of Burnham Market, which his wife had inherited from the Thurlow family; it had been the old widower's principal home for the past decade. The child arrived too late at night to stay at the house, and was lodged instead at the Pitt Arms – named after his aunt's family – nearby and, although Wilkinson, now in his late eighties, received him with kindness, his temper soured when another begging letter arrived from his son-in-law by mail.

Looking to the future, there was one particular career suited to active small boys and that was the Royal Navy. Captain Smith considered this route for both Sidney and Spencer, who was ten years younger; their elder brother, Charles, had already been sent to Dublin at his grandfather's instigation to become a page to Lord Harcourt, the Viceroy of Ireland. Those destined to become naval officers could enter in one of two ways: either to be taken to sea by a captain and rated as his servant, or as a 'first class volunteer', eventually to be promoted to midshipman until the examination for the commissioned rank of lieutenant could be passed; or through the Naval Academy at Portsmouth. Of these alternatives the former was the most popular because it kept the boy under the eye of the friendly captain, who could be expected to remain his patron throughout the important early years of his career.

So, when he was nearing the age of thirteen, Sidney Smith was sent to sea. King George III was, at this time, showing interest in the Royal Navy as a suitably strict upbringing for his own unruly sons – one of them, Prince William Henry, was to be sent to sea in 1779 – and it is probable that royal influence, exercised through the Queen, to whom Captain Smith was a junior courtier, had brought this about. He was a tough, cheer-ful, talkative boy, described thus at the time: 'though of small size, he was eminently handsome with clustering and curling black hair, dark, clear complexion and with a high colour ... He evinced an utter contempt of danger and a decision of charac-ter that, under proper training, warranted the most sanguine hopes of future excellence.'[3]

He joined his first ship, the *Tortoise*, an armed storeship of 32 guns, which he found at Deptford on the Thames in June 1777. She was commanded by an American, Commander Jahleel Brenton,* who had had to leave his home in Rhode Island because he was a naval officer and a loyalist. His command may have been a storeship but he manned her with the best seamen he could find – including fifty impressed from a return-ing East Indiaman – and handled her like a frigate: on their first day at sea, he fired on three passing ships, forcing them to stop and be searched.

From Portsmouth they were ordered to escort a convoy to New York and, on their return early the following year, young Smith was appointed to the brig *Unicorn*, and it was in her that he first experienced battle at sea. Off the American coast, she, in company with a forty-four-gun ship, the *Experiment*, chased the American thirty-two-gun frigate *Raleigh*; the brig, coming up with her, first fought a three-hour duel, sometimes yard-arm to yard-arm. The *Unicorn* suffered thirteen killed and many wounded, amongst them Sidney Smith, gashed by a splinter.

This was the most dramatic experience of an active cruise which included keeping prisoner 200 surrendered seamen from captured American privateers and riding out a storm, during which Smith was sent below to get a new sail from the locker on the lower deck; while he was below, the ship was struck by a squall, which laid her on beam ends so that he and his men were lucky to be able to scramble to the upper deck to help heave the guns over the side to right her.

In September 1779, Smith was appointed to the *Sandwich*, the flagship of the Channel Fleet. His first experience of a fleet action came at the end of the year when the Commander-in-Chief, the sixty-one-year-old Admiral Sir George Rodney,

* Father of the future Admiral Sir Jahleel Brenton, a famous fighting captain and naval historian.

sailed from Plymouth escorting a large convoy to Gibraltar, Minorca and the West Indies. On 8th January they fell in with a Spanish convoy and captured all twenty-three merchant ships and an escorting ship of the line. A week later, a strong Spanish squadron was sighted off Cape St Vincent and Rodney ordered the master of the *Sandwich*, who was responsible for ship-handling and navigation, 'Lay me alongside the largest ship you can see, or the admiral's, if there be one.'[4] Not only did the British outnumber the Spanish by two to one, but their bottoms were sheathed in copper – to protect against the wood-boring teredo worm in tropical seas – and so were faster. An Atlantic gale was blowing and night was coming on, but Rodney clung to the enemy. The fighting lasted all night; one Spanish ship of the line caught fire and exploded and five others struck their colours. At daybreak, the victorious British found themselves dangerously close to cliffs but could not lie under storm sails with their heads to the wind for fear of being blown ashore, so they had to make sail and plunge through heavy seas towards the open sea.

Not only had young Smith's alertness in the long battle been noted by the admiral but there had been another incident which became the talk of the fleet and which was remembered by another midshipman, the King's son, Prince William Henry, who was in the *Prince George*. Many years later, he – now the Duke of Clarence and soon to come to the throne as King William IV – wrote to Smith that he could 'recollect various exploits you have performed in the Navy, beginning with your having driven back to his quarters on the lower deck of the *Sandwich* a seaman in the action of Lord Rodney off Cape St. Vincent ...'[5] Had the man panicked and been sent back to serve his gun by the zealous midshipman?

The following September, Smith, having passed the examination for commissioning as a lieutenant, although he had not yet reached the obligatory age of nineteen, was appointed to the *Alcide*. In her he took part in Admiral Graves's abortive attempt of September 1781, to relieve Lord Cornwallis's army besieged in Yorktown, only to be driven off by an equal number of French ships engaged in reinforcing the American besiegers. But most of his time at sea was spent escorting convoys, intercepting suspicious ships and weathering storms. After one blow, he began a letter to his father: 'After having the lower

deck ports barred-in these four days on account of the bad
weather, the water is smooth enough today to … sit down and
lay the keel of a letter to you.'

After describing their departure from New York and joining
a convoy bound for Charlestown, he told how, at 2.00 a.m.:

> a *terrible* gale of wind came on, faster than we could get our sails
> furled; it carried away our fore and main topmasts, part of the
> fore-top and fore-yard, killed two men and wounded several
> others; the next morning we could see nothing of the fleet, the
> wreck beating alongside; the ship (from her ports and upper-
> works) making as much water as we can clear out of her with
> four chain-pumps, the wind (as it luckily was) driving us *along*
> shore, if it had come more to the S.E. we must all have gone *on*
> shore and, of course, *inevitably* have perished … I have now
> brought you up to the present hour, and I am not sorry that I have
> done, for she rolls so that my ink is spilled and my wrist aches.[6]

That was only one of their excitements. Soon afterwards, the
Alcide arrived at Barbados to find the island devastated by an
earthquake and a hurricane.

Such was Smith's personal success in the Navy that it was
decided in 1780 that Spencer, now aged eleven, should follow
him. He was to be given rough introductions to the realities of
war at sea. On an early visit to Portsmouth he was taken on
board the *Nonsuch*, which had just anchored 'in shocking order
and very much mauled in a night action with a French ship of
the line … the ship in a most disgusting *status quo* as a gazing-
stock for Portsmouth visitors, between decks she was in many
places like a Butcher's shop.'[7] Then, at the beginning of January
1782, he joined his first ship, the bomb ketch *Vesuvius*, which
was fitting out at Woolwich. He was given another sharp taste
of naval life when, within a month, his ship had dropped down
the river to the Downs anchorage off Deal. On 29th January
1782, he wrote in his diary:

> *Vesuvius*, Downs. Weather fresh breezes and clear. At 7 a.m., the
> *Roebuck*, 44, next ship to ourselves made the signal for a punish-
> ment by a yellow flag at the fore and one gun, every ship in the
> Fleet immediately sending on board her a boat, manned and
> armed, on the arrival of which the criminal was embarked in the
> *Roebuck*'s launch, stripped and made fast to a sort of gallows
> erected in it for that purpose. When all was ready he was towed
> away attended by all the other boats, alongside of every ship to

receive a portion of his punishment. The ceremony was not concluded and the procession returned until 3 p.m. when he had received 500 lashes, the *second* half of his sentence, which proved mortal, as he died on being handed in to one of the *Roebuck*'s lower deck ports either from pain, or cold, or both, having been 5 hours in a confined position almost immoveable.[8]

Spencer's budding naval career was interrupted by calls to London to attend the Queen and more visits to his grandfather at Burnham Market. Now he was accompanied by Sidney, but they never met another young naval officer, Captain Horatio Nelson, six years older than Sidney, whose father was rector of Burnham Thorpe a mile away, because he was at sea. Sidney also returned to sea and while his younger brother was on duty at an Order of the Garter ceremony in London in May, John noted, 'Intelligence at the Admiralty of an action having taking place in the West Indies between the British and French fleets commanded by Sir G. Rodney and M. de Grasse, in which the latter was totally defeated with the loss of 5 sail of the line ...'[9] A month later, he added, 'Indirect intelligence received of W.S.S. [Sidney] having been appointed by Sir G. Rodney to the command of *Fury*, 16, at Jamaica and sent with dispatches to N. America from there.'[10]

So came the news of the Battle of the Saints, so named after a group of small islands between Guadeloupe and Dominica, near which it had been fought between thirty-six British and thirty French ships of the line on 12th April 1782. When further news arrived, naval officers were interested to hear that Rodney had led his ships through a gap in the enemy line, breaking the established rule of fighting in parallel lines of battle and concentrating his fire on the ships he so enveloped. Five French ships of the line, including the Comte de Grasse's flagship, were captured but, when the French managed to get under way, Rodney had not followed and the majority escaped; nevertheless, it was hailed as a great victory. Sidney Smith had again caught the admiral's attention in action and, as a result, had been given command of the sixteen-gun sloop. The next that was heard of him was in February 1784, when he arrived at Spithead from the West Indies, now in command of the frigate *Alcmene*, of thirty-two guns. Within a month his ship had arrived in the Thames and when his younger brother, Spencer, joined the ship in Blackwall Reach and stayed on board for three nights, he gave him certificates of service at sea in both his commands 'with diligence and sobriety' and having been 'always obedient to command' in order to give him spurious 'sea-time' towards his naval seniority should he decide to make the Navy his full-time career.[11]

The first news to reach the brothers was of the death of their grandfather, Pinkney Wilkinson, at the age of ninety-two. The old man had not forgotten Mary, the boys' mother, in his will, leaving her £10,000 to be invested in property and held in trust so that she could benefit from the income. This he had stressed was 'for her sole, separate and peculiar use and not to be liable to the intermeddling control of her present, or any future, husband.'[12] The house and estate in Norfolk were left to Ann on which her husband, Lord Camelford, engaged his friend, the architect John Soane, who redesigned the hall in his own distinctive style.

In September 1783, Britain, France and Spain signed a peace treaty at Versailles recognizing the independence of the United States of America and so setting the scene for the future world order. As was usual when hostilities ceased, most ships of the Royal Navy were paid off – including the *Alcmene*, when she arrived at Portsmouth in February the following year – the redundant officers went home on half-pay, the seamen simply sent ashore and the ships were stripped down 'into ordinary' and moored to await another war. One option open to unemployed officers was to travel abroad to learn useful languages, and this Smith decided to do, thereby, 'further qualifying myself for my country's service'.[13] French and Spanish were, of course, the two most useful languages and although Smith had been taught to speak French by his mother, it was French that he chose. He selected Normandy for his stay in France, just as Nelson had gone to St Omer for the same purpose in October of the previous year.

But whereas Nelson keenly observed the social life of the French provinces and, before he could concentrate on learning French, fell in love with Elizabeth Andrews who was staying with her father, an English clergyman, at the same lodgings, Smith proved himself a natural intelligence officer. Visiting Caen he took advantage of a letter of introduction to the Duc d'Harcourt, the Governor of Normandy, who thought him a young colonel commanding a fashionable regiment and invited him to his chateau; here, he observed the social scene with a sharp eye and lost his heart at a dance, as he later reported to his elder brother Charles:

I fell in love with a *demoiselle,* whose name I do not know ... You see I let the heart go as it will ... It will never let me *marry* a Frenchman [sic], as her connections and *acres* are con- commitants, neither of which a *capitaine de vaisseau Anglais* ought to have any business with. I shall probably see my mistress tonight where I sup in consequence of an invitation produced by le Duc d'Harcourt's desire, *au colonel du régiment.*

But he also indulged in some overt espionage, as indicated in the same letter:

All the world here talk of the great works going on at Cherbourg, which are nothing less than building a breakwater two miles and a half from shore. His Most Christian Majesty, having found the want of a port in the Channel in the late war fit for the reception of large ships, is determined to make one at any expense ...

The project was therefore to make Cherbourg a naval base on the scale of Portsmouth so that this would naturally be of intense interest to the Board of Admiralty in London.

So, continued Smith, 'I went thither and, the day after, two more English captains of men-of-war arrived from Caen on the same errand ... ' He then watched and described in detail the technique by which huge wooden cones, 'built as strong as a ship'[14] and kept buoyant by necklaces of empty casks, were moored over the site of the breakwater then filled with rocks from lighters and the stone-filled cones sunk in position.

During his travels and occasional espionage, Smith emerges from his letters as a lively minded, hyperactive, talkative young man able to charm his way into any social circle, naval or mili- tary establishment. At Cancale, which his ship had once bombarded, he even turned his own experiences of action on that coast to good social advantage, explaining, that he had fallen in with a party of 'Frenchmen and Cancale *defendants* when we attacked their territories with Sir James Wallace', with whom he made friends. He told his brother Charles in a letter:

At the head of these troops we stormed an *auberge,* the good landlady of which, after some defence, surrendered at discretion ... we gave *her* quarter but none to her mackerel (the only thing we found in the house), one of the men brought some fire in a wooden shoe, with which we soon made the chimney roar, and boiled and ate away all together. I paid the piper, of course, after talking over old stories and then went to bed, leaving my new friends to puzzle their brains at what such a mixture of *milord Anglais* and *matelot*, common as I was, could be. My bed was very good and to my surprise the sheets bleached whiter than I had met with elsewhere; and I have since observed that the poorest house in France is not without a great stock of household linen.

The next morning I was conducted by one of my Cancale *quondam* enemies to the different places famous in the combat. He had picked up forty round shot and in the windmill, which I remember amusing myself with firing at (at our gun, as the Jacks say); 'Tis an ill wind that blows nobody any good, for he sold them as old iron for twenty sous apiece afterwards. There were also certain round holes in the window-shutters and doors of the houses and my attentive examination and English appearance proved my having had some hand in making them; so the old women, who had not forgotten the fright and flight they were put into, began to shew their implacability of temper with their tongues; I therefore mounted my horse to be ready to make my retreat good in case they should be inclined to pelt me with oyster shells by way of epilogue to the piece that was played six years before. If the action had commenced I should have had all the men on my side and perhaps some of the *young* women might not have been hard-hearted to a stranger. However, we parted very good-humouredly ...

So he rode on to the walled town of St Malo, noting, 'I saw with pleasure the inside of those batteries at St. Maloes, which had so often pelted us when we appeared off ...'[15]

On the brothers' return to London, they found little enticement to stay at home. Their elder brother, Charles, was staying with their mother at Bath so it was they who had to face their father's increasing instability. What his son Spencer described as his 'passion for low company' had led to the setting up of three establishments: one in Marylebone Street, which was seldom used and so sometimes available for his sons' lodging; another in Rotherhithe where he had 'formed a society according to his own heart, a *coterie* of Cuckolds and Bunters [vagrant women], where devotion and debauchery preside in turns' and another at Dover, a curious little castellated house near the shore, long thereafter known as 'Smith's Folly'.

Captain Smith tried his sons' patience by his demands. Sidney was often away, but when at home was able to make his father an occasional gift of money, which led to him being held up as an example to his younger brother. Spencer, whose allowance as a royal page he 'considered merely as a pension to be devoured by himself', was therefore exposed to the full force of his father's resentment when he called at Rotherhithe* for 'an inhospitable meal succeeded by a paroxysm of rage and storm; after some hours of unmerited abuse his fury subsided into pathetic complaints of being seduced to poverty and distress by other people's misconduct, by his children living upon him and consuming his substance without (W.S.S. excepted) contributing anything to the "stock", i.e. his privy purse.'

It was a nightmare household, with the dissolute Captain Smith presiding over 'a crew of dependents – book-keepers, labourers, chairwomen, etc., etc., and 3 ladies of a curious description', one being 'the favourite Sultana'. Spencer described this collection as 'a cloud of locusts', or, more specifically, as 'unworthy wretches, upon whom thousands are squandered, while food and clothing to a son, for whom he receives more than a sufficiency, is thought an exorbitant outgoing, and my quiet residence in his house construed into a crime; and the misbehaviour of his wife and children a constant cry.'[16] No wonder that his sons took any opportunity to distance themselves.

Sidney Smith's dabbling in amateur espionage during his visit to France proved addictive; it added an edge of adventure to tourism, exercised his professional knowledge and might

* His riverside visits were not always to his father for on 26th November 1787, he wrote in his diary, 'Attracted to Rotherhithe by a ship launch in the neighbourhood. The *Captain*, 74 guns, from Limehouse and a large East India ship (the *Triton*) immediately after from the opposite side of the River near Cuckold's Point – much confusion among the shipping occasioned by a strong easterly wind bringing up some hundreds of accumulated coasting trade, the channel fairly blocked from side to side and much damage done to hulls and rigging as the plot thickened with strong breeze and flood tide. The *Captain*, in going off, ran down a wherry of gaping spectators – a collier in the group nearly dismasted and a man chucked by the fall of a topmast, upon which he was, over several sail of vessels into the water.' A decade later, the *Captain* was to play a decisive part in the Battle of Cape St Vincent and win a knighthood and promotion for his grandfather's Norfolk neighbour, Captain Horatio Nelson.

well enhance his chances of promotion by a demonstration of
zeal. But Britain and France were at peace, chances of active
employment slim and his urge to roam was increasing. One
theatre that seemed full of excitingly dangerous potential was
the Mediterranean and particularly the North African littoral,
where piracy at sea and slavery ashore continued to affront the
trading nations of Europe. So, in 1787, he travelled through
Spain to Gibraltar and thence to Morocco, where the Sultan had
been threatening – verbally, at least – his northern neighbours;
indeed, Smith thought that war would follow.

So he crossed the straits into Africa on a journey devoted to
intelligence-gathering. Perhaps the Moroccans lacked experience of self-possessed young English gentlemen acting as spies,
or their courtesy prevented them from questioning his interest
in their seaports and warships. Unmolested, he completed his
tour as planned before embarking for northern Spain and there,
on the Portuguese border at Tuy, he wrote a letter to the
Secretary of the Admiralty. Explaining that he expected war
with Morocco and so had undertaken his journey 'in order to
acquire a knowledge of his coasts, harbours and force, so as to
be of use in case of such an event taking place; this knowledge,
so acquired, seems now to be called for by the Emperor of
Morocco having ordered his cruisers to be in readiness, if not
actually to capture British vessels.'

Smith then described the Sultan's naval force (seven frigates
and three rowing galleys) and that the most threatening bases
were four on the Atlantic, rather than the Mediterranean, coast.
However, he continued, the Royal Navy could not guard
against the threat to shipping on both sides of the straits of
Gibraltar with the single squadron then available. So he urged
the formation of a second squadron to be based on the
Portuguese coast at Lagos Bay and to consist of a fifty-gun ship,
frigates and some small, shallow-draught warships capable of
sailing over the sand bars which sheltered some of the
Moroccan harbours. Having suggested the strategy and tactics,
he came to the point:

> I am therefore on my return to England in the earnest hope that
> their Lordships will enable me to employ it to advantage in the
> protection of our trade by giving me the command of a force
> adequate to the destruction of his naval force, even in his

harbours ... I hope their Lordships will not consider this my infe-
riority of rank as an obstacle to grant me the honour I request but
rather trust that what I want in professional experience and
ability will be made up by *local* knowledge and zeal for the public
service; at the same time that they will pardon me if that zeal
carries me too far in thus making the proposition and offer to
myself.[17]

He had been effusively welcomed to London by his father,
who was living in Carrington Street, Mayfair. Smith 'fell in with
the gaieties of his station and the opportunities that were
offered him in the best metropolitan society', as an acquaintance put it, 'but in a manner neither vicious nor outrageous.
With the exception of some few passages of love ... he might be
pronounced a rather staid young man.'[18]

The threat of war evaporated and so his services were not
needed but his letter had caught the eye of their Lordships at
the Admiralty and his name noted. There was, however,
accepted alternative employment and that was to apply to the
Admiralty for long leave and then offer one's services as a
mercenary to a nation that was at war but not in conflict with
British interests. There had been recurrent war in the Baltic
between Russia and Sweden and as it was primarily a naval
war both combatants – particularly the former – offered
employment to experienced officers; indeed, the unemployed
Captain Nelson was to consider the option in 1790. The current
bout of warfare between the Baltic neighbours had broken out
in July 1788, when the Swedes, seeking to land an army to
advance on St Petersburg, had fought a major action with the
Russians; both fleets were obsolete and poorly manned and the
result indecisive so they withdrew to their bases to prepare for
the next round. The Swedish monarch, Gustavus III, was a
gentle, artistic but emotional man of forty-three, with star-
tlingly blue eyes and a weak face, known as 'King Charmer'.
He was inspired by high-flown ideals of patriotism but
distrustful of his own court, generals and admirals, fearful of
their ambitions or that they might have been infected by the
revolutionary ideas brewing in France.

The following year, Smith applied for and was granted six
months' leave to visit Stockholm and St Petersburg but was
required to give an undertaking that he would not enlist in the
service of any foreign power. Even so, he took the opportunity

to assess the prospects of employment, first with the Swedes.
Taking passage to Copenhagen, where the British ambassador
gave him a letter of introduction to the Swedish court, he chartered a sloop to carry him up the Baltic. But she proved
unseaworthy and had difficulty reaching the island of
Bornholm, where she had to be abandoned. There, the only
craft available was a Russian long-boat, undecked and twenty-
two feet long with a beam of seven feet. The only seaman he
could persuade to accompany him as his crew was a
Portuguese boy. The two of them set sail, making for the
Swedish base at Karlskrona, where he went on board the flagship of the Commander-in-Chief, the Duke of Södermanland.
His arrival caused a stir of excitement because several officers
remembered having met him in Morocco, where they had been
at the Swedish embassy and because he struck such a dramatic
figure. The duke was delighted by the energetic young
Englishman with his bright, intelligent eyes, aquiline nose and
shock of dark hair, so different from his own blond, phlegmatic
Swedish officers. His application was passed to King Gustavus,
who replied so fulsomely to 'Colonel' Smith that he must have
presented his qualifications without undue modesty. 'The great
reputation you have acquired in serving your own country
with equal success and valour', he began, 'and the profound
calm which England enjoys not affording you any opportunity
to display your talents at present, induce me to propose to you
to enter into my service ...' He then offered an employment
worthy of 'the élève of Rodney, Howe and Hood'.[19] Before
accepting, Smith would have to ask the Admiralty's permission
and he was able to persuade the British minister in Stockholm,
Robert Liston, to let him act as a King's Messenger carrying
despatches to London.

With the encouragement of the Duke of Södermanland in his
ears – 'Return as quick as you can and bring some of your brave
Englishmen with you, for we stand in need of officers ... I hope
that that Being, who watched over you in your little boat, will do
the same this time ...'[20] – he set out in January 1790. On landing
in England and after 'travelling night and day in open carriages
at the worst season of the year' to London, he was brought back
to reality. Imagining himself to be the carrier of vital news from
the Baltic, he was granted an initial interview by the Foreign
Secretary, the Duke of Leeds, whose attitude he found:

more polite than satisfactory ... I found, by my reception, that I had been egregiously mistaken since it was with difficulty that I obtained even the least degree of attention ... At the end of six weeks, I ventured to represent by letter, with all respect, that the most unqualified negative could not be more unpalatable to the King of Sweden, or more prejudicial to his Majesty's affairs, than this delay must be.[21]

Smith had also lodged a request to take a temporary commission in the Swedish Navy and no reply was forthcoming to this, either. If he waited in London longer, he realized that he would miss the fighting season following the thaw in the Baltic and so, without permission and without having attracted any further attention from the Government, he returned to Sweden. It was a long and stormy voyage and, too embarrassed to call at Stockholm, he made straight for the naval base at Karlskrona on his way to join the Duke and the King with their fleet in the Gulf of Finland.

Unwilling to admit to the crushing snub in London, he wrote to the British ambassador in Stockholm saying that he was on his way to tell the King 'the little I am authorised to say',[22] when in fact he had been authorized to say nothing. He used an even more inflated pretext to persuade the senior Swedish officers at Karlskrona that he was carrying important despatches for the King from the British Government and they gave him a fast cutter to join the Duke off Reval. He then continued in the commander-in-chief's despatch boat to join the King at Svenskund, where he arrived on 21st May. The fighting had already begun again and the Swedes had been worsted by the Russians, losing two ships of the line in an abortive attack on a moored Russian squadron.

Although he did not have permission to accept a Swedish commission, Smith decided to assume that he *had* and volunteered his services to King Gustavus, writing to the British ambassador, 'His Majesty has placed me on board a little yacht which follows his galley, the *Seraphim*, on board of which he remains in action. I shall probably not be able to refrain from doing the same. I hope that will not be considered as serving ... '[23]

The King was delighted to see the return of this stimulating and self-confident officer and promised him command of the 'light squadron'. Both Swedish and Russian fleets were divided

into heavy and light forces: the heavy composed of ships of the
line and frigates; the light, of smaller frigates (including some
that were rowed), floating batteries and galleys with oars
manned by crews, who could fight ashore as marines. At this
time the Swedes had twenty-five ships, which could put to sea
first because the ice in the Swedish ports melted before the
Russian ports on the far side of the Baltic were unblocked. The
Russians, however, had thirty big ships divided into three
squadrons, based on Kronstadt and Reval, with a final third in
reserve; the latter having been attacked so unsuccessfully by
the Swedes. The theatre of operations was the Gulf of Finland,
opening into the Baltic in the west and with the naval base of
Kronstadt and the Russian capital, St Petersburg, in the landlocked east. The Swedish strategic aim still remained the hope
of fighting the Russian squadrons separately and preventing
them from combining forces.

King Gustavus was in overall command but not only had
Smith been promised control of the light forces, he was also to
be the principal naval adviser. This aroused resentment among
Swedish officers, particularly when he attributed a catastrophic
epidemic among Swedish seamen to their ships being damp
because their timber was unseasoned and pickled with salt.
One officer, Captain Sillen, noted that:

> By the King and his staff he is regarded in an incomparable light
> and at table he is virtually the only subject of His Majesty's
> conversation. He retains all his English freedom of manner and
> says he is only here to satisfy his curiosity. Some pretend to know
> for certain that he ... merely intends to stay here for a while as a
> spectator – this, it seems to me, would certainly be the wisest
> thing he could do.

Another Swede, Captain Klint, described him as an 'adventurer' and did all he could to undermine Smith's authority and
countermand his orders until, finally, Smith turned to him and
silenced him by saying simply, 'My dear Klint, you don't
understand my position.'[24]

Up to this point the fighting had been indecisive but now it
was coming to a head. The first success was to the Swedes, who
swept aside the Russian light forces in the Bay of Viborg and
landed troops to prepare for the advance on St Petersburg, only
eighty miles distant. Then, on 3rd June, the Russian squadron

from Kronstadt attacked the Swedish line of battle and was reinforced next day by the Reval squadron. Outnumbering the Swedes by thirty to twenty-one, they drove them, together with their light forces, deep into the Bay of Viborg and blockaded them there for a month.

Smith fretted at the inaction, writing to the British ambassador in Stockholm, 'I dare say they think they block us up but I can assure them, so far as it depends on me, that we shall endeavour to make our way through them ... as I have not a greater opinion of the strength of a fleet from its being numerous.'[25] His own rôle was characteristic: after receiving a letter from the King about a success by his land forces – 'My hussars pounced upon the Empress's dragoons finely yesterday'[26] – he wrote of his own responsibilities at sea, 'I wish to amuse myself with attacking a wing, à la hussar, with a division which the King has ordered to be under my influence for that purpose.'[27] The King was flying the royal standard in the big galley, the Seraphim, and now he finally gave Smith what amounted to overall command of the light forces, writing an order on 13th June: 'Whereas I have instructed Colonel Sidney Smith, by word of mouth, concerning the operations which I have undertaken against the Russian coasting fleet in Viborg harbour – my commander and chiefs of divisions are therefore commanded to follow all such orders as the said Col. Sidney Smith shall give in my name.'[28]

The first orders were to clear Russian batteries from islands commanding the exits from the bay. The galleys and gunboats began to pull slowly through the wooded islands towards the open water of the Gulf of Finland. The light forces under Smith's command included 3 small frigates, 5 square-rigged bomb ketches, 20 galleys rowed and manned by some 4,000 marines and 72 gunboats each mounting a 24-pounder gun in bow and stern and rowed by 70 men. For a young officer brought up in ships of the line and frigates on the open sea, it was extraordinary to watch what he called 'the line of march' of his command as it moved under oars through the wooded archipelago towards the action. He described it himself:

Nothing can be conceived more sublimely beautiful than the picturesque scene around us, animated by this line of march, while the dead silence of the forests, which cover the shore and islands, was only interrupted by the splashing of the oars, re-

echoed through them. The exact order, the perfect proportion of
the intervals between the vessels, the lengths of the line, now
perfectly straight, and the end of it nearly out of sight from its
extent, now in various serpentine windings as the projection of
the shoals obliged the course to be partially changed, the masts
mingled with the tall forest trees ... all contributed to please the
eye, while the magnitude of the object for which this force was
destined and the probability of any immediate and desperate
conflict, contributed to awaken in the mind the grandest and
most awful ideas.[29]

The close-quarter fighting was often hand to hand and at the
point of the bayonet but the Russians used their guns to deadly
effect, as Smith wrote, 'the shot splintering the trees and
making showers of arrows, which killed or maimed all those
who were in their way'.[30] In one attack, Smith saved the life of
his critic, Captain Sillen, when he was hit in the arm, 'by
binding up the artery with a handkerchief tightened by a stick
to serve as a sort of tourniquet'. Taken back to a Swedish ship,
Sillen's arm was amputated and, when Smith asked him how
he was, 'he pointed to his hand, which was lying on the deck,
saying, "I see I am but poorly"'.[31]

At the beginning of July, King Gustavus, with Smith at his
side, decided to break out. First gunboats and then fireships
sailed from the bay but the Swedes were inexperienced in the
management and timing of such operations: one of the fireships
drifted back into their own line, destroyed two of their own
ships and threw their line of battle into confusion. Following
the big ships out of the bay came the light forces under Smith
with the King in the *Seraphim*, filled with apprehension and
drafting the wording of his own expected capitulation. He was
not alone in this expectation: the Russian admiral had had a
tent rigged on the poop of his galley to accommodate the
captive King in suitable comfort. Indeed, the *Seraphim* was
known to be the royal flagship and became the Russians' principal target and the King would probably have been captured
had not Smith persuaded him to take to a small boat and
escape.

But events did not fall out as expected. As the day drew on
into a long, pale summer twilight, darkened by smoke and
stabbed by gun-flashes, the galleys and gunboats fought, oar to
oar, much as the Venetians and Turks had fought at Lepanto

two centuries before. Sidney Smith had worked hard at training his guns' crews and had successfully galvanized them. As the Russian lines moved to the attack, the wind and sea got up, throwing them into disarray; Russian galleys shipped water, their rowers were called to the pumps and they drifted out of control, presenting easy targets to the Swedish gunners. At the end of that long, light night, the Russians had lost 64 ships, nearly 1,000 men killed by gunfire, or drowned, and more than 6,000 taken prisoner. The Swedes had lost only 4 ships and a few men.

Both sides lost and gained on that bloody day. The Russians had driven off the Swedish battle-fleet, which was never again to threaten them, but their own light coastal forces had been destroyed and that was enough to deter them from further maritime adventures in the Baltic; henceforth, Russia would concentrate on looking eastwards.

Once during the month in the Bay of Viborg, King Gustavus and Sidney Smith had been standing together on an exposed rock in a cold wind, watching the Russians through telescopes. Seeing that Smith was without a coat and looked cold, the King turned to a soldier and ordered, 'Give the colonel your cloak', to which the man replied with Scandinavian egalitarianism, 'I want it myself, sir.' So the King turned to a page and asked him to bring the colonel a cloak. This was one of his own, embroidered with the star of the Order of the Seraphim, at which the King remarked that if he had not called for the cloak because of the cold, Smith could have assumed that he was being invested with that order. 'It is not the Order of the Seraphim,' he added, 'but that of the Sword I destine for the colonel.'[32]

Soon afterwards, the King summoned his staff to gather around the royal standard, asked Smith to kneel and touched him on both shoulders with his sword to confirm the Swedish knighthood, the Order of the Sword. Weeks later, when the insignia was ready for a formal investiture, a truce had been agreed with Russia, the war was over and Sidney Smith had returned to England. However, at the request of King Gustavus, the ceremony was eventually performed at St James's Palace by King George himself on 16th May 1792, with full pomp. Moreover, Smith was given permission to use the title, becoming Sir Sidney, only to be mocked by his fellow-officers of the Royal Navy – including the currently unemployed

Captain Nelson – as 'the Swedish knight'. There was anger as well as resentment because, amongst the captains of Russian ships killed on 4th June, there were six British officers, currently surplus to the requirements of the Royal Navy, who had enlisted in the Russian service as Nelson himself had considered doing.

In the spring of 1792, Britain remained at peace, indeed William Pitt – the Prime Minister and Sidney Smith's cousin – had confirmed that the country would remain neutral whatever actions were taken on the Continent. In Sweden, Sidney Smith's patron, King Gustavus III, was assassinated. In France, the Revolution was gathering force, the monarchy seemed likely to fall and war with Austria and Prussia imminent. Meanwhile, the Foreign Secretary, Lord Grenville, was concerned about the Middle East, where the ramshackle but still powerful Ottoman Empire lay astride the British overland route to India. Meanwhile, John Spencer Smith, although only aged twenty-two, had been sent to Constantinople to join the British embassy to the court of Sultan Selim III. This was as much an intelligence mission as a diplomatic one and the problem was communications, which were insecure when they existed at all. It had been noted that his brother, Sidney, was not only an active officer with a penchant for intelligence work but seemed to have found favour with the King and so it was that, after discussion between the Foreign Secretary and the First Lord of the Admiralty, he was ordered to visit his brother to bring back his confidential report. He was also to take the opportunity of 'examining the Black Sea, Bosphorous, Sea of Marmora, Dardanelles, Archipelago and Ionian islands'[33] and for such purposes he would be allowed to take service with the Turkish Navy, as he had with Sweden's. He was given an advance of £1,500 for expenses and, with his customary enthusiasm, he set out on the long overland journey.

CHAPTER TWO

'An odd, eccentric man'

IN 1792, the two Smith brothers were reunited in Constantinople. Sidney was unaware that, in London, the Government was belatedly discovering his worth when a new crisis broke in the Baltic over what was seen to be the imminent threat of war with Russia following their capture of a Black Sea port from the Turks. But, ironically, the British officer closest to that scene of action was the one most urgently needed at the opposite side of the potential theatre of war. A large British fleet had been assembled under Lord Hood for despatch to the Baltic and it was realized that the only naval officer with practical experience of those waters, and without professional ties with Russia, was the maverick Smith. But he was now almost beyond the reach of communications.

Meanwhile, the progress of the Revolution in France was watched more with curiosity – sometimes with elation – than with fear. In June, King Louis XVI attempted to escape but was intercepted on the border at Varennes and forcibly returned to Paris. Yet, three months later, a new constitution re-established France as a monarchy and the political earthquake seemed to have stilled, if only briefly. It did not last and the Revolution rolled forward and the monarchy was doomed. When King Louis was executed in January 1793, and, when less than a fortnight later, France declared war against Britain, Smith was serving as a volunteer in the Turkish Navy as a cover for his espionage.

When news of the war reached him, 'this intelligence was to him like the sound of the trumpet to a war horse',[1] wrote a friend. It was obvious to him that a new theatre of war had opened in the western basin of the Mediterranean; it was exactly the spur to which he responded and he did so with customary verve. The news had reached him in the port of Smyrna, where several dozen unemployed British seamen were loafing on the waterfront. He immediately recruited them with the promise of a passage homeward, bought a lateen-rigged coaster, renamed her the *Swallow* and, with a crew of forty British seamen, set sail.

As they passed Sicily, the sombre panorama of the naval and military scene began to come into focus. The French Revolution had not swept the whole country; on the contrary, there was massive resistance to it across France, notably in the west, north-west and in the south, where Lyons, Marseilles and Toulon had declared for the royalists. The new republic counter-attacked and the royalists appealed for British help but before Admiral Lord Hood, who commanded in the Mediterranean, could react, Marseilles had fallen.

In August, one of the many British officers newly arrived in the Mediterranean, Captain Horatio Nelson, commanding the small ship of the line, the *Agamemnon*, questioned the master of a ship, lately sailed from Marseilles, which he had stopped at sea. Nelson wrote to his father that he had been told there were 'now only two descriptions of people in France – the one drunk and mad; the other, with horror painted in their faces, are absolutely starving.'[2]

That same month Lord Hood had been invited into Toulon and asked to help defend it against the advancing republicans. The naval base was eminently defensible, its dockyard sheltering beneath the great razorback ridge of Mont Faron and its two, almost landlocked, anchorages surrounded by little hills crowned with well-sited forts and batteries. All that was required was enough soldiers to man the perimeter of 15 miles and these Hood lacked, having only some 2,000 sailors and marines available for landing parties and 1,500 French royalist troops in the town. Reinforcements were summoned from allies, notably Spain and Naples but also from Piedmont, Sardinia and Malta. First to arrive were nearly 7,000 Spanish troops, and Captain Nelson was sent to Naples to persuade the Bourbon monarch, King Ferdinand IV, to help. Thanks to the friendship between him and the British ambassador, Sir William Hamilton, and his beautiful and vivacious wife Emma, the King agreed and, by October, about 5,000 Neapolitan

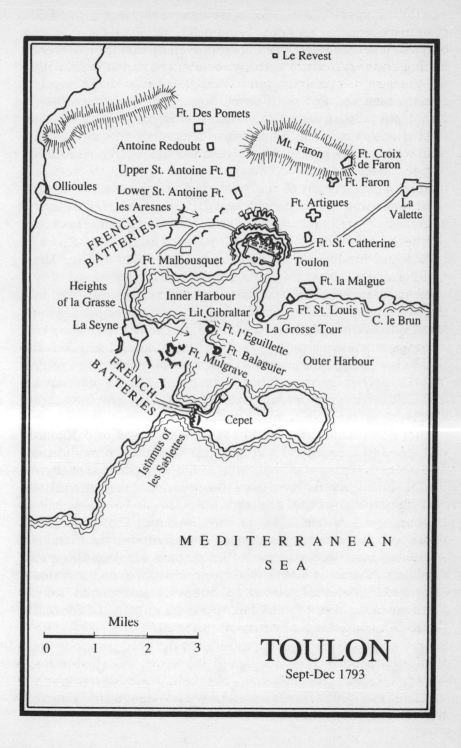

Le Revest

Ft. Des Pomets

Antoine Redoubt

Upper St. Antoine Ft.

Ollioules

Lower St. Antoine Ft.

les Aresnes

Mt. Faron

Ft. Croix de Faron

Ft. Faron

La Valette

Ft. Artigues

FRENCH BATTERIES

Ft. St. Catherine

Ft. Malbousquet

Toulon

Heights of la Grasse

Ft. la Malgue

Inner Harbour

Lit. Gibraltar

La Seyne

Ft. l'Eguillette

Ft. St. Louis

C. le Brun

La Grosse Tour

FRENCH BATTERIES

Ft. Balaguier

Ft. Mulgrave

Outer Harbour

Cepet

Isthmus of les Sablettes

MEDITERRANEAN
SEA

Miles

0   1   2   3

TOULON

Sept–Dec 1793

soldiers had arrived at Toulon. Yet even with these, and 1,500
Piedmontese, this provided Hood with only 17,000 men, which
was not enough to defend the perimeter. By that time, a French
republican army more than twice that size had arrived before
Toulon; not a polyglot force like the town's defenders but
Frenchmen charged with revolutionary zeal and ferocity. At
once, they began to attack. When the *Swallow* sailed into the
outer achorage at the beginning of December, the outlook was
dark and Hood was making preparations for possible evacuation.

Smith's first sight of the great port was promising, for the
two anchorages and the dockyard itself were thick with the
masts and yards of ships of the line and, ashore, gunsmoke rose
defiantly from the hilltop forts. Yet the defences were about to
crack and collapse. The defenders were not only outnumbered
by more than two to one, but were divided by degrees of enthusiasm, training and language. As few in the national
contingents spoke one another's language, they were given
separate sectors, or forts, to defend but were often unable to
communicate with their allies on either flank. Thus when the
French assaulted the Spanish, there was little thought of calling
for British reinforcements but, instead, for every man to run for
his life. British infantry fought fierce little actions on the heights
of Mont Faron, only to find themselves outflanked by the rout
of their allies and having to fight their own way back towards
the sea and the ships. It was ugly fighting on the edges of cliffs
and steep goat-tracks, and was made more ferocious by an
order to the republicans from the ruling Convention in Paris
that no quarter should be given.

Unknown to the allies at the time, but critical to their
prospects, was the presence in the French armies of a colonel of
artillery, Napoleon Bonaparte. A Corsican, stocky, sallow and
taciturn, Napoleon was nevertheless able to change his customary look of determination and thoughtfulness by smiling with
'a pleasing curl of the lip'. His approach to the conduct of the
siege was original. As he himself put it later:

> It was I who proposed the plan of attack that resulted in the
> reduction of Toulon. I regarded all the proposals (of the
> Convention) as totally useless and was of the opinion that a
> regular siege was simply not necessary. If from fifteen to twenty
> mortars, thirty or forty pieces of cannon and furnaces for red-hot

balls could be positioned where they could maintain fire upon every point of the greater and lesser roadsteads, then it was evident that the combined [allied] squadron would be obliged to withdraw ... That being so, I was convinced that the combined forces would prefer to withdraw the garrison.[3]

The key to dominance of the roadsteads was a promontory with two points, Balaguier and l'Eguillette. This commanded the anchorages, had been fortified strongly and its slopes shaved of scrub, so that it was known as 'Little Gibraltar'. On 18th December, at midnight and in pouring rain, the French assaulted the British and Spanish batteries there. Resistance was desperate and Bonaparte himself was slightly wounded by a pike-thrust in the thigh but the impetus was irresistible and the key to Toulon was taken.

A fortnight after Sidney Smith had sailed into the anchorage an urgent conference was held in the great cabin of Hood's flag-ship, the *Victory*. Bonaparte's capture of the commanding headland had been the decisive move and now it was only a question of time – and little time – before Toulon fell. There was no doubt of that and the attackers were now said to number 120,000. The allied troops had to be evacuated and the fleet itself would have to withdraw.

There was also the problem of the royalists in the city who could expect no mercy from the vengeful republicans. Whole families of local politicians, officials and any of the professional classes who had had dealings with the allies, had already crowded the waterfront hoping for rescue. Smith wrote:

This disagreeable scene was heightened and one's feelings tortured by the lamentations of women and children, who, with their husbands or fathers, were obliged to leave their homes and their property to save their lives under the certainty of a public execution if they escaped the massacre to be expected on an enraged and merciless enemy entering the town.[4]

There was another problem: the French warships in the dockyard. Toulon was the principal French naval base in the Mediterranean and, moored or in dock, lay 58 ships, including 32 of the line and 14 frigates. The revolution had already swept through the French fleet, many of its officers and warrant officers were already dead, or had fled, and most of the ratings still in the port sympathized with the republicans so that some

5,000 of them had had to be rounded up by the British and the royalists and imprisoned in moored ships. Therefore, the allies could only hope to man and sail away a small minority of those ships in seagoing condition.

For the past fortnight, Captain Smith, who, as an officer on half-pay, currently held no appointment in the Royal Navy, commanding only his own little ship, the *Swallow*, had been frustrated. Aware that his Swedish knighthood and impulsive tendencies had aroused resentment among his brother-officers, he was awaiting a passage to England to seek re-employment at the Admiralty and, while waiting, had been invited on board the *Victory* as Lord Hood's guest. He was there when a final council of war was held by the admiral with the Spanish admiral, Don Langara, and the commanders of the land forces. There was irritation among British naval captains that an unemployed officer on half-pay should be attending, to which Smith replied that the difference between them was that they had succeeded in getting commands of crews who were paid *for* them, but he paid for his crew himself. While they were gathered in the great stern cabin, Sir Sidney was quoted as having asked, 'What do you mean to do with all those fine ships of the enemy? Do you mean to leave them behind?'

'What do you propose to do with them?' Hood is said to have replied.

'Burn them to be sure.'[5]

No preparation for this had been made, but, a fortnight earlier, the same idea had struck Captain Horatio Nelson, while his ship, the *Agamemnon*, had been lying at Tunis. He had written to his naval mentor, Captain William Locker, in England, saying that he did not then fear the loss of Toulon but had added, if there was risk of that, 'at all events we can destroy the French Fleet and Arsenal in a very short time'.[6] That short time had now arrived. Lord Hood agreed not only to burn those ships, which could not be extracted, but also to burn the stores and magazines in the dockyard, and gave Smith command of a flotilla of gunboats and two Royal Navy captains, fourteen lieutenants, seven midshipmen and a surgeon. Although officially unemployed, it was the most significant command to which he had been entrusted on behalf of his own country. In one of two written orders, Hood told Smith, 'You must burn every French ship you possibly can.'[7]

The admiral also told him to ask Don Langara for help with the burning of ships within the dockyard basin, partly out of tact, for there had been tension between the two admirals since the Spaniard had claimed that he, and not Hood, should command the allied forces and had been rebuffed. So Smith boarded the Spanish flagship, the *Concepcion*, and asked Don Langara for the use of his gunboats, later noting, 'they were reluctantly granted me and as reluctantly followed me'.[8] As a result, Smith had last-minute doubts and told Hood, who replied, 'I am sorry you are so apprehensive of difficulty in the service you volunteered for ... It *must* be undertaken ... no enterprise of war is void of danger and difficulty – both must be submitted to.'[9]

As Smith's flotilla sailed, smoke and gun-flashes showed that fighting was now close to the city walls and the shores of the roadsteads. Before they reached shore, all but one Spanish boat had disappeared, leaving him with the *Swallow*, three British gunboats, a mortar-boat without ammunition, the *Victory's* pinnace and one Spanish felucca. Landing in the dockyard he found that the landward gates had been shut and barred but that, within, many of the royalists had thrown away the white cockades they had worn in their hats and substituted the red, white and blue of the Revolution. Prudently, Smith decided to take no action against them but concentrate on fire-raising. Other potential enemies now appeared: the convicts condemned to work as galley-slaves, many of them revolution-aries and expecting freedom when the republicans arrived. Usually they were chained to their benches in the galleys but, their guards having fled, they had begun to strike off their fetters and, although unarmed, they presented a threat. So Smith ordered the *Swallow* and one of the gunboats to lie off the galleys' moorings, where their guns could enfilade them if necessary.

The British demolition parties landed and set about placing combustibles and fuses in the storehouses and the ships along-side. Cannon-shot was already hitting the dockyard and, as Smith wrote later:

A great multitude of the enemy continued to draw down the hill towards the dockyard wall and, as night closed in, they came near enough to pour in an irregular though quick fire on us ... from the heights which overlook it. We kept them at bay by

discharges of grape-shot from time to time, which prevented
their coming so near as to discover the insufficiency of our force
to repel a closer attack.

While the charges, combustibles and gunpowder trains were
still being laid, a fireship, the *Vulcan*, was towed by Lieutenant
Gore into position across the main tier of moored French
warships. Her loaded guns could also bear on the galleys, from
which, as Smith wrote, 'the only noise heard among them was
the hammer knocking off their fetters, which humanity forbade
my opposing as they might thereby be more at liberty to save
themselves'. The enemy were already beating on the dockyard
gates as the British officers looked at their watches. 'In this situation we continued to wait most anxiously for the hour
concerted with the Governor for the inflammation of the trains.
The moment the signal was made we had the satisfaction to see
the flames rise in every quarter.'

Smith's lieutenants and their landing parties had done their
work well:

> Lieutenant Tupper was charged with the burning of the general
> magazine, the pitch, tar, tallow and oil storehouses and
> succeeded most perfectly, the hemp magazine was included in
> the blaze. The weather being nearly calm was unfavourable to
> the spreading of the flames but 250 barrels of tar, divided among
> the deals and other timber, inspired the rapid ignition of that
> whole quarter ... The mast-house was equally well set on fire by
> Lieutenant Middleton of the *Britannia*. Lieutenant Pater of the
> *Britannia* continued in almost daring manner to brave the flames
> in order to complete the work where the fire seemed to have
> caught imperfectly ... His situation was the most perilous as the
> enemy's fire redoubled as soon as the amazing blaze of light
> rendered us distinct objects for their aim. Lieutenant Ironmonger
> of the Royals remained with the guard at the gate till the last ...
> and was brought off safely by Captain Edge of the *Alert*, to whom
> I had confided the important service of closing our retreat and
> bringing off our detached parties.

As Captain Hare put a match to the powder-train that would
light the fireship, a flash ignited it prematurely and the *Vulcan*
erupted in flame. Hare was blown over the side, badly scorched
and, as the flames spread, Smith reported:

> the guns of the fireship going off on both sides, as they heated, in

the direction that was given them towards those quarters from whence we were most apprehensive of the enemy forcing their way in upon us, checked their career; their shouts and republican songs, which we could hear distinctly, continued till they, as well as ourselves, were in a manner thunderstruck by the explosion of some thousand barrels of powder on board the *Iris* frigate ... the concussion of air and the shower of falling timber ignited, were such as nearly to have destroyed the whole of us.

This was the first sign that anything had gone wrong. The French frigate had been lying in the inner roadstead and the Spanish had been ordered to sink her but had burned her instead, the explosion sinking two British gunboats, killing an officer and three ratings in one of them. Three Spanish officers who were working with Smith himself performed with competence and courage but reports from the main Spanish parties reported failure. They had been ordered to burn the French ships in the town basin but their boats had been prevented from entering by a boom across the entrance. Knowing that the Governor of Toulon had had the guns of the battery commanding the basin spiked, Smith joined the Spaniards in a second attempt to clear the boom. But by this time enemy infantry lined the docksides and volleys of musket-fire also crackled from the decks of the French flagship, which had been a principal objective of the fire-raisers.

So, abandoning the attempt, Smith and his men concentrated on the French ships of the line anchored in the inner roadstead, first setting fire to the 'seventy-fours', *Hero* and *Themistocles*. These had been used to imprison the republican sailors and it was thought that their guards had abandoned the ships and that the prisoners might have armed themselves. But the fire ashore and the explosion of the *Iris* had shaken their resolve and when Smith drew alongside and shouted to them in French that he would ferry them ashore if they promised to disarm and obey his orders, they submitted. A second explosion, even more violent than the first, blew a fountain of blazing wreckage into the sky but, as Smith put it, 'it is next to miraculous that not one piece of the many, which made the water foam around us, happened to touch either the *Swallow* or the three boats with me'.[10]

The whole harbour seemed to be engulfed in flame, its red glare reflecting off the clouds of smoke rolling across the city, the dockyard and the bay. The roar and crackle of flames and the exploding ammunition drowned the shouts and screams from the city, giving the British as ghastly a vision of hell as they could imagine. Colonel Bonaparte later described what he saw from a hillside about the harbour: 'The fire and smoke from the arsenal resembled the eruption of a volcano and the thirteen vessels burning in the road were like so many magnificent displays of fireworks. The masts and shapes of the vessels were silhouetted against the blaze, which ... formed an unparalleled spectacle.'[11] Smith concluded:

Having now set fire to eveything within our reach, exhausted our combustible preparations, and our strengths, to such a degree that the men absolutely dropped on the oars, we directed our course to join the fleet, running the gauntlet under a few ill-directed shots from the forts of Balaguier and l'Eguillette, now occupied by the enemy ... we proceeded to the place appointed for the embarkation of troops and took off as many as we could.[12]

Smith and his exhausted men, scorched and blackened by the fires they had lit, had concentrated on burning; they now concentrated upon the evacuation of the rearguard from the beaches. But the scene had become even more horrific through the night because, as expected, the population of the city panicked. Smith had foreseen this and, before volunteering to burn the ships and the dockyard, had offered to cover the evacuation with small gunboats, telling Hood, as he recorded later, that he was 'confident that I could keep any mob in order by grapeshot; and having less reason to be apprehensive of being set on fire by the enemy's red-hot shot and shells than the ships had, I knew I could keep my station so as to awe the town to the last and cover the embarkation.' But the time for that was now passed; the burning of the warships and stores had taken priority and not even Smith's grapeshot could have stemmed the panic that engulfed the town.

'The whole of this horrid scene is not describable,' wrote Smith. 'A few muskets fired in the town, perhaps from the windows, by some mad-headed republican, aroused a cry that their party had made a revolution in the town; the tumult and pressure on this alarm became such that many were forced into the water and drowned.'[13] Horrific accounts of the panic spread throughout the British fleet and boats were sent ashore to save as many as possible. A week later, Captain Nelson, now at Leghorn heard the stories and wrote to one of his brothers in England, 'Then began a scene of horror, which may be conceived, not described. The mob rose; death called forth all its myrmidons, which destroyed the miserable inhabitants, in the shape of swords, pistols, fire and water. Thousands are said to be lost.'[14]

As 1793 drew to its end, smoke hung over the town, dock-yard and empty anchorages of Toulon. Hood had led his ships to a new but temporary anchorage in Hyères Bay and there assessed the scale of the disaster. French royalists and the British had managed to save and sail away 4 ships of the line, 8 frigates and 7 corvettes. Smith and his men had burned or sunk 10 ships of the line, 2 frigates and 2 corvettes. But 18 ships of the line (including one of 120 guns), 4 frigates and 3 corvettes had not been destroyed and would now be wearing the republican flag. Most of the latter had been those the Spanish had been charged with sinking, or burning, and recriminations began. It was said that Don Langara had deliberately held back either because of his resentment at having to serve under Hood, or, it was rumoured, having reached a secret agreement with Robespierre and the Convention in Paris. Indeed, Robespierre himself was quoted as saying, 'The Spaniards, in consequence of this agreement, fled on all sides ... and left the English everywhere to bite the dust ... The ships which the Spaniards had to burn, they did not set fire to.'[15] Later, Bonaparte was said to have added, 'Sir Sidney Smith set them on fire and they would have all been burned if the Spaniards had behaved well. It was the prettiest *feu d'artifice* possible.'[16]

But, by any standards, Smith's achievement had been remarkable. He had destroyed what amounted to an entire battle-fleet, more than had been achieved in any action at sea that had won the victorious admiral honours and wealth. That this had been his own triumph was shown by his later remark, 'I volunteered it under the disadvantage of there being no previous preparation for it whatever.'[17] Yet although Hood wrote in his despatch to the Admiralty that Smith had 'very much distinguished himself',[18] blame was attached to him, too. Throughout the Royal Navy, the resentment engendered by his huge self-confidence, his Swedish knighthood and his habit of approaching the most senior commanders and Government ministers over the heads of his immediate superiors came to a head in specific criticism. Captain Cuthbert Collingwood, then commanding a ship in the Channel Fleet, wrote:

> Our miscarriage at Toulon is truly provoking, the more so as gross mismanagement alone could have prevented its being totally destroyed … No preparation was made for the destruction either of ships or arsenal; and at last perhaps it was put into as bad hands as could be found – Sir Sidney Smith, who arrived there a few days before and had no public situation either in the fleet or army, but was wandering to gratify his curiosity.[19]

Later, Collingwood's friend, Nelson, was to write that 'Sir Sidney Smith did not burn them all. Lord Hood mistook the man: there is an old song, "Great talkers do the least, we see." '[20]

Heat was added to the search for scapegoats because of the appalling aftermath at Toulon. Of its total population of some 28,000, nearly 15,000 had been taken off by the allied ships but a few weeks later only about 7,000 survived in the town. When the republicans first fought their way through the gates on 18th December, Colonel Bonaparte had been shocked by what he was to describe as 'scenes of such confusion that they would be difficult to describe'. Next day, the main republican army entered and, recorded Bonaparte, 'abandoned themselves to some excesses … which seemed authorised by promises made during the siege'. The slaughter in hot blood at the fall of the town and the killings in cold blood thereafter had been horrific in scale. Because most of the prominent royalists had escaped, the republicans took vengeance against those who expected to survive political upheaval. As Bonaparte himself recounted:

> It was proclaimed that everyone who had been employed in the arsenal while the English were in possession of the town must attend a roll-call in the Champ de Mars. These people were led to believe that this was so that they might be re-employed and so, confidently, nearly two hundred head workmen, inferior clerks and other junior employees attended and had their names registered. Thus it was proved by their own confession that they had retained their posts under the English government and the revolutionary tribunal, in the open field, immediately sentenced them to death. A battalion of Sans-Culottes* and Marseilles, brought expressly for the purpose, shot them.[21]

---

* Literally 'without knee-breeches' and therefore unfashionable, the slang expression for revolutionary irregulars.

Smith himself said that others were herded into the main square and cut down by grape-shot, after the first discharge, an officer shouting to the survivors, 'The vengeance of the French republic is satisfied – rise and go to your homes.'[22] As they did so, the guns, which had been reloaded, were fired again, which Bonaparte was hotly to deny. Certainly, the guillotine was set to work and, ten days after the fall of Toulon, the commanding republican general boasted, 'Every day since our arrival we have cut off two hundred heads.'[23] It was assumed that the number killed in the republican revenge was about 6,000.

With the loss of the great naval port and the prospect of the surviving French ships being ready to join those that had been at sea, Lord Hood had to seek a new base. He chose Corsica, where the sheltered anchorage at San Fiorenzo – or St Florent – in the north of the island would be well placed for the blockade of Toulon. There were French garrisons in the fortified towns of Bastia and Calvi, so major land operations would be necessary. The loss of Toulon, and hopes of using it as the springboard for a counter-revolution and a counter-offensive against the Convention, had been a total disaster but Smith's burning of half the French fleet had been some compensation. Whatever jealousy his contemporaries might show, his superior, Lord Hood, was well pleased and showed his satisfaction by giving him the honour of taking his despatches to London.

Smith arrived in London on 15th January 1794, and if he did not receive a hero's welcome, his reception by the Government was gratifying. The Admiralty was satisfied with his feat at Toulon and the First Lord, Earl Spencer, told him so, while the print shops were ordering copies of the dramatic aquatint of the scene being painted and engraved by Archibald Robertson. Several other artists were at work on canvases of the fiery scene. At soirées in London, Smith was pointed out as the first hero of the new war and his striking appearance was described as being 'decidedly handsome and, though not tall, of a compact, well-built, symmetrical frame with a dark and somewhat Hebraical countenance and a profusion of jet-black, curling hair'.[24]

There was a delay of a few months in finding him a new appointment and, as he had been on half-pay for two years and the expenses allowance from Lord Grenville for his mission to Turkey had proved far too modest, he was soon out of pocket.

Finally the Admiralty gave him command of the fine frigate
Diamond of thirty-eight guns, which was attached to the
Channel Fleet. This was heavily engaged in supporting royalist
insurrections in the north and west of France and the British
army under the Duke of York, which since 1793 had been trying
to save the Low Countries from French invasion with
diminishing success.

It was also gratifying when Lord Spencer chose this ship to
take him to Flushing on his way to Vienna and Major-General
the Earl of Moira, who was to command the 7,000 men sent to
reinforce for the Duke of York. The French were on the southern shore of the River Scheldt and one of their batteries fired a
few shots at the frigate, which fell short. Smith at once pointed
out the need for powerful, shallow-draft gunboats of the sort he
had commanded in the Baltic.

He also took advantage of the opportunity to lecture the First
Lord on the strategy and tactics necessary to win the war and,
in particular, operations on or against the French coast. Spencer
proved a tolerant and interested audience and on his arrival he
wrote to the Secretary of State for War, William Windham:

> I promised Sir Sidney Smith to write to you something about
> what he calls his ideas but my own ideas have really been so
> turned and twisted and tumbled about ever since that I protest I
> have been pretty nearly shaken out of my head. In general,
> however, I remember he said a good deal about the French coast-
> ing ships which, by their being very flat bottomed, can run into
> shoal water where none of our ships of war can follow them, and,
> of course, he is very desirous of having a fleet of flat-bottomed
> vessels at his command to go and break them all to pieces. He
> does not seem to think much of the scheme about Calais* but he
> has an idea that something might be done at Le Havre.
>
> He is certainly an odd, eccentric man but he is very clever and
> has a great deal of contrivance about him and if he could
> somehow be put into activity without giving offence to the more
> regular and orderly sort of Geniuses, who I believe all look upon
> him as a fellow of the College of Physicians does upon a Quack
> doctor, he might be of great service.[25]

Having been assured that this letter would be sent, Smith
followed it up with a long letter to Windham, in which he
declared that the most effective move against France –

* a seaborne raid

particularly to stave off an invasion of England – would be by 'a descent upon their coasts'. Repeating his view that Calais was the wrong place to attack, he continued, 'A ruler laid on the map from London to Paris shows the straight line of *shortest distance* to be by way of Dieppe, or Havre and Rouen and it is to be remembered that there is no chain of fortified places requiring regular sieges by that route.' Recalling his own visit to Normandy he believed that the Normans were generally hostile to the Convention and that moderate politicians might come forward to lead a rising so long as they were not first required to surrender to the British: 'my experience at Toulon has proved that this never can be expected if the *white flag* is shewn to them as an earnest of the return of the ancient system'.

He therefore proposed an attack on Paris itself:

An army on the two banks of the River Seine, using that river as its line of communication, having its baggage, battering train and magazines afloat under the protection of gunboats and consequently being unencumbered with horses and forage ... might move with facility and be less liable to total discomforture in case of failure, having a *floating fortress* to rally to. I am persuaded that an expedition of this kind, if it did not succeed to the full extent of the object might still do essential service: it would cut off one channel by which Paris is supplied with provisions ...

However, Smith did not immediately volunteer to command the gunboats, which he saw as the spearhead of such a river-borne offensive, for he had been hurt by criticism and lack of recognition. He gave vent to his bitterness for he saw that there was little prospect of substantial prize-money while cruising in the Channel and the North Sea:

I hope I may stand excused from stepping forward myself, which I am disinclined to do considering the little encouragement I meet with for such voluntary exertions. Besides, no man can serve in a situation to any degree of eminence without hurting his private fortune and I have unfortunately none to supply the demand incident to such a situation. If I had, I would most willingly sacrifice that as I do my time and my health; these, with a daring spirit and as much military experience as I could acquire by going wherever it was to be obtained, being all I can call my own, I devote them to my country's service, though, I confess to you, not so cheerfully as I have done hitherto. I have suffered such pecuniary embarrassment and distress since my return from Toulon as makes me, though reluctantly, impeach my country's Justice ... I content myself at present with a cruise in a frigate, the object of which, as it cannot affect the success of the war, does not afford even the prospect of that satisfaction which is the only repayment I can look to under the certainty of a lodging in the King's Bench prison* as my ultimate retreat.[26]

He continued in this vein at a length to try the recipient's patience. Lord Spencer was aware of Smith's talents and ordered exactly such a force of gunboats and fireships as he had proposed to be assembled for him to command. Meanwhile, the *Diamond* was kept under the direct orders of the Admiralty and, at the beginning of 1795, he was attached to the squadron of frigates commanded by Commodore Sir John Warren, which was carrying out a reconnaissance of the French coast. A report had reached the Admiralty that a French fleet under Admiral Villaret de Joyeuse had sailed from Brest and, if so, its destination was unknown and was important to discover. Warren was charged with this and he gave Smith the dangerous task of carrying out a close reconnaissance of the great French naval base on the Atlantic. The particular risk in this operation was that Brest itself and its inner roadstead could only be seen by penetrating the deep, almost landlocked natural harbour, commanded by hills and islands well fortified with shore batteries, at the head of which it lay. Warren urged caution and, knowing Smith's aggressive tendencies, warned him, 'Take care, Sir Sidney, to have no frigate-fighting!'[27]

Lying off Ushant, Smith spent the first days of 1795 disguising the *Diamond* as a French frigate and adapting his officers' uniforms likewise. Then, on the morning of 5th January, he steered for the harbour mouth astern of a large ship, also bound for Brest, and, rightly suspecting that this was a French warship, he hoisted French colours. But the tide was ebbing strongly and the wind was easterly, so neither ship could make way. The French ship anchored, as did the British frigate, both with the intention of approaching the port on the next tide. But Smith did not wait until morning; as soon as the tide turned, he weighed anchor and sailed past the bigger ship, seeing by the

* a debtors' prison in London

light of the moon that she was indeed a French ship of the line. Ahead, he saw two more ships at anchor, one of which he could see was a French frigate. He decided to pass them, too, to be lying off Brest at daybreak so that he could make a quick, close observation of the port before running for the safety of the open sea. He passed near to the two enemy ships, 'observing the precaution in passing to give all orders in a low tone of voice that the enemy might not hear us speak English'.

As the sun came up he saw that no more enemy warships lay in the roads off the harbour. His mission completed, he put his helm over to run for the harbour mouth. His sudden change of course alerted the captain of a French corvette, bound for the port, and he immediately put about, making signals of interrogation. The two French warships at anchor took alarm at this, hoisted their topsail yards and began to make sail. Ahead, the ship of the line was also under way and steering a course to cut off the *Diamond*. Smith continued in his report:

> My situation was now extremely critical ... I saw by the course of the line-of-battle ship had taken, her intention to cut me off in my passage between her and the rocks so that I could not effectuate it. There seemed no alternative but to remove their alarm ... I accordingly steered directly within hail of this ship ... and, to avoid being questioned in any way that might embarrass me to answer, I began the conversation in French with the captain, who was in the stern gallery.

It was apparent that the French ship was partly disabled and pumping out water from leaks, so Smith declared that he had come to offer assistance, and realizing that his ship would not be recognized, added that he belonged to a French squadron in Norwegian waters. The captain thanked him but said he had men enough to man the pumps; indeed, Smith could see them 'crowded on the gunwale and quarter, looking at our ship'.

Only the enemy ship – named *Le Caton*, as he was told by her captain – now stood between him and the open sea. The *Diamond* now lay across her stern – the position necessary to rake the ship from stern to bow with a broadside through the windows of her stern cabins – and his guns were double-shotted, their crews closed up. Smith considered:

> I should be able to preserve my present position under her stern so as to rake her repeatedly ... My guns were, of course, ready

pointed but I reflected it was useless to fire, since I could not hope to secure the ship and carry her off from the two others ... The utmost we could do would be to give her a most destructive raking fire and sail away; this my men were both ready and eager for but I overruled the proposition, considering the carnage must have been shocking from the effect of our guns, double-loaded, enfilading a crowded ship within half a pistol-shot; and conceiving it both unmanly and treacherous to make such havoc while speaking in friendly terms and offering our assistance.[28]

Smith's two pursuers, seeing that he had stopped to hail *Le Caton* had hauled away, so with a polite farewell to the French captain, he, too, made sail and steered for the harbour mouth and the open sea.

By a combination of Smith's enthusiasm and his relatively humane imposition of discipline, with flogging kept to a minimum, his frigate had now become what was described as 'one of the most perfect specimens of a vessel of war in the British Navy'. His expected orders arrived in March and they were exactly what he had wanted. He was to command an inshore squadron consisting of the *Diamond*, two smaller frigates, a sloop, eighteen gunboats, six fireships, a floating battery and two tenders. His task would be to harry French coastal shipping and support counter-revolutionaries when and where he could. There followed, throughout the year, a succession of brisk little actions in which he put his preaching into practice, sending his gunboats inshore after French ships that had supposed they could shelter from the British frigates within shoals along the coasts of Normandy and Brittany, while others were driven on to the rocks.

In September, he chased a corvette and reported that:

she endeavoured to elude our pursuit in the labyrinth of rocks before Treguier but the attempt proved fatal to her as she struck on the Roenna and soon filled and fell over; we ceased our fire immediately and set our boats to save the crew ... We were not fortunate enough to save more than nine; they reckon about twenty perished, besides the captain, who was washed off the wreck a few minutes before our boats reached them; her name was *L'Assemblée Nationale* ...[29]

When other ships were driven to take shelter under the shore batteries at La Hougue he pressed home his attack under fire from red-hot shot and in his despatch took the unusual step of naming a rating who had been killed, Thomas Gullen – 'one of the best quartermasters in the ship'.[30]

The fighting ashore, which had broken out fiercely again, was savage, no quarter being given or expected. In June, Admiral Warren escorted a 'secret expedition' of some 6,000 royalist troops to be landed in Quiberon Bay to support the counter-revolution. This was covered by the main fleet under Admiral Lord Bridport, and Smith was ordered to make diversionary attacks along the coast to the east. It was an ugly war as became apparent as soon as landing parties went ashore. The *chouans*, as the indigenous royalists called themselves, were being recruited and armed but were under no illusions as to the brutality ahead. One surgeon's mate from the British 'seventy-four' *Robust*, noted in his diary, 'The Chouans flocked from all quarters to join the emigrants army; brought in a party of Republican prisoners and put them to death. One of the head Republicans, an officer, was hung on the ensign staff.[31] Such entries became routine. But the expedition ended in disaster and, less than a month later, the survivors re-embarked and returned to Portsmouth; 700 of the *émigré* soldiers, who had surrendered and could not be evacuated, were executed by the republicans.

The harrassing continued throughout the autumn and winter and, in March 1796, Smith led one of the most dashing attacks of all, following a convoy of nine French ships into the harbour of Herqui on the Brittany coast, which was defended by heavy guns mounted on the rocky headland commanding the approaches. His men stormed the batteries and spiked the guns while others burned the ships in the harbour. The lieutenant, who had led the assault up the cliffs, was sent to London with Smith's despatch to the Admiralty and the captured French colours to present to the Board. It was the sort of neat, melodramatic action that thrilled the British public and, the London theatre being quick to respond to popular news, an operetta called *The Point at Herqui, or British Bravery Triumphant* was hastily written and performed at Covent Garden.

A month later, the *Diamond* was cruising in the Baie de la Seine in search of more targets of opportunity. Her captain was now well known to the French, who had nicknamed him – or so he liked to say – 'The Lion of the Sea'. They knew he had been the fire-raiser at Toulon who spoke perfect French and was therefore probably, at best, close to the royalist *émigrés* in England and, at worst, himself a spy. His name was known in Paris, too. The Reign of Terror seemed to have ended with the execution of Robespierre and his henchmen in the summer of 1794 and, just over a year later, Napoleon Bonaparte, whose tactical insight had brought about the fall of Toulon, had snuffed out a counter-revolution in the streets of Paris with his grape-shot. But the war continued with even greater ferocity and that colonel was now the foremost soldier in the Directory – the governing body that had succeeeded the Convention – as Commander-in-Chief of the Army of the Interior. With his leadership combining discipline with revolutionary zeal in the French Army, all Europe – including the Brtitish Isles – felt at risk as, indeed, it was.

On 18th April, the *Diamond* was in sight of the bluffs above the port of Le Havre at the mouth of the Seine, the route by which Smith proposed striking at the enemy's capital. There was little wind, so he decided to make a reconnaissance in the ship's boats and, accordingly, after dark, these were manned and armed and, as several of the frigate's officers were either sick or had been left ashore, Smith himself took command. His particular objective was the *Vengeur*, a privateer lugger, which had successfully preyed upon British shipping in the Channel, boarding ships in convoy at night but continuing under British escort, without suspicion until they could make a dash for a French port. Two days before, while cruising off Le Havre, he had sighted her at anchor in the inner roads but the water was too shallow to allow the frigate to run alongside for boarding so he determined to 'cut her out'.

With Smith in the boats were three lieutenants, six midshipmen and twenty-four ratings; the officers armed with their swords; the others with cutlasses and pikes and pistols and tomahawks thrust into their belts; in case the enemy ship could not be sailed away and had to be burned, sulphur matches were taken aboard. There were two unusual members of the raiding party: one was Smith's secretary, Midshipman John Wright, who seemed oddly old and sophisticated for that lowly rank, and a French *émigré*, a twenty-five-year-old lieutenant in a royalist regiment, who had survived the disaster at Quiberon the year before, François de Tromelin.

The four ships' boats, with Smith himself commanding from

a Thames wherry, pushed off into the darkness and, at half-past
two on the morning of the 19th, entered the roadstead off Le
Havre. It was a dark night with a light onshore breeze as they
pulled towards the anchorage with muffled oars. Then the mast
of the *Vengeur* was sighted and, when the boats were half a
pistol-shot from her side, a challenge was shouted from her
deck; the British seamen tugged their oars with all their
strength, the boats ran alongside and, led by Captain Smith,
they sprang aboard. There was a sharp, hand-to-hand fight on
deck; the French quickly surrendered and were hustled below
under hatches. In the cabin, Smith, sword in hand, found the
lugger's four officers, just woken by the noise and loading their
pistols, and he politely asked them to surrender – 'Vous pouvez
être assuré, Messieurs, que je ne suis pas ici sans force suffis-
ante pour vous faire soumettre, et je vous engage fortement de
rendre vos armes de suite.'[32] – which they did. Then it was
discovered that one of their men had cut the anchor cable and
that the lugger was drifting. Hurriedly, the British made sail
but the wind had dropped, the tide had begun to flood, the
only anchor to be found was a light and inadequate kedge, and
the *Vengeur* began to drift into the mouth of the Seine.

There was still no wind, so the *Diamond* could not move to
help and those on board could only watch the slow and
inevitable progress of events. The four boats took the lugger in
tow but could make little impression against the current, so
that at daybreak they were off Honfleur across the estuary from
Le Havre. The alarm was sounded ashore and a French
corvette, armed luggers and boats filled with soldiers were
rowed out from Le Havre. Realizing that fighting was
inevitable, Smith sent his prisoners ashore on parole and
prepared for hand-to-hand combat.

The first attack was beaten off but more armed boats were
sighted leaving Le Havre. From the deck of the *Diamond*,
Lieutenant Pearson, who had been left in command, watched
helplessly as the distant action began: the French boats circled
the outnumbered British and Pearson heard the sputter of
shooting, but there was no wind and the frigate's sails hung in
loose folds. The fighting was fierce – muzzle flashes in the
smoke, the plunging of oars and sudden clashing of cutlass
blades – but, despite Captain Smith's exhortations, it was
obvious that the outcome was only a matter of time. One British

seaman had already been killed and several wounded, and there was fear of what might happen next because rescue was out of the question. No quarter had become the custom in fighting ashore – although, at sea, chivalry usually survived – but this action was being fought between the banks of the Seine; the savagery of the civil war was a possible consequence. In any case, if François de Tromelin were captured he would certainly be shot.

After three-quarters of an hour, there was a lull and, as the enemy still barred their escape, Smith ordered his boats to close up and addressed their crews. He told them that rescue was impossible and that the only course open to them was to surrender. However, Lieutenant de Tromelin would be doomed if he were recognized, so he had to pass himself off as Smith's servant, John Bromley, a French-Canadian. Smith himself later described events:

> My brave fellows collected round me, on the enemy's closing on us, swearing to die fighting by me ... the servants behaved admirably and the boys acted like men ... the enemy prepared to board us, sword in hand, refusing us quarter with insults and imprecations. Our firm posture checked them and my harangue to their chief relented their fury and turned their resentment into admiration. It was acknowledged that we could not get away and that further resistance would not avail but we were determined to die with arms in our hands if they would not give us quarter and this determination saved us.[33]

So Smith again shouted across to the commander of circling French boats. This proved to be Captain Le Loup of the corvette, to whom Captain Sir Sidney Smith surrendered his sword.

CHAPTER THREE

'Fortune's wheel makes strange revolutions'

WHEN THEY SAW the victorious French tow the captured *Vengeur* and the British wherry into Le Havre, the watchers on the deck and in the rigging of the *Diamond* were not unduly worried. If Captain Smith had not been killed, they were confident that he could be exchanged for one of several French captains held captive by the British. So a boat flying a white flag of truce was sent into the harbour to enquire after their captain and his men. They were received with formal courtesy and waited for a written reply from the commanding officer at Le Havre addressed to the frigate's senior officer. This announced that four British seamen had been killed in the action and one officer wounded, a midshipman hurt in hand and thigh. As for the captain, 'Mr. Sidney Smith est prisonnier de guerre et traité avec tous les regards dus à son grade ... Soyez persuadé, monsieur, que vos frères d'armes trouveront dans la générosité Francaise tous les soins dus à leur état et à leur situation.'[1]

Lieutenant Pearson, who was now in command of the *Diamond*, was relieved and wrote a report on the affair to the Secretary of the Admiralty. However, next day, he had to write a postscript to Lord Spencer telling him that he had been told by the skipper of a French fishing boat that Captain Smith had been 'ordered off to Rouen, most likely on his way to Paris'.[2] This was ominous because the Directory knew that Smith had been responsible for burning half their fleet at Toulon and General Bonaparte had even nicknamed him, 'Capitaine de Brulot'. Despite the fact that he had been a British naval officer acting under his admiral's written orders, he had been on half-pay, held no official appointment in the fleet and had been condemned as an arsonist.

The worst fears were realized when, some days later, copies of the Paris newspaper *Moniteur Universal* reached London. This reported:

At last we have got Sidney Smith, this English incendiary who burnt our ships at Toulon, the same man who had tried on several occasions to set fire to the buildings and ships in Le Havre and promised Pitt to reduce our ports and our fleet to a heap of ashes. While his ship, the *Diamond*, was moored in the estuary after putting the *Vengeur* out of action, she was attacked by a number of small vessels which had been sent to intercept her and obliged to surrender with her captain and crew. That Smith intended to set fire to the town is beyond doubt for a stick of sulphur was discovered only a few months ago under one of our frigates under construction in the shipyard ... As we have not got in Le Havre a severe enough prison in which to keep him, we are sending him under strong escort to Rouen, pending the decision of the judiciary in respect of all the attempts of this monster. We understand that the Directory has just given orders for him to be taken to Paris as an incendiary.[3]

As Smith sat in the coach, rocking down the road to Paris, he could reflect on one piece of good fortune. All but two of those captured had been thrown into the local prison before being marched off to the fortresses where prisoners of war were held. However, these two were the most important: Midshipman Wright and his servant John Bromley, alias the royalist officer, François de Tromelin, whose true identity remained concealed from their captors.

John Wesley Wright was, at twenty-six, old for a midshipman and this might have suggested that he was not quite what he seemed. A few months before, Smith had noted the quiet, dark-haired young man as having potential as an intelligence officer, because of his courage, flair for languages, skill with a pencil and his worldly, cosmopolitan air. He was of Lancastrian ancestry but had been brought up in Minorca, where his parents had been living. At the age of ten he had, apparently, been nominally listed as an ensign in an infantry regiment, but had then been transferred to the Royal Navy as a volunteer to begin training to become an officer and, in 1780, took part in the defence of Gibraltar during the great siege. Returning to England, he continued his education for two years at school in Wandsworth, near London, and then found

work in a City merchant's office. This took him to Russia and
he lived in St Petersburg for five years, becoming fluent in
several languages, including Russian and French. On returning to England, he was introduced to Sir Sidney Smith, who
recognized abilities he particularly valued and persuaded him
to resume his naval career, joining the *Diamond* as captain's
secretary and rated as a midshipman until he could take the
lieutenant's exam.

Through the gates of Paris clattered the cavalcade and its
cavalry escort and through the narrow streets of tall, leaning
houses until they halted outside a grim, Gothic gateway. Smith
asked where he was being taken.

'A l'Abbaye, monsieur.'

'Ah!' he replied nonchalantly, 'c'est fameuse, je crois, dans
votre histoire, n'est ce pas?': This was probably an oblique
reference to the September massacres of 1792 when more than
300 prisoners had been massacred there.

In the l'Abbaye de St Germain – as its name implied,
medieval monastic buildings converted into a prison – he,
Wright and Bromley were locked into dark, stone-walled
rooms. 'I was led to a gloomy room, round which I cast my eye,'
Smith was to recall, 'and was shortly left alone with a single
gendarme, whom I thus addressed, "*Nous sommes camarades a
present – co-prisonniers.*" '[4] Yet Smith was not unduly dismayed
for he expected an exchange with a French prisoner in England
to follow as a matter of course. So, on 30th April, he wrote a
cheerful letter to his father, saying that he was 'in better health
than usual from having nothing to fatigue me and in excellent
spirits, finding amusement in the novelty of my situation; the
whole is like a very interesting play, "the characters, dresses
and scenery entirely new"; but whether tragedy or comedy, I
cannot yet pronounce ...' He declared that his treatment had
been 'very generous', concluding, 'Separation and confinement
is all we have to complain of but the fortune of war is imperi-
ous and I learn patience every day by the practice.'[5]

Meanwhile, Smith used his enforced leisure to write letters,
one of which was to the Secretary of the Admiralty in the hope
of releasing somebody else from prison. One of his seamen in
the *Diamond*, Patrick Begley, who had been court-martialled for
desertion and imprisoned and his former captain now put
forward extenuating circumstances, asking that, having served

part of his sentence, he should now be released; the recommendation was acted upon.

Conditions in l'Abbaye were not rigorous, for it had not been designed as a prison and Smith and Bromley were allowed to share a sitting-room overlooking the street, while Wright remained in solitary confinement. It was while staring out of the window that they became aware of an unusually brightly lit window high in a house opposite. They then noticed that at the back of the room within, a sheet had been rigged like a screen, where it could not be seen from the street, and that the light came from a projector, or 'magic lantern'. As they watched, this began to throw large letters on to the screen and these spelled the words: *Qui êtes vous?*

Then the letters began to be projected in alphabetical order and were then slowly repeated. In order to reply, Smith tore a page from an old prayer-book he had found in the room and, with soot from the fireplace, drew on it a large letter A. He held this to the window while pointing at the top of one of the bars. He then drew each letter of the alphabet, indicating which section of the bars represented it until he had completed a simple system of signalling; if seen from below, he could pretend to be swatting flies. At daylight next day, they saw three young women in the room, who looked across to them and smiled. Having no idea who they were – they might equally be royalist sympathizers, or *agents provocateurs* – Smith nicknamed them after the Muses: Thalia, Clio and Melpomene. The two men discussed messages to be transmitted and decided that the first essential, if a chance of escape should arise, would be money. As the only friend they knew in Paris was the Sardinian ambassador to London, the Chevalier de Revel, who had commanded the Sardinian troops at Toulon, and who was thought to be visiting the city, they signalled, 'We want money. Ask Revel.'[6] Soon afterwards a doctor called to examine Smith and, while he was taking his pulse, slipped a roll of gold coins into his palm.

Arrangements for the exchange of officers could be expected to take several weeks. Hopes of this appeared to be well founded because the Admiralty, without waiting for negotiations to begin, sent a French officer of equivalent rank, a Captain Bergeret, late of the frigate *Virginie*, to Paris on parole in the expectation that Smith would be returned; but the

Directory was not interested in an exchange and Captain Bergeret returned to imprisonment in England.

It had now become apparent that he was not considered a prisoner of war. There were two reasons for this. One was that his captors at Le Havre had sent a report to Paris, claiming that their prisoner had been trying to repeat his fire-raising at Toulon, as seemed proven by finding a stick of sulphur in his boat. The other was that he was known to speak French and to be on friendly terms with French *emigrés* in England. The British and their allies were employing a twin strategy against France: trying to combine their own naval and military operations with aiding the internal counter-revolution, by means of subsidies, arms and attempts to subvert republican officers and officials. Working with the royalist espionage organization, the *Agence de Paris*, the British spymaster, William Wickham, could employ the Royal Navy to ferry royalist agents to and from France. To Smith's captors, it seemed self-evident that he and his secretary, Wright – both French-speakers, who had been serving on the Channel coast where counter-revolutionaries had been active – must have been involved.

The French had been quick to spread reports of Smith's complicity in espionage, which were repeated in London newspapers, eager for sensational news. On 7th May, the *Morning Post* reported that 'The Directory *affirmed* that as Sir Sidney *was taken out of his Uniform*, he could *not be considered as a prisoner of war*, but as a Spy and therefore not to be exchanged.' The *Anti-Jacobin* sprang to his defence, claiming that the Directory itself had acknowledged Smith to have been captured armed and in uniform; he was therefore considered eligible for exchange. That report was, however, to prove as illusory as the other.

The reality of his predicament became clear when Smith was formally charged under the Act of Accusation with attempting to set fire to the town and docks of Le Havre. The charge was signed by Paul de Barras, a member of the Directory – the ruling *junta* of five Directors – and this could amount to a death warrant. Then orders arrived for Smith, Wright and Bromley to be transferred to another prison, the Temple, which was used for housing condemned prisoners; the royal family had been imprisoned there and King Louis himself had left there for the guillotine set up at the gates of his own palace. Was he, too, about to be put on trial for his life? It began to seem probable;

indeed, Bonaparte was to recollect that, at that time, there were
plans to put Smith on trial and execute him. Another possibility was that their signals to the Muses across the street had been
seen and that they were being transferred to a more secure
prison.

The Temple was a sinister place, a medieval *donjon*, the core
of a fortress built by the Knights Templars in 1222 as their
stronghold in Paris. Now, as a prison, the tall, square keep with
towers at each corner, capped by conical cupolas, stood in a
compound surrounded by a high wall, measuring about a
hundred and seventy-five yards by a hundred. Within, the
stone walls, narrow passages and spiral staircases and small,
deeply sunk windows could cow the most optimistic arrivals.
Smith was taken to a room that had been occupied by the royal
family two years before and told that he was to be held *en secret*,
in solitary confinement, although John Bromley would still be
allowed to attend him. Once a day, he would be allowed to
walk in the courtyard under armed guard when it was clear of
other prisoners.

Aware that he was in far deeper trouble than he had
thought, Smith wrote to the 'Citizen Minister for the Navy',
insisting that he had been a naval officer carrying out orders
and maintaining that it was 'the usage of war to burn what
cannot be taken' and that he should not be treated as an arsonist. Soon afterwards, he heard that a French naval officer,
Admiral Richery, had just returned to Rochefort after a
successful raid on Newfoundland, where he had burned much
of the fishing fleet in their harbours. So, after seven months'
imprisonment, he again wrote to the minister complaining
that, 'Had Admiral Richery been captured by my compatriots
during, or returning from his so well prepared and daringly
executed expedition, I ask whether you really think, in all
good faith, that he would have been detained in solitary
confinement in the Tower of London?'[7] The letter had no
effect, for no other reason, perhaps, than the fact that he was
a prisoner of the Department of Justice and not the Ministry
of Marine. His imprisonment continued as rigorously as
before.

In July, Smith had written to Windham, the Secretary of State
for War, asking his help in arranging an exchange. Six weeks
later he received an encouraging reply, saying that he was in

touch with those within France who might be able to help. In
October, he wrote a grateful acknowledgement, saying how
surprised he was that:

> a letter of that nature can have passed the Jaws of all the
> Cerberuses and the Eyes of all the Arguses by which I am
> surrounded, so as to arrive in the innermost recesses of this Tomb
> *with the seal unbroken* is a matter of mystery to me. It is useless and
> would be impolitic to enquire into that too much. Your ability in
> contriving to find such able and faithful agents calls forth my
> admiration ...'

He said that he had not been ill-treated and 'the very strict-
ness of the orders given regarding me ... procures the
respectful attentions of all who are about me.' But the Temple
was getting crowded with a new influx of royalist prisoners
and the resulting 'noise and noxious effluvia have taken away
my chief consolation', which had been 'tranquillity and good
air'. But guards could be friendly, as he wrote, 'I have, however,
occasionally had a sly conversation with the officers, who
compose my guard, some of whom, having been prisoners in
England and under no obligations to the hospitable inhabitants
of Hampshire, made it a point to testify their gratitude and to
mark their disapprobation of the difference that has been
shown in my case.'[8]

That Windham had an agent able to pass such letters to Smith
was suggested in his next letter when he gave the latest news of
the war. Telling Smith of successes by the Austrians against
France and that Spain had declared war on Britain, he added
that his letter might reach him 'before any free communication
may be allowed'. Finally, he wrote that the Earl of Malmesbury
was engaged in negotiations with the Directory in Paris and
had been instructed to demand 'an explanation of the causes of
your detention ... an outrage so contrary to the laws of war',
adding, 'I cannot entertain a doubt that your present close
confinement must soon end and that before long you may even
be restored to that service which has suffered very sensibly by
your absence.'[9]

But soon it became apparent that Windham was over-
optimistic. In December, Smith answered Windham's next letter,
which, he wrote obliquely, had arrived 'by the return of the
same conveyance', no doubt secret. He was grateful for Lord

Malmesbury's efforts, of which he knew, and those of Henry
Swinburne, who was also in Paris, leading a British mission to
discuss the exchange of prisoners. Two of the Muses, who
proved to be daughters of a Madame Launey, visited
Swinburne but, fearing that involvement with Smith's case
might jeopardize a more general exchange of prisoners, he
refused to see them; however, they left notes for him from
Smith hidden in walnut shells and this prompted Swinburne to
give them money to be smuggled into the prison. Finally he
agreed to call on them at the lodgings, to which they had now
moved, up four flights of stairs in a house in the Rue de la
Corderie opposite the Temple. They proved to be far less
prepossessing than he had imagined but he had, in any case,
decided that he could do no more to help, refusing a suggestion
from London that all exchanges of prisoners be delayed until
Smith was released. Smith was magnanimous in his letter to
Windham, simply saying of Swinburne and Malmesbury that
'their strenuous representations have not, however, as yet
produced the smallest amelioration in my situation.'[10] Now his
only allies were in London, and they were few: Windham
himself and the politician Edmund Burke. As for the Admiralty,
Lord Spencer had offered to exchange 1,000 French prisoners
for Smith but the Directory had demanded 4,000. Although Sir
Sidney had offered to capture them all back within a week
when released, the Admiralty had refused the offer and one
member of the Board, Rear-Admiral Sir William Young, spoke
of Smith bringing his troubles on himself through 'impru-
dence'. 'A good preparation for abandoning a man',[11] noted
Windham in his diary.

There seemed to be no alternative but to make the best of
imprisonment. Smith's cell was high in what he called 'the
Tower of the Temple' on a floor reserved for important state
prisoners; below were political prisoners and below them,
criminals. An advantage of being so high was that, from his
small, heavily barred window, he could see over the perimenter
wall to the tall, huddled houses of Paris beyond. To his amaze-
ment he again saw a brightly lit window where the Muses
reappeared and resumed their signalling. Smith and de
Tromelin, acting as his Canadian servant, Bromley, were still
separated from Wright, who remained in confinement. De
Tromelin had been acting the part of the servant with style,

dressed as a 'buck-skinned, booted and spurred English jockey' and amusing the gaolers with his attempts to speak French. Indeed, it was noted:

> he acted so well, that he almost overdid his part; for, in frater-
> nising with the turnkeys he would sometimes get drunk with
> them and, in making love to the Governor's daughter, he
> promised her marriage ... The prisoners seemed as if they were
> acting a comedy ... Sir Sidney repeatedly scolded this jockeyfied
> emigrant with great unction and gravity; and so well did they
> both play their parts that Sir Sidney confesses that he sometimes
> ceased to simulate and found himself forgetting the friend and ...
> rating his valet soundly.[12]

Now the two of them decided that they must take a risk and try to contact de Tromelin's wife, who was in France; some days later, she showed herself at the Muses' window. The next move was for de Tromelin to meet her. Although she could watch from the window as her husband walked in the prison courtyard, it would be too risky for her to visit the Temple under any pretext, particularly as she was exceptionally beautiful and might be recognized by royalist prisoners. But the Governor, Citizen Lasne, and his wife, had taken a liking to John Bromley and agreed to his going on errands from the prison on parole because in his Newmarket jockey's dress he would not pass unnoticed in the streets of Paris if he tried to escape. So it was easy for François de Tromelin and his wife to meet briefly. However, sooner or later, they would be seen together and he appeared to be so much her social inferior that a cover-story had to be agreed: that Madame de Tromelin was a single girl madly in love with Captain Smith, of whom she had read, and was bribing his servant to take love letters to him.

This was only one of several schemes afoot. Through the Muses' signalling and messages from Madame de Tromelin, Smith heard that General Louis de Frotté, the leader of the *chouans* in north-west France, was trying to help him and that Colonel Louis-Edmond Picard de Phélippeaux, an engineer officer who had been on the staff of the Prince de Condé, and who, after being captured in the Vendée, had been rescued on the eve of his execution, was now in Paris to organize the escape of three royalists also in the Temple. With him were the two agents who had effected his own escape: Boisgirard, who had been engaged as a dancer at the Opera, and Hyde de Neuville, a descendant of the great Earl of Clarendon,* who had taken the *nom de guerre* of Charles l'Oiseau. The latter had agreed to include Smith, Bromley and Wright in the escape from the Temple.

L'Oiseau's courier was a girl, who regularly visited the prison on various pretexts, and she had agreed to help on one condition: 'I will serve Sir Sidney Smith with great pleasure because I believe that the English Government intend to restore Louis XVIII to the throne. But if the commodore is to fight against France, and not for the King of France, Heaven forbid that I should assist.'[13] Then the plan ran into difficulties when one of the three royalist prisoners decided that, as he had only been sentenced to one year's imprisonment, he would prefer to serve that time rather than run the risk. The other two agreed to continue but the escape was suddenly cancelled without any explanation; Smith himself thought that it might have been betrayed by one of the three.

L'Oiseau planned a new escape for which a tunnel would be dug from the house where the Muses signalled, beneath the street and under the prison wall. The royalist girl had lodgings in the house and l'Oiseau let it be known that he was in love with her and that was the reason for his frequent visits. In fact, he was busy tunnelling. As he drew closer to the outer wall of the Temple, he realized that breaking through, or tunnelling beneath, required a professional mason. One was recruited by Madame de Tromelin but was not told of the nature of the work until he reached the cellar. Realizing the risk he would run, he bravely agreed to work on condition that his family were provided for should he be arrested.

When the tunnel reached the outer wall of the prison, the mason had to chip at the stone and, to drown the noise, a little girl of seven was recruited to parade up and down the street above beating a tin drum. The exercise yard within the walls was at a lower level than the road outside and, as the final stones were dislodged, one rolled into the yard almost at the feet of a sentry. The alarm was sounded and the tunnel discovered but when they searched the cellar, all they found were

* His father had fled to France after the defeat of the Jacobite rebellion at Culloden and settled at Sancerre.

heaps of excavated earth and *tricolore* cockades for the escaped prisoners to wear in their hats.

Governor Lasne visited Smith in his cell and remarked, 'Commodore, your friends are desirous of liberating you and they only do their duty. I also am doing mine in watching you more narrowly.'[14] Soon after Smith was invited to dine with him and the latter noticed how his guest was looking longingly out of the open window to the busy street outside. Noting the governor's worried look, Smith said, 'I know what you are thinking of; but fear not. It is now three o'clock. I will make a truce with you till midnight; and I give you my word of honour, until that time, even were the doors open, I would not escape. When that hour is passed, my promise is at an end and we are enemies again.'

'Sir,' replied Lasne, 'your word is a safer bond than my bars and bolts: till midnight, therefore, I am perfectly easy.' After dinner, the two men walked to the door, Lasne opened it and said, 'Commodore, the boulevard is not far off. If you are inclined to take the air, I will conduct you thither.'[15] Later, when Smith had returned from his walk, the governor continued:

> If you were under sentence of death, I would permit you to go out on your parole because I should be certain of your return. Many very honest prisoners, and I myself among the rest, would not return in the like case. But an officer, and especially an officer of distinction, holds his honour dearer than his life. I know this to be a fact, commodore, therefore I should be less uneasy if you desired the gates always to be open.

Later, on reflection, Smith agreed: 'My keeper was right. Whilst I enjoyed my liberty, I endeavoured to lose sight of the idea of my escape and I should have been averse to employ, for that object, means that occurred to my imagination during my hours of liberty.'[16]

But that liberty was not to last. Governor Lasne was replaced by a stern Jacobin named Boniface and Smith's captivity became as rigorous as it had ever been. However, on 1st February, 1797, the threat of trial on a capital charge was suddenly lessened when his custody was transferred from the Department of Justice to the ministry of Marine. Soon afterwards, the Minister of Marine, Pléville le Pelley, visited him in prison and, in the course of conversation, Smith asked him for a definition of liberty. As the minister floundered, Smith contin-

ued, 'I am not surprised that you cannot define it but I, who
grew up with the concept of liberty with my mother's milk,
have no difficulty in doing so – it is the absence of constraint.'[17]
The minister could only agree.

One change did arise from the meeting: Smith was able to
insist that both Wright and Bromley could be included in the
list of prisoners of war eligible for exchange. Five months later,
the order arrived stating that: 'John Bromley, servant of Sir
Sidney Smith, should be removed from the Temple, to be
conducted from brigade to brigade to the port of Dunkirk, and
from there across to England.'[18] De Tromelin said that he would
never leave Smith, who insisted that he comply because he
would be more use in achieving his own escape outside than
within. Wright was not on the list but, in any case, he let it be
known that he would not leave without Captain Smith.

When the time came for John Bromley to leave, he bade an
emotional farewell to the gaoler's lovelorn daughter, and Smith
gave him money and a certificate of faithful service. The royalist officer then left Paris under escort of republican soldiers
and, on 22nd July, embarked at Dunkirk for England. Some
weeks later, Smith received a letter from his father saying that
Bromley had been to see him and his estranged wife and that
he had been paid eighteen months' wages. This was to cover
the plan for de Tromelin to return immediately to France,
where his wife still waited in Paris.

Life became slightly easier. Now that Bromley had gone,
Wright was allowed to keep Smith company. Meanwhile,
Boniface, too, was coming to like Smith. One reason for the
governor's trust was that Smith had been approached by a
fellow-prisoner – an *agent provocateur* – with a plan to escape,
telling him that at a certain hour he had arranged for doors to
be left unbolted. Although suspecting him, Smith agreed but, at
the appointed time, looked into the yard and found his suspi-
cions confirmed by the sight of a file of soldiers loading their
muskets in the yard below. Smith and Wright went to bed
instead and asked the governor to remove the prisoner for
being a disruptive influence. On another occasion, a riot developed in the streets around the prison and Boniface gave Smith
and Wright loaded pistols because, he feared, the mob might
try to massacre royalist prisoners; in the event, the great doors
held and the Englishmen returned the pistols.

Then, on 5th December 1797, they heard sounds of gunfire and were told it was the firing of salutes to welcome General Bonaparte back from his victorious campaign in Italy; having acquired the Low Countries, the Rhineland and the Adriatic islands in exchange for Venice, he had finally signed a peace treaty with the Austrians at Campo Formio in October. Thinking that he might react chivalrously towards an old adversary from the battle of Toulon, Smith wrote him a letter asking him to persuade the Directory to treat him as a prisoner of war. Boniface, perhaps hoping that he himself might benefit by offering his services as a courier, agreed to take the letter to the general's house in the Rue de la Victoire, so re-named after his recent victories. But General Bonaparte refused to receive either Boniface, or his prisoner's letter.

So Smith wrote another letter, perhaps in pencil, this one on a wooden shutter of his window in the hope that it would be read, repeated and would eventually reach the ears of General Bonaparte. He wrote in French:

> One has to admit that Fortune's wheel makes strange revolutions but, before it can be truly called a revolution, the turn of the wheel must be complete. Today you are as high as you can be but I do not envy you your happiness because I have a still greater happiness and that is to be as low in Fortune's wheel as I can go, so that as soon as that capricious lady turns her wheel again, I shall rise for the same reason that you will fall.
>
> I do not write this to distress you but to bring you the same consolation that I have when you reach the point where I am. You will occupy this same prison – why not you as well as I? I did not expect to be shut up here, any more than you do now.
>
> In a partisan war it is a crime in the eyes of one's opponents to do one's duty honourably as you do today, and, in consequence, you embitter your enemies against you. No doubt you will reply, 'I do not fear the hatred I arouse in them. Has not the voice of the people declared for me?' That is well spoken. Sleep in peace. Before six months have passed, if not today, you will learn what the reward is for serving such masters, the reward for all the good you have done them. Pausanias wrote long ago, 'He who has placed all his hopes on the friendship of the public has never come to a happy end.'
>
> But, of course, I do not have to convince you that you will come here because to read these lines you must be here. I assume that you will have this room also because the gaoler is a good man: he gave me the best room and will do as much for you.[19]

It was a masterpiece of psychological warfare. Even if
Bonaparte did not hear of it immediately – and he was making
plans to leave Paris for the next act of his career of conquest –
the words had found their way into the newspapers. One day
he would hear them and they would surely haunt him. He was
already aware of the capture of *Capitaine de Brulot* but, in his
superstitious, Corsican way, he might never be able to rid
himself of the mocking eyes of the Englishman, even when they
were behind the bars of one of his own prisons.

Perhaps Smith aroused such strong feelings in the French
because there was something Gallic about him: his easy
command of their language; his Gascon swagger and gallantry;
his Mediterranean looks; and, of course, the fact that he was an
aggressively hostile Englishman. Royalist Frenchmen were
willing to die for him and several Frenchwomen who saw him
in the Temple are said to have fallen in love with him. One of
them, an adolescent girl from an aristocratic family, sent him
innumerable love letters, signed 'Isabella'. Some Jacobins, too,
were charmed by him but others wanted to kill him. During his
imprisonment, word was sent to the Admiralty that French
prisoners of war held at Portchester Castle, near Portsmouth,
had been overheard plotting to murder him in the Temple by
sending him a gift of poisoned tea.

Despite his defiance, the prospect seemed bleaker than ever.
The British Government seemed to have abandoned attempts
to negotiate his release and the three principal royalist prisoners in the Temple had gone – two deported to Guiana and the
third released – so that Charles l'Oiseau appeared reluctant to
risk his life to rescue two Englishmen.

However the governor and Madame Boniface had taken a
liking to Smith and, like Lasne, sometimes allowed him out for
the evening on parole. He would walk down the long Rue du
Temple and through the old aristocratic quarter of the Marais
towards the Seine. Occasionally, he would take Boniface out
drinking but, early, in 1798, when he was alone, or with John
Wright, he would sometimes dine at a small restaurant in the
Rue Honoré, run by a Madame Lequin, an Irishwoman married
to a Parisian. Another regular customer was a Scot named
Keith, who had been an associate of Harris, the agent for the
banker William Boyd, who had supported King Louis XVI
financially and, as a consequence, had had to leave France.

Keith's presence had attracted the attention of the counter-espionage police, who had positioned an informer there, an Englishman named Thompson, who had been allowed to continue teaching English in Paris on condition of performing this service. Smith was too conscious of the probable presence of such agents to betray unwittingly any hopes, or plans he might have, but a visiting ship's captain named Breenan was less discreet and Thompson's patience was rewarded by over-hearing him say that he had asked to find a ship to take Sir Sidney Smith to England.

The informer's report reached Pléville Le Pelley on 15th February as he was about to leave for a meeting at Lille, so he hurriedly sent the Chief of Police, Dondreau, an urgent warning:

> I have just received private information, my dear colleague, that Captain Sidney Smith, detained at the Temple, will escape within ten days; and that he is being allowed the privilege of going out to sup in town because he was seen yesterday evening in a house in the Rue Honoré at the corner of the Rue Richelieu. I beg you to order that a guard should be set to watch him and another to watch the gaoler and prevent him from granting leave of absence until I have been able to obtain more complete and certain information respecting this prisoner and his secretary.[20]

For Smith, after nearly two years of imprisonment, life had settled down into the boredom of routine, relieved by occa-sional outings into the streets of Paris but rarely by new plans for escape. For General Bonaparte, however, activity was intense. Since his return from Italy, he had been commanding the Army of England waiting on the Channel coast for an opportunity to cross and invade. But, increasingly, he had real-ized that this was beyond the capability of the *Grand Armée* while the British dominated the sea: it would have to be post-poned. But there was an infinitely more exciting idea with even greater possibilities. On 9th February, Charles de Talleyrand, the Directory's Minister for Foreign Affairs, had received a memorandum from the consul in Alexandria, Charles Magallon, proposing the annexation of Egypt.

Then, on the day that the police spy overheard Captain Breenan speak of finding a ship for Captain Smith's escape, Talleyrand presented the Directory with his own plan to invade Egypt, develop it as a French colony and open the way to India.

On the 23rd, General Bonaparte wrote his memorandum to the Directory admitting that the invasion of England was impossible at present and should be postponed, but proposing other options, among them the invasion of Egypt and the conquest of the East. This need only be a prelude to an attack on England, he stressed, and told the Directory, 'To go to Egypt, to establish myself there and found a French colony will take some months. But as soon as I have made England tremble for the safety of India, I shall return to Paris and give the enemy its death blow.'[21]

While Bonaparte was persuading the Directory – and they, for their part, were beginning to wonder whether such an adventure would also be advantageous in removing this over-ambitious general from Paris – Sidney Smith was told to be ready for escape. Then, early on the morning of 24th February 1798 a *fiacre* – a four-wheeled cab – drew up at the gates of the Temple. Ignoring sinister, cloaked figures with the watchful looks of police agents standing nearby, two men in uniform alighted – leaving a third within and fourth seated beside the driver – and stepped confidently up to the doors, knocked and were admitted to the prison. There, the two, who could be seen to be an officer in the Voltigeurs and a staff captain, presented a written order to the gaoler on duty, who told them to wait while it was shown to the governor. He read the order, which was written on the headed paper of the Ministry of Marine, dated 'Paris, 5th Floreal, Year VI' and bore the signature of Pléville Le Pelley. He read:

> The Minister of Marine and the Colonies to Citizen Boniface, Head Gaoler of the Temple.
>
> The Executive Directory having ordered by its decree of the 28th Ventose, enclosed herewith, that all English prisoners of war, without distinction of rank, should be collected into one prison, I charge you, Citizen, to consign forthwith to the bearer of the present order, Citizen Etienne-Armand Auger, Commodore Sidney Smith and Captain Wright, prisoners of war, to be transferred to the general prison of the Department of Seine-et-Marne, at Fontainebleau.
>
> You are enjoined, Citizen, to observe the greatest secrecy in the execution of the present order, of which I have informed the Minister of Police, in order to prevent any attempt to rescue the prisoners whilst on their journey.[22]

The two officers were kept waiting while Boniface considered the order, then sent for his clerk and ordered him to transcribe it in the prison register. Finally he emerged to tell them that he would comply. Smith, who was reading a novel in Spanish, and Wright, were summoned from their cells and faced the two officers, neither of whom they recognized. When told that they were being transferred to another prison, Smith asked where they were being taken. When told it was Fontainebleau, he suggested that, to save time, their clothes and books could be packed and forwarded later. 'It's not far,' Smith said to Madame Boniface, who had joined the others in the hall, 'You will come and see me, I hope?'[24] Then he presented money to several of the warders and shook hands, while Captain Auger signed for the two prisoners.

As they were about to leave, Boniface announced that, as an extra precaution, he would give the party an escort of six armed guards. At this, Auger declared, 'Citizens, between soldiers the word of honour is enough. Commodore, you are an officer; so am I. Give me your parole and we can do without an escort.'

'Sir,' replied Smith, 'I swear on my honour to accompany you wherever you wish to take me.'[25]

That was enough for Boniface and he shook hands with his prisoners as they were led out to the carriage. As the cab door was opened for him, Smith looked up at the driver and the man beside him. Under the broad brim of the man's hat, he met the eyes of François de Tromelin. Then the door was shut, Boniface waved and they were away. Then and only then did he see the face of the fourth figure in the corner of the carriage; it was Colonel Phélippeaux. He told him that 'Captain Auger' was Boisgirard, the dancer and royalist agent, and the Voltigeurs captain was one of Phélippeaux's officers, Le Grand de Palluau. The watching figures around the prison gates had all been royalist agents, Hyde de Neuville, Sourdat, Laban and Viscovich, a Venetian, all of them armed, ready to rescue Smith and Wright by force if the trick failed.

'Drive faster!'[26] shouted Le Grand. The driver cracked his whip, the *fiacre* lurched forward and turned a corner too sharply, hit a bollard, broke a wheel, slewed into a fruit stall and hit a child. A shouting crowd surrounded them, calling for the police. This was no time or place to linger and Phélippeaux threw open a door and told the others to follow him. As they scrambled out, pushed through the crowd and ran, Le Grand turned and threw the coachman a coin – realizing, too late, that it was not a republican coin but a gold, royalist *louis*.

They ran through narrow streets towards the river and the bridges. All but one crossed, Boisgirard, who turned towards the Opera, where he was to dance that evening. On the far bank, they stopped in the Rue de l'Université and entered the house of the Clermont-Tonnerre family. There they found a group of men playing whist, amongst them General Frotté's aide-de-camp, de Lamberville, who explained all. When the French royalists had decided that Smith and Wright could not be rescued, Madame de Tromelin had changed their minds, saying that not only was Smith their ally but that he had saved her husband. Two principal royalists, the Comte de Rochecotte and General Frotté had given an escape plot high priority and de Lamberville had been told to organize the escape route, while Phélippeaux would arrange the actual escape. Viscovich, who was a spy working in the Ministry of Marine, was eager to avenge the destruction of the Venetian Republic by Bonaparte the year before. When his minister had been about to leave for Lille, he had signed several sheets of headed writing-paper in case there were urgent orders to be executed. He had been able to steal one of these and on this Phélippeaux had forged the order of transfer.

They stayed the night in the house in the Rue de l'Université in the company of a royalist politician, named Pasquier, who was in hiding. Early the next morning, Smith and Wright left with Phélippeaux on their journey to the coast. They had no passports or travel documents, and first there were guards and barriers to be passed – the most dangerous of which were at the gates of Paris. Phélippeaux had arranged that they would travel in a carriage, which had just arrived from Nanterre, furnished with a permit for the return journey. But, as the carriage drove through the narrow streets, it struck a wall and was slightly damaged, giving the passengers the excuse to get out before reaching the barrier. While the guards were examining the carriage and questioning the driver and postillion, they slipped past and boarded it once it had been allowed through.

On the road to Rouen, they listened for the clatter of pursuing hoofbeats, or a shouted challenge, but none came. Indeed, the governor of the Temple, content with duty done, was unaware of any escape. That day, he completed the written formalities, noting the transfer to Fontainebleau of 'Commodore Smith' and 'Captain Wright' in time for the weekly inspection by the prison authorities. The prison doctor, who had got to know Smith, was interested to hear of the transfer and when, on 2nd May, he happened to be dining with a senior prison official, he asked how Smith was faring in his new quarters. The official had not heard of his move and visited the Temple that evening to check. It seemed to be true enough, for the documentation seemed in order, but he was piqued that he had neither been consulted, nor informed. Then it struck him that the order for release might have been a forgery and Smith might have escaped, so next day he sent a messenger to Fontainebleau to confirm that he was there. When the messenger returned with the news that he was not, the alarm was raised.

Gallopers were sent to alert all the gates of Paris, checkpoints on the main roads and to the Channel ports, and descriptions of Smith and Wright were circulated. But the fugitives were already in Rouen, safe in a royalist's house while forged passports were prepared. After their years in prison, they longed to walk in the open and rashly did so only to find themselves faced with a barrier, where guards were demanding and examining identity papers. Having none, Smith whispered instructions to Wright, telling him to walk ahead and, when stopped, to start searching his pockets. This he was doing when Smith strolled up to the guard, nodded towards Wright and remarked, 'Je reponds pour le citoyen, je le connais.' 'C'est bien, citoyen,'[27] replied the guard and waved them both past the barrier.

Finally the passports were ready and, dressed in rough seamen's clothes, they crossed the Seine and made their way to Honfleur, where a small fishing boat had been chartered. Setting sail, they navigated the estuary, where they had fought the Le Havre gunboats two years before, and were soon on the open sea. It was only then that one of the Honfleur fishermen recognized the fugitives because he had once been on board the *Diamond* and was heard to whisper, 'Je connois celui-là, c'est l'Amiral Schmit.'[28] But Smith had always been generous to French fishermen, whom he regarded as a prime source of intelligence. Besides, he had given him a tot of rum, so nothing more was said. At last, out in the Channel, a ship's sails were sighted and then the British ensign. They ran alongside the *Argo*, a frigate of forty-four guns, commanded by Captain James Bowen, who welcomed them on board. On 7th May, they were off Portsmouth, went ashore and immediately set out for London.

Next morning, having arrived in the capital, Smith hammered on the door of the house where his mother was lodging, rushed up to her bedroom and introduced Colonel Phélippeaux to her as the man who had rescued him. Next he reported to the Admiralty and was at once received by Lord Spencer, who sent him along Whitehall to see the Prime Minister, William Pitt, and the Foreign Secretary, Lord Grenville, before his return ended triumphantly with an audience with the King. The impact of the news of the escape of 'The Lion of the Sea', as Smith had been called in the newspapers, was euphoric for there was a need for heroics after so much grim news over the past year when the French had triumphed everywhere.

In France, General Bonaparte heard the news of the escape at Toulon, where he had arrived – two days after Captain Smith had reached London – to supervise the embarkation of his expeditionary force of 55,000 men, there and at three other ports. His mind was filled with dreams of Egypt and eastern conquest, and he cannot have entertained any inkling of the possibility that Sidney Smith's warning, written on a shutter in the Temple prison, could have any relevance; indeed, he may not yet have heard of it. But his military secretary, Fauvelet de Bourrienne, was to write, 'Such a seemingly ordinary escape, yet one that was to wreck the most gigantic projects and the most audacious plans.'[29] Two days later, Bonaparte sailed for Egypt.

Meanwhile, Sir Sidney Smith was being lionized in London as the hero of the hour. The celebrated miniaturist Maria Cosway engraved a sketch of him as a prisoner in the Temple – by a French artist named Hennequin – showing him seated at a barred window, book in hand, turning his handsome, serene profile towards a shaft of sunlight. Apocryphal stories were attributed to him about ghastly scenes in the Reign of Terror, which had, in fact, ended almost two years before his capture. They might, however, have had some basis in fact. One told of him seeing aristocrats being led from the Temple on their way to the guillotine, filing through the hall towards the doors and the waiting tumbrils, amongst them 'a pretty and interesting girl';[30] as she passed a doorway, a gaoler whisked her inside and hid her in a well until she could make her escape.

There was even a vaguely romantic story of another sketched portrait of Sir Sidney in prison being sent to a girl, who was in love with him but identified only by the initials M.V. Attached was a long, sentimental verse:

> By your request, dear maid, I dare to send
> This faint resemblance of my gallant friend;
> Sketched in the Temple's gloomy prison walls:
> Where (deaf to justice and to honour's calls)
> Gallia's fell despots, prompted by their fears,
> Held him in bondage, full two ling'ring years;
> Elate with hopes to bend his constant heart,
> Now to harsh threats, now they resort to art.
> Mistaken wretches! Gallant Sidney's soul
> Was ne'er one instant under your control:
> Your arts and threats could only serve to bind
> The ties of honour stronger in his mind ...
> The fair recipient replied in similar style:
> What though nor arts nor terrors could control
> The dauntless energy of Sidney's soul
> Yet in the mimic semblance is exprest,
> The pensive languor of a captive's breast.
> Not so he looked, when terrible in war,
> His gallant deeds were bruited from afar! ...
> For, ah! how sweet in liberty to rove,
> Amid the greetings of a nation's love! ...
> In youth's gay morn he boasts a deathless name,
> And lives triumphant in the arms of Fame![31]

Much as Captain Smith was flattered by such sentiment, he had suffered two wasted years when even more flamboyant praise had been heaped upon other officers, amongst them Admiral Nelson. He was impatient to return to war and realize his ambitions, made more specific and personal by his prophecy to General Bonaparte.

CHAPTER FOUR

'Ardent in his imagination'

THE FEAR OF invasion that had followed Bonaparte's appointment to command the Army of England was replaced by fear of
the unknown. The *Grande Armée* had struck its camps along the
cliffs and downs across the Channel and was now at Toulon but
that did not necessarily mean that the danger was past. The
whole Mediterranean littoral was at risk because, for the past
year, the French had been in undisputed command of that sea,
or the enemy might burst through the Straits of Gibraltar into
the Atlantic and descend upon Ireland, which was simmering
with revolt. The entry of Spain into the war as an ally of France,
which Smith had heard about from Windham while in prison,
had tipped the balance against the British at sea and the fleet
had been withdrawn from the Mediterranean at the beginning
of 1797. True, Admiral Jervis had worsted the Spanish fleet off
Cape St Vincent soon after the evacuation, but the Royal Navy
suddenly seemed to have been hamstrung by serious mutinies
in ships at Spithead and at the Nore. Despite this, the British
had defeated the Dutch at Camperdown and, the mutinies
having been settled, were back in fighting trim. But the initiative remained with the enemy and their aggressive genius,
General Bonaparte.

News from the Mediterranean and its shores came either
from returning merchant ships, or from overland travellers. So
it was known that in French and Italian ports there were
enough transports and warships to take an invading army
anywhere in the world. On 27th April, *The Times* declared that
its destination was likely to be either Portugal, or Ireland; in
either case, the enemy could, and must, be held at the Straits of
Gibraltar. Or, they might be bound for Naples, Sicily, the

Levant, Egypt, or Constantinople, so it would not be enough to blockade the Straits. A squadron of warships strong enough to fight the fleet now known to be at Toulon – including many that Smith had been unable to burn in 1793 – should be sent into the Mediterranean on the armed reconnaissance, or to block their way into the eastern Mediterranean.

For some there was no doubt who would be chosen for this task and Lord Grenville wrote to the First Lord of the Admiralty, 'The officer to command such a squadron should be Sir Sidney Smith, not out of partiality for him, but thinking that his name is better known to both Russians and Turks, and his character better suited to act with them than many of the other officers, whom, possibly, you would prefer for a Channel cruise! ... As the work of the officer appointed would be largely diplomatic, it would be expedient to give him plenipotentiary powers.'[1] To Grenville, Smith seemed a natural choice because not only was he brave and intelligent, sophisticated and aggressive but, since his escape, he had become famous, and a national hero was needed to restore morale.

But Spencer had some doubts, for he was aware of the resentment amongst naval officers over Smith's apparent conceit and high-handed manner, his use of a foreign title and what they saw as his persistent self-publicizing; but he also knew of his contacts in Constantinople and that these could be used more directly. A squadron entering an almost landlocked, hostile sea, where it was vastly outnumbered by its enemies, required the highest possible standards of discipline and understanding between the captains and whichever officer was in command. So he turned to the other possible choice: Rear-Admiral Sir Horatio Nelson, whose initiative, imagination and leadership had also marked him out for the meeting of exceptional challenges.

At the time of Smith's capture, Nelson – then a captain – had been in the Mediterranean. After the taking of Corsica, where he had landed his ship's guns for the sieges of Bastia and Calvi, he had fought a celebrated duel with a huge French ship, the *Ça Ira*, making his name as a fighting captain. Commanding the last British ship to leave the Mediterranean, he had joined Jervis in time for what became known as the Battle of Cape St Vincent, where he had achieved national celebrity. The opposing fleets had met in mist and seeing that the Spanish were in two divisions and that the British, sailing on an opposite course, would not be able to turn in time to drive between them, he had acted without orders. Putting his helm over, he had steered for the head of the second Spanish division and fought it with his single ship, halting it in its track until Jervis and the main fleet could join the action. Not only had his ship survived, but he had boarded and taken one enemy ship and then led the boarders on to the deck of a second from the deck of the first, prompting admiring jokes about 'Nelson's patent bridge for boarding first-rates'.[2] For this he had been knighted and promoted rear-admiral, and his renown was such that when, five months later, he had led an attack on Tenerife, which had failed and cost him his own right arm, this was seen as a glorious failure rather than the disaster it was.

Like Sidney Smith, Horatio Nelson was as ambitious and hungry for fame as he was imaginative and daring. Both officers were not only admired but loved by their men; Nelson, who was learning tact and diplomacy to combine with his natural generosity, was also admired and loved by officers. The Spencers had recently entertained Sir Horatio and Lady Nelson to dinner and been charmed by them and by their apparent love for each other, Lady Spencer remarking that 'his attentions to her were those of a lover'.[3] Despite the loss of his arm and his conviction that his naval career was finished, the Admiralty decided otherwise, appointing him a subordinate commander to Jervis, the newly ennobled Earl St Vincent, in the Mediterranean Fleet. His flagship was to be the seventy-four-gun *Vanguard* and on 10th April 1798, she sailed for Lisbon, the base from which St Vincent was blockading the Spanish fleet in Cadiz. It was for the commander-in-chief to decide whether to take the bulk of his fleet into the Mediterranean himself, or to detach a powerful squadron. On 29th April, Spencer had written a long memorandum to St Vincent, giving him the latest news of the Toulon preparations and advising:

> The appearance of a British squadron in the Mediterranean is a condition on which the fate of Europe may at this moment depend ... If you determine to send a detachment into the Mediterranean, I think it is almost unnecessary to suggest to you the propriety of putting it under the command of Sir H. Nelson, whose acquaintance with that part of the world as well as his activity and disposition seem to qualify him in a peculiar way for that service.[4]

So, on the day Smith arrived in London from Paris – and several days before Grenville recommended him for the Mediterranean mission, unaware that the Admiralty had already made up its mind to choose another – Horatio Nelson sailed eastward from Gibraltar into the unknown. Under his command were three 'seventy-fours' with a promise of ten more to come, as soon as reinforcements arrived from England – and two frigates and a sloop, commanded by captains, whom St Vincent described as 'choice fellows'[5] and whom Nelson would soon call his 'band of brothers'.[6]

At the same time that Nelson sailed into the Mediterranean an extraordinary piece of intelligence reached London, that a large party of *savants* – an odd mixture of scientists and artists – had been reported as joining the mysterious French expeditionary force embarking at Toulon. It continued:

They have an immense amount of printing equipment, books, instruments, chemical apparatus, which suggests a very long absence. Among the books one notices above everything travels to the Levant, Egypt, Persia, India, Turkey, the Black Sea, the Caspian ... Greece. They are taking a dozen geographical engineers, military engineers, mathematicians, astronomers, chemists, doctors, artists and naturalists of every sort; two professors of Arabic, Persian and Turkish, and all have gone on board without knowing where they are going.

Guesses baffle everyone. Some say a conquest of Egypt and cutting the Isthmus of Suez is contemplated in order to undermine English commerce with India; others think the operation will be a long one because another fleet of boats in pieces has been shipped for transportation to Suez in order to have a fleet in the Red Sea in fifteen days; others again suppose that English possessions in India are to be attacked by land having crossed the desert ... with 30,000 men. It is said that Bonaparte will probably command the expedition.[7]

So thick a cloud of mystery overhung the preparations at Toulon that, despite some obvious clues, one scientist wrote home to say that their destination might equally well be Asia, Africa or America. The reality was even more bizarre than the report. When Bonaparte, accompanied by Josephine, reached Toulon on 9th May, both the inner and outer roadsteads and the sea beyond were thick with the masts of ships. There lay 13 ships of the line, 42 frigates and smaller warships and 130 transports. On board were some 17,000 troops, the same number of sailors and marines, 1,000 field guns and 700 horses. Nor was this all, for other convoys were preparing for sea at Genoa, Civita Vecchia and Ajaccio, bringing the total to nearly 400 ships and 55,000 men.

The solders were mostly from l'*Armée d'Italie*, conscripts who had been tempered by victory into a formidable force, motivated by revolutionary zeal and lust for plunder. They did not know where they were going, but Bonaparte addressed them in high, heroic style:

> Officers and soldiers, two years ago, I came to take command of you. At that time you were on the Ligurian coast in the greatest want, lacking everything, having even sold your watches to provide for your needs. There, all was given to you in abundance. Have I not kept my word? Well, let me tell you that I have not done enough yet for the fatherland, nor the fatherland for you. I shall now lead you into a country, where by your future deeds you will surpass even those that are now astonishing your admirers, and you will render to the Republic such services as she has a right to expect from an invincible army. I promise every soldier that, upon his return to France, he shall have enough to buy himself six acres of land![8]

Bonaparte and Josephine went on board Admiral Bruey's huge flagship, a ship of 120 guns, which had been in action with Nelson three years before when named the *Sans Culotte*; now, offering a clue to their destination, she had been renamed l'*Orient*. The admiral's cabins had been sumptuously furnished, one as a library, and there they met the bemused *savants*. There were 167 members of what was called the Commission on Sciences and the Arts, including 19 civil engineers, 16 cartographers, pharmacists, mathematicians, botanists, mineralogists, astronomers, architects, zoologists and archaeologists led by Gaspard Monge, a Jacobin scientist. After accompanying her husband on his inspections, Josephine returned ashore to wave farewell to the armada as it slowly assembled and sailed in a stiff breeze.

The same wind, as it strengthened into a gale and blew the huge convoy south-east, also struck Nelson's little squadron as it passed Sardinia, scattering it across the spume-streaked sea and dismasting his flagship, the *Vanguard*. When the storm abated, his other two ships of the line closed with the flagship to help with repairs but the frigates and the sloop, on their captains' initiative, returned to Gibraltar. Then, on 7th June, the promised reinforcement of ten 'seventy-fours' arrived and Nelson was ready for action, only to find that Toulon was empty and that nobody knew where the great expedition had gone. Without frigates to scout, Nelson had to rely on whatever scraps of intelligence could be gathered from passing ships, and on his own intuition.

Meanwhile, in London, Sidney Smith was fêted – according to a contemporary's description – as 'the first lion of the day'.[9] He told the story of his escape to fashionable gatherings and a pantomime based on his adventures, *The Lucky Escape, or The Return to the Native Country*, was presented at Astley's Theatre. King George summoned him to a private audience at Buckingham House and, in an inspired gesture, ordered that the French prisoner of war, Captain Bergeret of the *Virginie*, who had been vainly offered to the Directory in exchange for Smith, could now return to France whenever he wished. News of Admiral Nelson's mission was anxiously awaited and speculation as to Bonaparte's destination was intense, it being noted that, six years earlier, while Sir Sidney Smith was in Constantinople, he had written to Lord Grenville forecasting probable French designs on Egypt and had repeated the warning while commanding the *Diamond* off the French coast.

Nothing was heard from the Mediterranean but reports of Nelson's failure to find Bonaparte, and rumours of his fleet appearing off Naples, Corfu or Constantinople, for it was known that they had not escaped into the Atlantic. The summer passed and then, on 2nd October, the news reached London that Admiral Nelson had found and destroyed the French fleet. He had caught it at anchor in Aboukir Bay between Alexandria and the Nile delta. Sailing into battle at sunset, his ships had steered either side of the anchored French line, demolishing their ships in succession. Next morning, ten French ships of the line had been captured, one – the colossal *l'Orient* – had blown up and two had escaped. Surveying the bay strewn with wrecks, wreckage and scorched corpses, Nelson simply said, 'Victory is not a name strong enough for such a scene.'[10]

This had been the climax of his three months' of chasing Bonaparte around the Mediterranean; blinded by lack of scouting frigates, and so failing to save Malta from being seized from its archaic occupants, the Knights of St John, and looted; passing the huge French convoy in the night – at twice its speed – and arriving off Alexandria before they did and finding the harbour empty; leaving the Nile delta two days before the French arrived and returning only after the French army had been put ashore. But now, at last, an apocalyptic victory had been won and London, then the whole British Isles, went wild with joy. But while church bells rang, oxen roasted on spits, glasses were raised and country folk invented a new dance called 'The Vanguard, or The Breaking of the Line', some contingency planning was occupying those in Whitehall. Lord Grenville, in particular, was concerned about what might happen next. The French fleet was certainly destroyed and, in the popular imagination, the French army was now marooned ashore to die of thirst in the Egyptian desert. However, it *was* ashore and, presumably it would march on Cairo and take it; the city was defended by its strange Ottoman rulers, the Mamelukes, a warrior cast descended from Caucasian slaves, whose wild cavalry was unlikely to withstand the disciplined volleys of Bonaparte's infantry, or the grapeshot of his field artillery.

So, assuming that the French could occupy Egypt, what next? The country was ostensibly part of the vast, ramshackle Ottoman Empire, ruled from Constantinople and spreading from the borders of Austria to Persia. The Turks – the dominant force – could field an enormous army of brave, fierce soldiers, formidable in individual combat but without the drill and fire-power that made the best European armies so formidable. Lord Nelson – as he now was – might well sweep the eastern basin of the Mediterranean clear of the surviving French ships but the French army could still rampage ashore, carving its way through the Ottoman Empire, either eastward towards India, or northward and westward, through Constantinople, into the defenceless eastern regions of Europe.

Therefore, there was an urgent diplomatic task to stiffen Turkish resistance to any French incursion and, at all costs, to prevent them from becoming allies, for there was a history of alliance between Paris and Constantinople. King Louis XIV had suggested to the Turks the cutting of a canal through the isthmus of Suez. Since the beginning of 1796 when Robert Liston – Sir Sidney's diplomatic friend in Stockholm – had left

Constantinople, where he had then also been ambassador, Spencer Smith had taken over as minister plenipotentiary to the Sublime Porte.* There were still problems of intelligence-gathering and communication and, remembering how well his brother, Sidney Smith, had performed in these rôles, Grenville suggested he should, after all, be sent into the Mediterranean, as he had suggested earlier, and he wrote to Spencer, 'I think I have begun to alter my mind about Sir Sidney Smith ... I think that until the French are actually driven out of Egypt ... there still remains something to be done.'[11] He had a diplomatic mission in mind, whereas Lord Spencer was planning a naval appointment for him in the same theatre of operations, and so it was that a dual rôle was suggested and decided upon. Sir Sidney would be both joint minister plenipotentiary with his brother and senior naval officer in the Levant.

At the beginning of October, Smith was appointed to command a ship of the line, the *Tigre*, a former French prize taken by Lord Bridport three years earlier. She mounted 80 guns and had a complement of 640, including 125 marines, but this was no ordinary ship's company for her captain had been allowed to pick his men and not only from the Royal Navy. As might have been expected, about 40 came from the *Diamond*, including Midshipman Beecroft, who had been wounded in the fight off Le Havre, and the coxswain, and he also asked for his former secretary, John Wright, now a temporary lieutenant. At his recommendation, Grenville had decided to send a military mission to Constantinople to advise the ramshackle Turkish army, and 76 officers were assembled, headed by Lieutenant-Colonel George Koehler with the temporary rank of general. To these Smith was able to add French royalists, who had helped him escape from Paris: Colonel Phélippeaux, François de Tromelin, Le Grand and Viscovich, the Venetian. He invited the *chouan* commander, General Frotté, to join him but the invitation was declined because of the call of duty in Normandy, but he asked Smith to take his half-brother, Charles de Frotté; in the event, the general was arrested by the Directory, while negotiating under a flag of truce, and executed, as was the Comte de Rochecotte, who was betrayed by one of his own agents. The

---

* The term applied to the Ottoman government, originating from the name of the great ceremonial gateway to Baghdad.

Frenchmen were delighted to be with Smith, of whom Le Grand wrote, 'I am happy in frequent opportunities of seeing Sir Sidney Smith, who is a brave and generous-hearted man with a fine countenance and eyes that sparkle with intelligence.'[12]

In London, Smith had been dining with his rich and rakish first cousin, Lord Camelford – their mothers were sisters – who was also a captain in the Royal Navy. Camelford was a trouble-maker, who had shot dead one of his lieutenants in cold blood for refusing to obey an order; now he was in command of the frigate *Charon*. It was galling that the young peer's high-living was, in part, due to his mother having inherited the mass of the fortune left by her father, Pinkney Wilkinson, while her sister's sons struggled to maintain the standard of living their position required, Sidney having spent beyond his means during his summer in London while helping to support his *emigré* friends. In some ways the two were men after each other's heart. Camelford was currently involved in a wild, unofficial idea of attacking the Spanish empire in central America by operating on both sides of the isthmus, much as had been the aim of the disastrous expedition to Nicaragua, on which Lord Nelson had almost died nearly twenty years before. Both men were fasci-nated by coastal raiding and inshore fighting with gunboats and now Smith was able to arrange for Camelford to accom-pany him to Constantinople with a cargo of ordnance, so that they could man Turkish-built gunboats to harass the French at the mouth of the Nile. It was decided that he should also bring out some of Koehler's military mission.

The naval, military and diplomatic missions to Constantinople were to sail with the blessings of both the Admiralty and the Foreign Office. Grenville, accompanied by Camelford, travelled to Portsmouth to dine on board the *Tigre* at Spithead with Smith, who, on 21st October, received his orders from Spencer:

> to put to sea without a moment's loss of time in the ship you command and to proceed with all possible despatch off Cadiz and, putting yourself under the command of the Earl of St. Vincent, Admiral of the Blue and Commander-in-Chief of His Majesty's ships and vessels in the Mediterranean ... follow his Lordship's orders for your further proceedings.[13]

If St Vincent was not off Cadiz, Smith was to join him at

Gibraltar. Smith also received from Grenville his diplomatic commission to act as 'joint minister plenipotentiary' to the Sublime Porte. He sailed at the end of the month.

The double mission was unusual, and probably unique, so Spencer wrote a long letter of explanation to St Vincent, saying that the Government planned to harness the furious Turkish reactions to the French invasion of its Egyptian territory:

Of these, it appears to His Majesty's Ministers most urgent to make the most and with a reference to the habits of acquaintance which a residence in Constantinople had given him, as well as his near connexion with our Minister there, it has been judged expedient to send out Sir Sidney Smith ... His speedy arrival in the Dardanelles with these instructions you will immediately perceive to be of great consequence ...

I am well aware that there may perhaps be some prejudices, derived from certain circumstances which have attended this officer's career through life, but from a long acquaintance with him personally, I think I can venture to assure your Lordship that added to his unquestioned character for courage and enterprise, he has a great many very good points about him, which those who are less acquainted with him are not sufficiently apprised of, and I have no doubt that you will find him a very useful instrument to be employed on any hazardous or difficult service ...

Should the arrangement of the force to remain for the present in the Levant, to cooperate with the Turks, lead to there being only one or two ships of two decks on that service, it may be most advisable that, from the local and personal acquaintance Sir Sidney is possessed of with the Turkish officers, he should be the senior officer; but I have given him to understand that, if a large force should be thought necessary, his standing on the list [the *Navy List*] will not admit of it, there being so many captains of distinguished merit, who are his seniors.[14]

It was a delicate, complicated situation but Spencer's letter seemed to make it clear and leave no reason for resentment among more senior officers.* Yet Smith could be a difficult man, perhaps because, having dealt on intimate terms with British ministers and foreign royalty, he sometimes seemed to

---

* A parallel in the Second World War was when Lord Louis Mountbatten – still a substantive captain – was appointed to command combined operations with the temporary ranks of vice-admiral, lieutenant-general and air marshal and to be Supreme Commander in South-East Asia as an acting full admiral.

patronize naval and military officers, who were highly conscious of the deference expected from those of junior rank. Even an admiring friend could write that 'he had much of the deportment of the courtier in his carriage and a little of the *petit-maitre* in his appearance ... He was ardent in his imagination and fluent in his speech. These are sometimes dangerous gifts.'[15] But his friends and his ships' companies loved him and his dynamism. One of his sailors remarked upon his appearance and manner: 'Sir Sidney was a weaselly man – no hull, sir – none; but all head, like a tadpole. But such a head! It put you in mind of a flash of lightning rolled up into a ball; and then his black curly nob – when he shook it, it made every man shake in his shoes.' Asked if Smith was handsome, the sailor replied:

> Blest if I can tell! You know, sir, as how we don't say of an eighteen-pounder when it strikes the mark at a couple of miles or so, 'That's handsome', but we sings out, 'Beautiful!' though, after all, it's nothing but a lump of black iron ... All I can say is that he was most handsome when there was most to do.[16]

This charismatic, difficult, original man was about to meet the formidable old admiral who embodied the conventional qualities of duty, obedience and courage. Lord St Vincent, now aged sixty-three, had been with Wolfe at the taking of Quebec nearly forty years before, and had been weathered by the battle and the breeze into a sturdy, stooped oak of a man. He could be ruthless but there was a twinkle in his eye and he had been the first to congratulate Nelson on disregarding his own orders to bring success at the Battle of Cape St Vincent. He might warm to Nelson, with his easy, direct manner and Norfolk accent, but might not take kindly to a man with lordly manners, however brave and professional he might be. Indeed, he already knew of Smith's reputation, and, on hearing Lord Grenville's suggestion of sending him to the Mediterranean earlier in the year, had written to the Secretary of the Admiralty, Evan Nepean, trying to dissuade him. The content and tone of the First Lord's letter to St Vincent had shown that he, too, was aware of possible problems, and events showed that his apprehension was justified.

Smith met St Vincent ashore at Gibraltar, the latter annoyed that his objections had been disregarded, but, as was to be expected from the old professional, he was briskly businesslike.

He had received a letter from Grenville, stressing Spencer's decision that when Smith arrived in the eastern Mediterranean he was to 'take command of such of his Majesty's ships as he may find in those seas, unless, by any unforeseen accident, it should happen that there should be among them any of his Majesty's officers of superior rank.'[17] St Vincent told him that Lord Nelson was thought to be at the Sicilian port of Syracuse, having left Captain Hood in command of a small squadron blockading the French army's transports in Alexandria, and that he could take these ships under his command. Smith asked the admiral if one of these could be the *Theseus*, commanded by a friend, Captain Richard Miller, an American.

All seemed settled. Smith should first deliver despatches to Captain Alexander Ball, who was blockading the French in Malta. He should then sail north to meet Nelson at Syracuse, give him despatches and St Vincent's letter explaining the new command arrangements, the admiral adding that they would thereafter communicate only in code. He also gave him a new cypher book and a copy for Nelson. He then handed Smith his sailing orders, which concluded that, after delivering the two sets of despatches, he was to make for Constantinople with all possible speed.

On 11th December, the *Tigre* was off Malta and Smith heard from Captain Ball that Nelson was not at Syracuse but at Naples, where his flagship was being repaired. So he wrote to St Vincent explaining that, having left the despatches for Nelson with Ball for forwarding, he himself was pressing on to Constantinople. To confirm the command arrangements already agreed, he added that, on arrival, he would, as Grenville had written, 'consider himself to be in command, assuming the other captains were his juniors'. Smith also wrote a tactful letter to Nelson, congratulating him on 'the most perfect naval victory that ever was gained by any country in any age', enclosing copies of his orders and explaining that he had been chosen for the task because of his brother's diplomatic success in Constantinople 'rather than to any undue preference of me to older and better officers, who have the honourable advantage of distinguishing themselves under your orders'.[18] He then steered for the Dardanelles and Constantinople.

Sidney Smith was, of course, unaware of what either Nelson,

or Bonaparte, had been doing, or thinking, since the great battle in Aboukir Bay on 1st August. He was unlikely to have any apprehensions over Nelson's reaction to his arrival because he knew him slightly and that he was generous-minded. Now that his victory was won he could surely only be grateful that another officer had come out to share the burden of blockade and patrolling.

But Nelson had changed. In the battle he had been wounded by a flying fragment striking a glancing blow on his forehead, slashing it open, causing concussion and temporarily blinding him with blood and dangling skin. The wound itself had responded to treatment but had left him with headaches and a short temper; indeed, it was eventually to be suggested that there had been damage to frontal lobes of the brain, causing changes in temperament and even character (or that this effect had been caused by what would come to be known as post-traumatic shock). He arrived at Naples on 22nd September, stressed and drained, and there he was nursed by the voluptuous wife of Sir William Hamilton, the British ambassador. He had been away at Malta for the second half of October but had now returned to Naples, where he heard of the euphoric reception of the news of his victory in London. There was one disappointment and an acute one. Jervis had been created Earl St Vincent for the battle, which Nelson had been instrumental in winning, but now this infinitely more important triumph, which could be expected to change the course of history, had only won him a barony. Emma Hamilton had written to him in her effervescent way, 'If I was King of England, I would make you the most noble, puissant Duke Nelson, Marquis Nile, Earl Alexandria, Viscount Pyramid, Baron Crocodile and Prince Victory.'[19] A final touch to his heightening and conflicting emotions was that he, a married man with a step-son also a naval officer in the Mediterranean, was falling in love with Lady Hamilton.

Meanwhile, disaster had overwhelmed Naples. After his arrival at the court of King Ferdinand IV of the Two Sicilies, Nelson had so inspired the boorish and unintelligent monarch and his over-emotional, intelligent but neurotic Queen, to take the initiative against the French, who were marching south and had taken Rome. So the King led his own army, recaptured Rome without difficulty and had then been routed by the

French counter-offensive. The liberal intelligentsia of Naples rose against him and, with the arrival of the French vanguard, the monarchy had been overthrown and a republic proclaimed. On 21st December, Nelson himself had had to rescue the royal family from the *Palazzo Reale*, embark them in his flagship and take them through a violent storm to Palermo, where they arrived on Boxing Day. Now he heard that Captain Sidney Smith, whom he regarded as something of a braggart for using his Swedish title, had taken command of his own ships off Alexandria.

There may have been an earlier prejudice against Smith. Although he had been in the Atlantic and Caribbean when the Smith brothers had visited Pinkney Wilkinson at Burnham Market, he would doubtless have heard of their begging mission to their rich grandfather. When he himself had spent five years at his father's house in the neighbouring village of Burnham Thorpe, he knew Wilkinson's successor at Westgate Hall, Sir Mordaunt Martin, and would have heard the story of the feckless Captain Smith and his two young emissaries. In any case, Nelson was now sensitive to any imagined slight and the thought of Smith taking ships from his command was intolerable. Lord Spencer and Smith himself could not have been more tactful in explaining the latter's dual appointment but, although Smith had been ordered to place himself under St Vincent's command, there was no specific mention of him coming under Nelson's, only that he could not assume command of other ships when more senior officers were present. Hearing of Smith's arrival from St Vincent was enough for him to take umbrage.

So, on the last day of 1798, Nelson wrote to St Vincent:

My dear Lord, *I do feel, for I am a man*, that it is impossible for me to serve in these seas, with the squadron under a junior officer – could I have thought it! and from Earl Spencer! Never, never was I so astonished as your letter made me. The Swedish knight, writes Sir William Hamilton, says that he shall go to Egypt and take Captain Hood and his squadron under his command. The Knight forgets the respect due to his superior officer: he has no orders from you to take my ships away from my command: but it is all of a piece. Is it to be borne? Pray grant me your permission to retire and I hope the *Vanguard* will be allowed to convey me and my friends, Sir William and Lady Hamilton to England.[20]

But Nelson was careful to obey the orders to the letter, and, on the same day, he wrote to Sir Sidney, acknowledging the situation, and assuring him, 'I will most strictly comply.' It was a polite but formal letter, worded so as to remind Smith that he was his superior officer: 'I must desire that you will lose no time in proceeding to Alexandria to take command of the blockade, etc., which I shall direct be delivered up to you.' But, even here, his natural generosity broke through, for he added, 'From my heart, I wish you every success.'[21]

Finally, on 1st January 1799, he wrote to Lord Spencer confirming that he had ordered Captain Troubridge to 'deliver up to Sir Sidney Smith the blockade of Alexandria and the defence of the Ottoman Empire by sea; for I should hope that Sir Sidney Smith will not take any Ship from under my command without my orders; although Sir Sidney, rather hastily in my opinion, writes Sir William Hamilton that Captain Hood naturally falls under his orders.'[22] This might seem to have been a petty dispute but had demonstrated two problems which bedevilled the exercise of command: the slow communications, which were often overtaken by events; and the personal antipathies that could be set up by professional and social resentment.

With time to brood on board ship, such resentments festered and took on a malign force of their own and such was this case. Lord St Vincent was unwell and irritable; he distrusted Smith as an over-sophisticated and highly political officer and felt that he had been tricked into giving him authority, which had been taken away from Nelson, to whom he wrote early in 1799:

> I am not well and have great cause for dissatisfaction from higher quarters. *He* (that is Sir Sidney) has no authority whatever to wear a distinguishing pendant [of a commodore commanding a squadron], unless you authorise him, for *I* certainly shall not ... I foresee that you and I shall be drawn into a *tracasserie* [wrangle] about this gentleman, who, having the ear of ministers and telling his story better than we can, will be more attended to.[23]

Nelson also brooded, his resentment against Smith aggravated by his own problems: his infatuation with Emma Hamilton developing into a sexual liaison; his guilty irritation with his loving wife in England and his anger with his step-son, Josiah Nisbet, who was serving under his command and had showed his natural reaction to the affair with Emma. Although the question of naval command seemed to have been settled with St Vincent stressing to Smith the importance of regarding himself as being under Nelson's direct command, there was the question of Smith's diplomatic title. Although he may not have thought of it before, he also resented Smith's rôle as 'minister plenipotentiary' in Constantinople. He had corresponded affably with Smith's brother, who now called himself Spencer Smythe, but still the antipathy showed; at the end of January, he wrote to Captain Ball: 'The Earl St. Vincent has ordered Sir Sidney to put himself immediately under my command, which I suppose the great Plenipo will not like; however he has brought this upon himself.'[24]

When letters arrived from Smith himself, he looked for signs of insubordination and, imagining he had found such when Sir Sidney was writing as a diplomat and therefore as an equal, he reported this to Lord Spencer, complaining of:

> those parts, which as the captain of a man-of-war to an admiral commanding the squadron in the Levant, are not so respectful as the rules of our service demand from the different ranks in it. No man admires Sir Sidney's gallantry and zeal more than myself, but should recollect how I must feel in seeing him in the situation, which I thought would naturally fall to me.[25]

Later, he wrote again to St Vincent that 'whilst you do me the honour of giving me the command of the detached squadron, *I will be* commander of it and suffer no, not the smallest interference of any captain, however great his interest may be';[26] the word 'interest' being the contemporary term for professional favouritism from men of influence and power.

The two men corresponded from opposite points of view. Nelson was mostly in Palermo, sitting up late in stuffy cardrooms, drinking champagne while Lady Hamilton gambled, and probably liverish from the unaccustomed rich food, taking offence at supposed slights. Smith, however, was unaware of the resentment he had caused and delighted by his success in galvanizing the sluggish Turks to start collecting an army on the island of Rhodes for a counter-offensive against the French. Nelson was infuriated to receive a letter from Smith written in anything less than a subordinate officer's respectful tones, realizing that he could always claim to be writing it as

the diplomat rather than the naval officer. So he wrote to
Smith:

> Your situation as joint Minister at the Porte makes it absolutely
> necessary that I should know who writes to me; therefore I must
> direct you, whenever you have ministerial affairs to communi-
> cate, that it is done jointly with your respectable brother and not
> to mix naval business with the other; for what may be very
> proper language for a representative of his Majesty, may be very
> subversive of that discipline of respect from the different ranks in
> our service. A representative may dictate to an admiral, a captain
> of a man-of-war would be censured for the same thing; therefore
> you will see the propriety of my steering clear between the two
> situations.[27]

Angry echoes had reached Whitehall, for St Vincent had
written to Lord Spencer giving him an inaccurate and
prejudiced account of the problem:

> An arrogant letter written by Sir Sidney Smith to Sir William
> Hamilton ... has wounded Lord Nelson to the quick ... who,
> besides, feels affronted by his embassy and separate command,
> which compels me to put this strange man immediately under his
> Lordship's orders, or the King may be deprived of his important
> services, and those of many valuable officers, as superior to
> Sidney Smith, in all points, as he is to the most ordinary of men.
> I experienced a trace of the presumptuous character of this young
> man during his stay in Gibraltar, which I passed over that it
> might not appear to your Lordship I was governed by prejudice
> in my conduct towards him.[28]

In fact, Smith had written a tactful letter to Hamilton, setting
out the naval and diplomatic tasks he had been given and never
suggesting that he was to take command of more senior officers' ships. Yet Nelson, while civil and correct in his dealings
with Smith, could not resist belittling him to his own friends as
'the Great Sir Sidney', or 'The Turkish Admiral'.

Sidney Smith had arrived in the Golden Horn in the *Tigre* and
reached Constantinople on Boxing Day. Welcomed by his
brother, he had been taken to an immediate audience with
Sultan Selim III, who had been in power for nine years and was
now aged thirty-seven, to put his signature to the treaty of
alliance with the Ottoman Empire and Russia, which had just
been negotiated. Disregarding Bonaparte's disingenuous

pretence of invading Egypt on the Sultan's behalf to unseat the untrustworthy Mameluke rulers, the Sublime Porte had already declared war on France. This meant that Smith would take command of any Turkish, or Russian, warships in the Levant. The Sultan now also gave him command of all Turkish naval and military forces then being mobilized to fight the French, making him a member of his inner council, the Divan. For his part, Smith presented the Sultan with gifts from King George III: twelve portable brass three-pounder cannon for carrying on camel-back, a model of a ship of the line, the *Royal George*, and paintings of naval battles. Smith divided his time between his ship and the former Venetian embassy, where Spencer Smith was now installed, and he sent a detachment of marines ashore to guard it.

As a personal favour, Smith then asked if the Sultan would release forty French prisoners held in the galley-slaves' dungeons. This was granted and Lieutenant Wright was sent to supervise their release and their repatriation to Toulon in a ship commanded by Midshipman Beecroft. In a letter to the prisoners, Smith compared his own magnanimity with the treatment he had suffered in Paris, writing of 'the sacred rights of prisoners of war. That title will always be respected by me; the bad example of your Government not having the smallest influence with me.'[29]

In Constantinople, Smith at last heard the news from Egypt. Having evaded Nelson on passage to Alexandria, Bonaparte had arrived on 1st July and hurriedly landed his army on open beaches to take the city, while, against his advice, the escorting fleet had anchored in Aboukir Bay fifteen miles to the east. When Nelson arrived on 1st August and destroyed that fleet, the French army was already in Cairo. They had marched across the scorched desert, suffering agonies of thirst and of despair at the sudden isolation from everything familiar in this hot wilderness, from which death in battle, or suicide, seemed the only escape. But Bonaparte rallied them with his oratory, their bands played *La Marseillaise* and they staggered on. Finally, on 21st July, 25,000 Frenchmen faced the glittering Mameluke cavalry and a vast rabble of their servants and armed peasantry on open melonfields, from which could be seen, 10 miles away through the afternoon heat-haze, the great tombs after which would later be named the Battle of the Pyramids.

Giving the order to form squares, Bonaparte proclaimed, 'Soldiers, forty centuries look down upon you!'[30] The gallant horsemen were no match for drilled infantry squares, six to ten ranks deep, firing volleys, rank by rank; two hours later, the melon-fields were strewn with their brilliantly costumed corpses.

Elated by victory, the French were disillusioned by their conquest. Instead of fertile fields, watered by the Nile, and opulent cities of minarets and fountains, they found desert, poisoned wells, fetid villages and even the famous cities of Alexandria and Cairo to be crumbling heaps of ruinous tenements around outcrops of ancient archaeological splendour. The officers were as appalled as the men and criticized the concept and the conduct of the expedition to Bonaparte's face; yet he held his army together. Even when news of the destruction of his fleet in Aboukir Bay reached Cairo, Bonaparte would countenance no defeatist talk: he was a soldier not a sailor; his army was intact; in any case, he had planned a long stay in Egypt.

The campaign had become an extraordinary compound of heroism and horror, of intellectual endeavour and savage reaction. Bonaparte imposed military and civil law, French shopkeepers set up in business in the streets of Cairo, a French-language newspaper was published and the army learned to ride camels to form a *Régiment de Dromedaires*. At the same time, official decapitation – almost on the scale of the Reign of Terror – became an act of policy in the city and, it was reported, when there was a complaint of debauchery and venereal disease being beyond control in the Cairo barracks, 400 prostitutes were rounded up, beheaded and thrown into the Nile. Beyond the capital, Egyptian peasants and French patrols were being killed in atrocity and counter-atrocity. Yet *L'Armée d'Egypt* became as stylish as *L'Armée d'Italie* had been and orders were written on paper headed with either elaborate allegorical engravings of the Nile river-god cradling a cornucopia against a background of crocodiles and pyramids, or Fame, carrying a laurel wreath, flying above an angel inscribing a tablet with a list of victories to add to those already carved on an obelisk. Meanwhile, those who wrote them spent each night tormented by mosquitoes and lice.

Gradually, the French settled into Cairo, becoming more

tolerant and efficient, putting down any signs of insurrection swiftly with only a few executions of ringleaders. They installed street lighting and began a regular stage-coach mail service with Alexandria. They introduced printing, minted coins and built windmills for raising water from the Nile; schools and hospitals were founded. The *savants* got to work, mapping the country, studying its geology, natural history and archaeology while assembling data and drawings for the massive work they planned, *Déscription d'Egypte*. Bonaparte had studied the Koran on the voyage from Toulon and, to placate the Egyptians, professed his admiration for Islam; currying favour reached an extreme, when he declared that the entire French army would convert and that he would build a mosque that would accommodate them all at prayer. When the mullahs told him that the converts would have to be circumcised and foreswear alcohol, he persuaded them to grant the army associate membership of the faith and tolerate their wine. However, one undistinguished divisional commander, General Jacques Menou, did publicly convert to Islam, taking the additional name of Abdallah, and was appointed Governor of Cairo. Bonaparte himself tried wearing Arab dress with a scimitar in his sash, but realizing he looked ridiculously theatrical, changed back into uniform.

Immediately after the Battle of the Pyramids, Bonaparte sent General Desaix in pursuit of the Mameluke leader, Murad Bey, with a division of less than 3,000 men up the Nile and into unknown territory. On foot, on camelback and by boat, they slowly ascended the great river to find, instead of their elusive enemy, the great temples of Ancient Egypt, up to their capitals in sand. Soldiers of the French Revolution showed a sense of history by carving their names on pillars commemorating the feats of pharaohs 3 millennia before their own time. Desaix never caught Murad Bey and Bonaparte himself failed to catch the other Mameluke leader, Ibrahim Bey, who retreated eastward into the desert of Sinai and then Syria beyond.

In Constantinople, still unaware that he had ruffled so many feathers, Sidney Smith and his brother discussed plans for a counter-offensive with the Sultan in Constantinople. It was agreed that, while an army was assembled on the island of Rhodes, the French could be harassed in Egypt. Smith had permission from the British Government to recruit 1,000

Albanian mercenaries to man gunboats in the Nile delta. He proposed to launch amphibious attacks on their outposts when the river rose in its summer flood; the *Tigre* had brought out a team of English shipwrights, who were already instructing Turks, not only in the building of gunboats but ships of the line. In preparation for the offensive, his French royalist friends had taken commissions in the Turkish army: Phélippeaux as a colonel; de Tromelin, using his *nom de guerre*, as Major Bromley, de Frotté also a major and both Le Grand and Viscovich becoming captains. Although Boisgirard was still dancing at the Opera in Paris, Smith exercised his patronage by commissioning him as a colonel and having his pay forwarded to his private bank account.

Then, early in 1799, Smith was shocked to read a newspaper report that Lord Elgin, the ambassador to Berlin, had been appointed ambassador extraordinary to the Sultan of Turkey, over the heads of the Smith brothers, who had not been forewarned. The brothers were as bewildered as the Sultan and, seeing their own position undermined, explained to the Turks that this was a political appointment that did not invalidate their own positions; nevertheless, it was a major blow. Until they were superseded, if, indeed, they ever were, it would be prudent to press ahead with their offensive against the French.

Soon afterwards, the instructions arrived from Nelson, ordering Smith to Alexandria, where Troubridge would hand over responsibility for the blockade. He arrived off the Egyptian coast early in March to find that while Troubridge had been effective – when forty empty transports tried to leave Alexandria for their home ports in Italy, he burnt them and returned their Italian crews to shore – his attempts to destroy the French frigates and transports still within the harbour had failed. He handed over to Smith two ships of the line, the *Theseus* and the *Lion*, telling St Vincent in a letter that he had 'left Sir Sidney everything that he could want that he may not be able to say the blame lays on Lord Nelson if he should not succeed'. He was even more hostile to Smith than Nelson, adding, 'Sir Sidney talks so large as a member of the Divan and Plenipo that he makes me sick.'[31]

When Troubridge sailed, Smith gave him a letter for Lord Spencer outlining his own plans for action against Bonaparte, making use of the vast Turkish army and the gunboats manned by the Albanians. Smith had in mind a twin approach, offering Bonaparte a choice between continual harassment at sea by the British and on land by the Turks, or evacuating Egypt with his army on parole by what Smith called a *pont d'or*. Yet, while the latter option was in line with Smith's political instructions to effect the removal of the French from Egypt, the offering of a 'golden bridge' of escape to the enemy would go against all Nelson's ideas of total, decisive victory. He wrote sharply to Smith that 'this is in *direct opposition to my opinion* which is *never to suffer any one individual Frenchman to leave Egypt* – I must therefore *strictly charge and command you* never to give any French ship, or man, leave to quit Egypt.'[32] He was smarting at Sidney Smith having signed the treaty with his brother in Constantinople and for hoisting the broad pendant of a commodore – the senior captain of a squadron – without his permission, complaining about it at every opportunity. He wrote to St Vincent:

> I shall, my Lord, keep a sufficient force in the Levant for the service required of us, but not a ship for Captain Smith's parade and nonsense – Commodore Smith, I beg his pardon, for he wears a broad pendant – has he any orders for this presumption over the heads of so many good and gallant officers with me? Whenever Sir Sidney went on board the *Tigre* in state, as he calls it, the *Royal Standard* was hoisted at the mast-head and twenty-one guns fired. The Turks, however, who love solid sense and not frippery, see into the Knight and wonder that some of Sir Sidney's superiors were not sent to Constantinople: but I have done with the Knight.[33]

While Troubridge had been cruising off Alexandria and firing ineffective broadsides at the harbour, Bonaparte had headed in the opposite direction, chasing Ibrahim Bey east-ward. To alert the Turks, Smith sent Lieutenant Wright to the old crusader port of Acre on the coast of Syria, the stronghold of the Ottoman governor of the Levant littoral from the Nile delta to the Turkish border, Djezzar Pasha, whose name meant, appropriately, 'The Butcher'. Bosnian by birth, he had, when young, sold himself into slavery to a Mameluke and became a tax-gatherer for his master, embezzling, absconding and making his own way with such ruthlessness that, finally, he took over the huge Levantine province and its capital at Acre. Although now past sixty, he was a powerfully built, emotional

man with a high opinion of himself and a reputation for
cruelty.

On his march east, Bonaparte and an army of 13,000 had first
encountered Djezzar's fortress of El Arish and a nearby
encampment, defended by nearly 3,000 Mamelukes and
assorted soldiers from the Ottoman province. The French
stormed the camp in a night attack, then surrounded the fort
with artillery, bombarded it at point-blank range and forced its
surrender. About a third of the defenders were killed and, of
the survivors, the Mamelukes were released and the rest given
the choice of fighting for the French, or following the army as
prisoners of war. In the fort, the French found much-needed
provisions – for they were again marching through desert – and
also a room filled with men dying of plague.

The advance into Syria, a vast territory stretching from the Red
Sea to the Taurus mountains and eastward beyond the River
Tigris to Persia, was the further realization of Bonaparte's dream
of eastern conquest. The expedition up the Nile might be more
exotic but this was the way to both Constantinople and Vienna
and also to India. He sent messengers to the Shah of Persia,
requesting permission to march through his territories, and to
Tippoo Sultan – 'The Lion of Mysore' and ally of the French in
India – warning him of his approach. The news of the loss of the
French fleet, which Nelson had already sent to India, could be
disregarded because the French army was still in existence.

The advance continued, with the vanguard commanded by
General Jean-Baptiste Kléber, a huge, bluff Alsatian, aged forty-
six, who had made his name suppressing revolt in the Vendée.
He was admired by his men as much as Bonaparte was, by now,
distrusted as an exciting but over-confident commander, who
was as likely to lead them to disaster as to triumph. The army
marched east then northward along the low, sandy coast, trail-
ing clouds of dust: 10,000 infantry in 4 divisions, 800 cavalry,
1,400 gunners, riding their horses and limbers, about 100 men
of the *Régiment de Dromedaires*, then the commissariat, a few
savants, some women and, finally, escorted by mounted troopers, the shuffling column of ragged prisoners.

The town of Gaza – again crumbling, flat-roofed houses and
the domes and minarets of mosques – fell without a fight on
24th February. On 7th March a letter reached Smith from
Djezzar's chief of staff, telling him:

After losing the castle of El Arish, Djezzar's soldiers have defended practically nothing. The same soldiers abandoned Gaza ... Among them reigns the greatest disorder and fear of the French, so that at every instant we expect to hear of another reverse, or even to be shut up in Acre, which will offer little resistance if the troops have no more courage ... I hope that in your generosity you will never abandon a friend and ally.[34]

But the French had reached the walls of Jaffa three days before. The castellated towers and walls built by the Crusaders looked formidable and when Bonaparte sent a summons to surrender, it was ignored. Batteries were mounted and, on 7th March, opened concentrated fire on a curtain wall to beat down a breach. At 2.00 p.m., Bonaparte was told that the breach was practicable and the assault was launched. Watching French officers were first admiring of the resolution with which the storming parties rushed the breach and then appalled by what followed. The assault required a sustained ferocity that could not be quickly slaked, so that, as Bonaparte himself was to record, 'The soldiers' fury was at its height: everybody was put to the sword; being sacked, the town experienced all the horrors of a city taken by storm.'[35] Defenders trying to surrender were bayoneted, women were raped and murdered, even the old and children were slaughtered in the bloody hysteria. During that first terrible night, more than 2,000 were killed.

Next morning, it was seen that several thousand surviving defenders had barricaded themselves into a caravanserai and, having seen what had happened in the city around them, were preparing to die fighting. Two young French officers – one of them Bonaparte's step-son, Eugène de Beauharnais, the son of Josephine's first husband, who had been guillotined during the Reign of Terror – approached under a flag of truce. The Turks agreed to surrender on condition that their lives were spared, to which the officers agreed. So the Turks piled their arms and were escorted out of the city. When Bonaparte was told that he had now acquired about 3,000 more prisoners of war, who would have to be fed, he asked, 'What do they want me to do with them?'[36]

The answer came next day. The prisoners were marched to open land in front of Bonaparte's tent that would have been suitable for a parade-ground and there surrounded by French infantry. Then Bonaparte was told that some of the garrison of

El Arish, whom he had released, had been found under arms at Jaffa, so breaking their parole, and this gave him a pretext. He already knew that he could not feed this number of prisoners and he could claim to expect that, if released on parole, they would take up arms again. He spared the commander of the Jaffa garrison, ordered that 300 Turkish artillerymen, who had been trained by French officers, be incorporated into his own army and that Turkish officers should be kept prisoner. Then he wrote to his chief of staff, General Berthier, to 'order the adjutant-general to take all the gunners and other Turks captured with arms in their hands at Jaffa to the sea shore and to have them shot, taking precautions that none shall escape'.[37]

So, on 9th March, 800 prisoners were roused and marched to the beach, a French eyewitness recording that 'they shed no tears; they uttered no cries; some, who were wounded and could not march so fast as the rest, were bayoneted on the way';[38] and there they were shot. The only chance of escape was to swim so hundreds ran into the water, where they were shot, or were drowned. French soldiers launched boats to follow and kill all those who had managed to reach rocks offshore.

Some of the French were appalled, as was a young paymaster, André Peyrusse, who wrote to his mother:

That execution finished, we wished to persuade ourselves that ... all the other prisoners would be spared ... But we were soon disillusioned when, next day, twelve hundred Turkish gunners, who for two days had lain without food before the tent of the General in Command, were taken to be executed. The soldiers had been carefully instructed that powder was not to be wasted and they had the ferocity to stab them to death with bayonet thrusts.[39]

Amongst those killed were children, who had clung to their fathers, and the prisoners who had marched with the army from El Arish. When it was over, Peyrusse wrote, 'This example will teach our enemies that they cannot count upon French good faith; and, sooner or later, the blood of these three thousand victims will be upon us.'[40] In hot and cold blood, the massacres in the city and on the beach had taken, according to French records, 4,441 Turkish, Egyptian and Moroccan lives. Bonaparte wrote to General Marmont, who was commanding the garrison at Alexandria, 'The capture of Jaffa has been a brilliant affair. Four thousand of Djezzar's best troops and the best gunners of Constantinople had to be put to the sword.'[41]

He was satisfied that an effective message had been sent to Djezzar and the defenders of Acre. When Jaffa surrendered the commander had been spared but most of his garrison had been slaughtered. Bonaparte had sat at his writing-table within ear-shot of the terrible sounds of the mass executions and wrote to Djezzar, saying that he had no wish to shorten the life of an old man and that the real enemies of them both were the Mamelukes and the English so they should unite against them, otherwise, 'I shall march in a few days against Acre.'[42]

CHAPTER FIVE

'A little revenge'

LEAVING ALEXANDRIA, AFTER firing broadsides at extreme range and to little effect at the French shipping packed in the harbour, Sidney Smith steered the *Tigre* east, along the desert shore, past the sand-bars and swamps at the mouth of the Nile. As usual, he enthusiastically gathered intelligence, sending a boat close inshore to identify French outposts and putting Lieutenant Wright ashore on a secret mission: 'landed at a short distance from Alexandria in the night-time, not openly as a British naval officer but bearded, moustachioed and shawled *à la Turque* and for the express purpose of gathering valuable information'. Before vanishing into the darkness, he warned the boat's crew about the need for security: 'Men, beware of your words!'[1]

Next night he was picked up and, having reported to Smith, was sent ahead to warn the garrison of Acre of the approaching French.

The *Tigre* passed El Arish, Gaza and Jaffa, the ghastly scenes ashore only suggested by an occasional column of smoke. To the east, beyond the sandy shore, distant, shadowy hills became visible, darkening as they neared the coast and reaching it with the great bluff of Mount Carmel, 2,000 feet above the sea. On 15th March, they cleared its headland with the little fishing port of Haifa below, and saw a long beach curving northward to a walled city on a headland. This was Acre.

Djezzar Pasha's capital was ancient. In Roman times it had been known as Ptolemais and it had been named St Jean d'Acre by the Crusaders, who had captured and lost it twice after sieges of dreadful carnage. Beyond the building of minarets, it remained much as King Richard I of England had known it. Acre cowered behind great limestone walls built across the neck of the peninsula, facing north and east with a massive square keep at the angle, known as The Devil's Tower because of a legend linking it with Judas. Behind the walls were the domes and minarets of the mosques and the flat-roofed houses of its 15,000 citizens. The city was laced with streets so narrow that laden camels often could not pass but, immediately behind the Devil's Tower, the halls, cloisters and courts of the great mosque and Djezzar's palace were luxuriously spread, the tufted tops of palm-trees in their gardens sprouting above the rooftops. On the seaward walls there was another tower, the Fly Tower, named after Beelzebub, the Lord of the Flies, a short mole and watergate but the small harbour was silted so that ships had to anchor offshore in an exposed roadstead and, in a storm, run for the shelter of Mount Carmel. Beyond the walls, market gardens and orchards had been planted on the rolling ground to either side of two streams that flowed from the hills to the sea; an ancient, arched aqueduct brought water from a mountain spring.

The *Theseus* was already lying off Acre, where she had arrived three days before, and Captain Miller came on board the *Tigre* to report on the state of the defences. He and Colonel Phélippeaux had inspected the medieval walls and bastions and found them crumbling and virtually undefended, although there were a few cannon facing the sea. The French engineer had managed to convince Djezzar, who seemed to have worried mostly about the fate of his wives and concubines, of the danger. Immediately the garrison and gangs of labourers were put at his disposal and they began working to strengthen the walls, mount guns and bring up ammunition. There were some 4,000 men under arms – Turks, Syrians, Kurds, Albanians, Bosnians and Negroes – all of them under Djezzar's direct, personal command.

The *Tigre* anchored off Acre on 21st March and Smith at once landed marines and seamen from his 2 ships of the line – 800 were eventually ashore – together with some of his ship's guns, which were mounted on the ramparts. He posted pickets beyond the walls and, at night, had fires and lanterns lit to illuminate the approaches and sent out scouts to give warning of the French.

The strategic importance of Acre had become increasingly clear to both Smith and Bonaparte: while the British

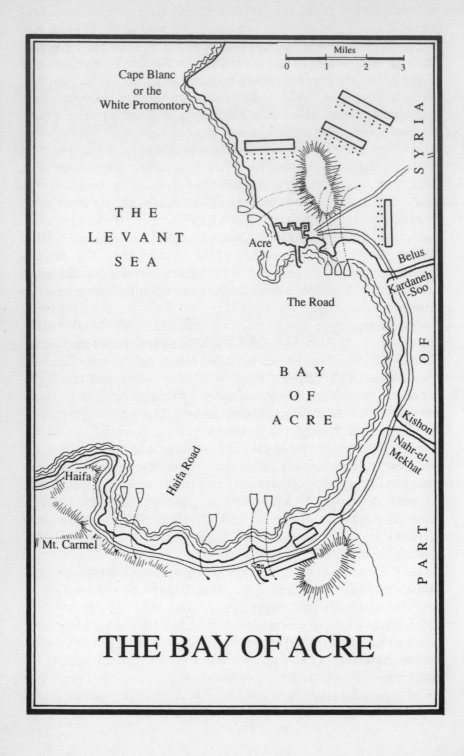

THE BAY OF ACRE

commanded the sea, the city could not be by-passed because the allies could land an army there in the rear of the French. But Bonaparte believed it would fall as easily as Jaffa for here, too, his army outnumbered the defenders by about three to one and the walls were no defence against siege guns. Then, the first sign that it might not be so easy came on the day after the mass executions ended outside Jaffa: French doctors reported that a soldier showed the symptoms of bubonic plague.

It may have seemed like divine retribution but it was almost certainly as result of infection from El Arish, where the garrison had been infected. Now the horrifying news spread through the ranks and four soldiers shot themselves in the belief that they were suffering from it. Bonaparte had risen to the occasion, visiting the improvised hospital at Jaffa, taking his time in talking to sick soldiers and helping to carry the body of one who had just died. This helped reassure his tired and frightened men but he realized that it made a swift advance even more important: he must take Acre before the plague took hold. Also, his diplomacy had been more successful in Syria* than in Egypt, and he had engaged the sympathy of the powerful Druze tribes, who, anxious to be rid of Ottoman rule, had promised him 15,000 fighting men when he had taken Acre. Once Acre had been taken, the only fortified city ahead was Aleppo – and that was far from the sea and British ships – so the road to Constantinople would be clear, and so would the road to Damascus and India.

Leaving the thousands of Turkish corpses rotting on the beach outside Jaffa, the army struck camp on 14th March and headed north, the dust turning to mud as it began to rain. The main army marched along the axis of the road, its right flank guarded by a division, on a parallel line of advance; this was commanded by the leonine General Kléber who was worried by the loss of nearly a week at Jaffa and considered the massacre of the prisoners not only barbarous but certain to alienate other Islamic nations.

Next day, the vanguard occupied Haifa and, from the summit of Mount Carmel, Bonaparte looked across the wide bay to Acre on its headland. Before a sea mist came down, he could see, off the point, two ships of the line at anchor and

* covering modern Israel and Lebanon as well as Syria

several small craft but nothing to suggest serious opposition. Vast stocks of wheat, rice, biscuit and olive oil had been captured at Jaffa together with cannon, powder and shot. The heavy siege artillery, which would be necessary if major fortifications were encountered, was on its way from Egypt by sea.

Meanwhile, Smith had sent his boats to reconnoitre the shore north and south of Acre. Sighting the French vanguard, mounted on donkeys and escorted by the *Régiment de Dromedaires*, making its way northward from Haifa, he ordered a thirty-two pounder carronade to be mounted in a launch and sent it to be ready offshore at daybreak. Before the French had even seen the launch, grapeshot swept the shore and they fled inland to the safety of Mount Carmel; henceforth, the approach march was kept to the inland road from Nazareth to Acre. That night the French heard firing out at sea and two coasters flying the *tricolore* put into Haifa. Next morning, the British arrived in ships' boats, boldly pulling inshore to cut them out; but, as they tried to board, the French fired from the dockside, driving them off, killing four midshipmen and eight seamen and taking twenty-two prisoners. At first, Bonaparte was delighted but then he was told some ominous news. First, the masters of the coasters reported that the other ships in their convoy, laden with the siege artillery, had been captured at sea by the British. Then, from the prisoners he learned that the officer in command at Acre was Captain Sir Sidney Smith, whom he had encountered at Toulon and in Paris. Bonaparte now knew of the warning Smith had written on a shutter in the Temple prison and, as a Corsican, having been brought up in the tradition of superstition and the blood feud, it had disturbed him.

The French army made camp on the plain of Acre just beyond the range of guns on its walls and sited its own batteries where they could concentrate their fire on the Devil's Tower. An officer, Captain Mailly, was then sent into Acre under a flag of truce to demand surrender, having been told to take careful note of the defences he saw. He was thrown into prison by Djezzar. So the chief engineer, General Sanson, accompanied a night patrol trying to inspect the walls but Smith's pickets sighted them in the light of watch-fires and drove them off. However, he had seen nothing to counter reports that the defences seemed no stronger than garden walls and there was no dry moat. These defences seemed to present nothing for which siege artillery would be needed and could presumably be demolished by the guns they had, which could fire nothing heavier than twelve-pound shot.

Smith, to whom the tyrannical Djezzar deferred, prepared his defence. Marines and British gun-crews were deployed amongst the garrison along the walls and particularly around the Devil's Tower. Meanwhile, the *Tigre* and four gunboats, captured from the French, were anchored to the east of the town, where they could enfilade an assault, and the *Theseus* anchored on the other side to cover the northern walls. On the 24th, an armed storeship, the *Alliance*, arrived with orders from Captain Troubridge to discharge her cargo and return to him immediately but, putting operational necessity before tact, Smith took her under his own command and sent her to join the gunboats covering the beaches to the north of the town.

On the 23rd Smith sat at his desk in the stern cabin of the *Tigre* and wrote to St Vincent, reporting his arrival at Acre, where 'the presence of a British naval force appeared to encourage and decide the Pasha and his troops to make a vigorous resistance',[2] the harassing of the French on the coast road and the capture of their siege guns at sea.

Three days later, while Bonaparte watched from a hillock known as King Richard Coeur de Lion's Mount, his batteries opened fire on the Devil's Tower to cover the digging of trenches as close as possible to the walls. On the 26th, Djezzar's men launched a wild sortie but French discipline told and they were driven back within the walls. As the smoke cleared, Bonaparte could see that a breach had been blown and he summoned his generals to discuss whether an assault would be possible. 'Of course the breach is practicable,' said Kléber sarcastically, 'a cat could easily get through.' As for the trenches, he continued, 'They are all right for you, General, but, as for me, they hardly reach up to my belly.'[3] Bonaparte accepted that the breach was impracticable and ordered that a heavier, more concentrated bombardment would open at dawn in two days' time.

Under Smith's direction the breach had been blocked with stones and baulks of timber and more guns brought up to cover its approaches; the ships and gunboats were moved closer inshore and a brass eighteen-pounder cannon mounted on the lighthouse at the end of the mole. At dawn, French officers could be seen gathering on King Richard's Mount and then were hidden by smoke as the guns of the besiegers and the besieged opened fire. At noon, the French guns fell silent and, as the smoke cleared, Bonaparte examined the walls through his telescope: the breach seemed much wider. Kléber refused to comment on its feasibility but Bonaparte gave the order for an assault. Sappers raced forward, carrying scaling ladders, followed by twenty companies of Kléber's grenadiers.

The British on the walls cocked their muskets and gripped their cutlasses, but the sight of the advancing columns, bristling with bayonets, unnerved the Turks and they ran. But the French faltered for they had, for the first time, seen the dry moat – fifteen feet deep and twenty feet wide – that they had not expected below the walls. The sappers climbed down their ladders but those who reached the foot of the thirty-foot walls on the far side found the ladders were not long enough to reach the breach in the walls. The grenadiers, reaching the edge of the moat had no ladders to descend into it and as they stood, hesitating, were cut down by grapeshot from naval guns out at sea. Djezzar rallied his men, who, sensing success, ran back to the ramparts and flung grenades and rocks on to the French trapped in the moat. The assault was stalled and French bugles sounded the retreat. As a French general wrote when it was over, 'This was the day when Acre should have fallen'[4] and as a captain noted in his diary, 'Many of us were of the opinion from that moment that we could never take the place.'[5]

With the dry moat strewn with French corpses from the first assault, the sight and smell of putrefaction beset those manning the walls. They had to accept the stink but there was one peculiarly ghastly sight below them. This was a gorgeously uniformed French general, who had been killed in the attack, when the Turks had stripped and mutilated his body and hacked off his head. One British seaman, Daniel Bryan, captain of the foretop in the *Tigre* – described as 'an elderly man ... and rather deaf' found this particularly offensive but, when he asked why nobody buried the corpse, was told, 'Go and do it yourself.' He did.

Bryan, carrying a pickaxe and shovel, was lowered down the face of the wall by other sailors, who tried to dissuade him, even offering to go themselves but were told, 'No, you are too young to be shot yet. As for me, I am old and deaf and *my* loss would be no great matter.' Then, as an eyewitness account put it, 'His first difficulty was to drive away dogs. The French now levelled their pieces – they were on the instant of firing at the hero! It was an interesting moment!' The sailor called out, 'Mounseers, ahoy! vast heaving there a bit will 'e? And belay your poppers for a spell.' His message was understood and 'an officer, perceiving the friendly intentions of the sailor, was seen to throw himself across the file. Instantaneously the din of arms, the military thunder, ceased; a dead, solemn silence prevailed.' So he dug in the rubble and then 'shaking what was so very lately a French general very cordially and affectionately by the hand, he reverently placed him in his impromptu grave...' Then, setting a slab of stone at the head, 'Dan, with the peculiar air of a British sailor, took a piece of chalk from his pocket and tried to write, 'Here you lie, old Crop.'* Finally, 'he made his best sailor's bow and footscrape to the French, shouldered his implements and climbed over to his own quarters ... This he did to the cheers of both parties.'

Back on board ship, Sir Sidney sent for Bryan and the following conversation was said to have followed: 'Well, Dan, I hear you buried the French general?' 'Yes, your Honour.' 'Had you anybody with you?' 'God Almighty, sir.' 'A very good assistant indeed,' replied Smith and then said to an officer, 'Give old Dan a glass of grog.'[6]

At the end of March, a gale blew and the two ships of the line had to run for shelter in the lee of Mount Carmel. French sappers had failed to blow in the counterscarp – the outer side of the moat – but blew up the aqueduct where it reached the walls, so filling the moat with rubble. They fired red-hot shot into the breach in the hope of burning the timber barricades but Phélippeaux had anticipated this and covered them with bales of cotton soaked with water. Again the defences held fast.

While Smith was storm-tossed out at sea, Djezzar took advantage of his absence to indulge in one of his favourite customs. The French had heard grim stories about him, Berthier their chief of staff, telling stories of the Pasha's habit of flaying unfaithful wives and personally beheading courtiers who offended him. Now he lived up to his reputation and French prisoners – one report was of 30, another of 400 – were tied in

* an executed man

sacks and thrown into the sea, amongst them Captain Mailly, who had assumed that his flag of truce would protect him. As Berthier recorded: 'A quantity of bags were perceived on the shore: our soldiers opened them and – Oh, crime! they found the bodies of unfortunate men tied in pairs, enclosed in the sacks by order of the Djezzar.'[7]

Another assault was launched at dawn on 1st April and it, too, failed miserably, every member of the storming party being killed or wounded, amongst the latter being Eugène de Beauharnais. Two days later, the British ships were able to return to their positions on either side of Acre to find the French had made the most of their absence by extending their siege works. Their trenches had crept to half a pistol-shot of the walls and it was clear that the sappers were trying to drive a mine beneath the Devil's Tower. Counter-mining was impossible because of a mass of ancient foundations and the fact that no pick-axes were available. So it was decided to launch a sortie by British marines and seamen to drive the miners away and destroy their shaft.

This was to be commanded by Major Thomas Oldfield of the Royal Marines from the *Theseus* and Lieutenant Wright, who was now second lieutenant of the *Tigre*. The Turks were to make diversionary sorties on either flank but, as the time approached and a strict silence was enforced among the waiting columns, they began yelling war cries so that the French were alerted. Even so, the British scrambled down from the breach, and charged, their impetus carrying them through heavy fire to the mouth of the mine. Wright entered first at the head of a party of pikemen and, finding that no demolition party had been able to follow him, pulled down the timber props so that the roof caved in. As he emerged, the French counter-attacked and both he and Major Oldfield were hit. When the British regained cover, they could see the bodies of both officers from the walls.

Then, it was said, Smith:

> called to one of his men, a gigantic, red-haired Irish marine named James Close. Pointing to the mass of carnage that lay sweltering in the ditch below, where the slightly wounded and the actually dying were fast hastening into mutual corruption under the burning sun, Smith said, 'Close, dare you go there and bring us the body of poor Wright?' 'What darn't I do, yer honour?' was the immediate reply and, exposed to the musketry

of the enemy, wading through blood and stumbling over dead bodies and scattered limbs, he, unhurt, at length found Wright, not killed but only wounded, and he brought him away from these shambles of death. The French spared him for the sake of the heroism of the act.[8]

Other marines seached for Major Oldfield, believing the body to be that of Colonel Phélippeaux and that Bonaparte had ordered that it be brought in for identification. French and British reached him at the same time. The British, thinking him dead, tried to drag his body away by the neck-cloth, while a French grenadier hooked a halberd into his side and hauled the other way. The neck-cloth broke and the French collected the body only to find that he was still alive. He was identified as a British officer and, when he died soon afterwards, was buried in the French camp with military honours. Meanwhile, the Turks had returned to the walls carrying sixty severed French heads.

Both sides sought reinforcements. Smith had asked of the Sultan that the Turkish army, which had been assembling on Rhodes, should be sent as urgent reinforcements and also ordered the frigate *Charon* to bring guns and ammunition from Constantinople. There was more help to come from the east, for the Sultan had ordered an army of 20,000 to march from Damascus to the relief of Acre. When French scouts reported that the army had crossed the River Jordan and was near Nazareth, Bonaparte sent Kléber's division against it, following himself with another division and a battery of artillery.

Bonaparte was too impatient to enjoy sieges and at Acre he found himself at a disadvantage. Although he had defeated the only Turkish army between himself and Constantinople, and had heard that Damascus might be ready to surrender, he was in no position to take advantage of this. He had no base nor supply depot within reach, from which his army could be replenished, and reinforcement by sea was barred by the British, who could themselves bring seaborne support to the besieged city. For this reason, he had lost his siege artillery and had had to call for more to be sent from Egypt to Jaffa and then hauled overland. He had not enough men to contain Acre and continue the advance with his main army, so the city had to be taken; if not, none of the options in his grand strategy would be possible. But the sort of warfare that seemed to be developing inland, which would require the chess game of forced marches, strategic deployment and the springing of tactical surprises, was the sort in which he excelled.

As the French reached the Jordan there was a succession of sharp actions in which, each time, they were hugely outnumbered and in each of which their discipline broke the whirling cavalry charges. There was again the expected booty – engraved scimitars, embossed shields, inlaid muskets and embroidered saddle-cloths – and, when it had been collected, the Jordan valley north of Lake Tiberius was found to be cleared of Turks. Supremely confident, Kléber and the 2,000 men of his division sighted a huge encampment beneath Mount Tabor. He had hoped to launch a night attack but was too late and the sun was already up when they were seen and the camp stirred into action. The French formed squares just in time to face a torrent of cavalry; some said there were 25,000 mounted warriors. The squares held for 10 hours and thirst, hunger and fatigue were beginning to achieve what the cavalry could not, when a distant cannon-shot echoed round the rocky hills: it was Bonaparte's column marching to their relief. The cavalry's dash turned to panic and they spurred away towards Damascus. Bonaparte slept that night at Nazareth.

This sort of victory was expected of Bonaparte and news of what he called the Battle of Mount Tabor was broadcast throughout the Levant. But Acre still had to be taken and Bonaparte returned to the siege. Back at the camp, where his men were miserable with dysentery, plague, heat, flies and the stink of death that hung over the walls of Acre like the gunsmoke and haze of dust, he decided that action was the only solution. The siege guns had, he had heard, been landed at Jaffa but, without waiting for them to be dragged over the hills to Acre, he ordered another, immediate assault. Early on 24th April, a mine was blown beneath a corner of the Devil's Tower and grenadiers guards again charged the breach. But, as Peyrusse wrote home, 'It was clear that it was impossible to penetrate it. The enemy, installed at the top of the tower and hidden behind the battlements, flattened our troops with rocks, shells and hand grenades. However, since nothing could turn back our troops, the Turks resorted to powder kegs which they threw on them. All our men were suffocated although a few managed to run away half-burned.'[9] These kegs were called 'stink-pots', filled with sulphur and mealed gunpowder that gave off choking fumes. So another attack was ordered for the following morning. This time, the French broke into the ground floor of the Devil's Tower, but the Turks above tore open the ceiling to hurl down grenades and again the French were expelled.

Now the siege artillery was arriving and Bonaparte wrote to his staff in Cairo that he expected Acre to fall on May 5th, or 6th. The fourth and fifth assaults on May 1st and 4th – this at night, the attackers illuminated by lanterns lit by the defenders in front of the breach – and another on the 6th, also failed because Bonaparte had, in his impatience, committed them before his siege artillery was in position. Defending the breach, the Turks were at their best, showing their individual courage and ferocity, driven by their fear of the French and their religious fervour. When they suddenly collapsed into panic – as they sometimes did – there was always a file of British marines or gun-crews, of sailors ready to fight with their customary resilience.

Smith himself seemed to be everywhere. From the *Tigre* he directed naval operations and conducted his correspondence with Constantinople, his superiors at sea and with London; he was constantly out and about in the city and was usually on the walls when an assault was expected, demonstrating that he was as physically active as he was mentally agile. With his interest in espionage, guerrilla and psychological warfare, he was ashore and outside the defences as well. Such an occasion was to be recalled by one of his officers, Midshipman Richard Janverin. A small group had crept forward from the walls, when one of them sighted French sharpshooters in front of their trenches. 'I see them lying down under the ridges of sand, Sir Sidney,' he was warned, 'and they will put a ball through you before you can say Jack Robinson.' Having been sighted, there was no question of crawling back to the walls and Smith ordered, 'Now, boys, the devil take the hindmost!' and ran. Janverin added that Smith had got to the breach 'before his companions were half way.'[10]

Here, as in Egypt, Bonaparte was also confident in his use of psychological warfare. He had distributed leaflets in Arabic proclaiming himself the defender of Islam, he who had already destroyed the power of the Pope in Rome and of the Knights of

St John in Malta. He also circulated a proclamation to the Christians (and to the emir of the Druze, the unorthodox Islamic sect persecuted by other Moslems), that he was the successor to the Crusaders as a defender of the Faith. However, Smith had acquired examples of both and reprinted and distributed each to the opposite side, so that Moslems saw him as a Christian champion and Christians as a Moslem. As result, the Islamic Druze leader forbade his men to fight for the French and allied himself to the British. To cap it, Smith himself signed leaflets printed in Constantinople with the Sultan's offer of a free passage to France for any soldier who surrendered and had bundles of them thrown into the besiegers' trenches.

Furious at having met his match, Bonaparte published accusations against Sir Sidney. He accused him of having deliberately sent the French prisoners he had freed at Constantinople back to France in a plague-infested ship – Midshipman Beecroft had, in fact, rejoined the *Tigre* after this mission and reported that he had landed them all in good health at Marseilles – and that he had condoned Djezzar's murder of his French prisoners, concluding: 'His proceedings during the whole of his cruise have been those of a madman.'[11]

Within the walls of Acre, the defenders were running short of ammunition and anxiously watched the western horizon for the relief fleet from Rhodes. Smith galvanized the defence: on the walls to meet a new assault, on board his ship, in conference with Djezzar and by letting his energetic uniformed figure be seen throughout the city. Then, on 2nd May, he suffered a loss of which he wrote to St Vincent, 'Our grief for this loss is excessive on every account': Colonel Phélippeaux, the engineer, had, as Smith put it, 'fallen a sacrifice to his zeal for this service: want of rest and exposure to the sun having given him a fever, of which he died.'[12]

The French had driven a new mine under the Devil's Tower but because the siege guns were not all sited, Bonaparte postponed the next assault for twenty-four hours and, during that time, the defenders, digging a counter-mine, broke into it and destroyed it. Although no new breach could now be blown, the assault was ordered and one French column refused to attack. Finally, on 7th May, all the heavy guns had been mounted in the batteries and yet another attack was ordered but only after a two-day bombardment. Then, that day, the fifty-first of the siege, the sails of the Turkish troop transports from Rhodes and their escort of corvettes at last came over the horizon, their Turkish commander, Hassan Bey, having been delayed because his original orders had sent him to join Smith in Egypt. It was obvious that once reinforcements and, more importantly, ammunition were put ashore in the city, it could probably hold out longer than the besiegers. So Bonaparte ordered an assault that evening.

This time, the French artillery fire 'suddenly increased tenfold'. Guns in the British ships and the brass cannon on the lighthouse returned fire but with less effect because, under cover of night, the French had thrown up earthworks close to the breach to protect themselves. That night they built protective breastworks close to the walls 'composed of sandbags and the bodies of their dead, built in with them, their bayonets alone being visible above them.' The attack began before dawn, the French clambering over the rubble that half-blocked the moat and gaining the top of the Devil's Tower so that, Smith reported, 'daylight showed us the French standard on the outer angle of the tower'.

The next day, the 8th, was, as Smith said, 'a most critical point of the contest' because his reinforcements were to be landed and 'an effort was necessary to preserve the place for a short time till their arrival'. He had some 800 marines and seamen ashore, mostly manning guns, and now he led them to the breach, where he found 'the heap of ruins between the two parties serving as a breastwork for both, the muzzles of their muskets touching and the spearheads of the standards locked'. Djezzar suddenly became alarmed that if Smith were killed the defence would collapse and, as the latter reported to St Vincent:

Djezzar Pasha, hearing that the English were on the breach, quitted his station, where, according to ancient Turkish custom, he was sitting to reward such as should bring him the heads of the enemy and distributing musket cartridges with his own hands. The energetic old man, coming behind us, pulled us down with violence, saying if any harm happened to his English friends all was lost. This amicable contest as to who should defend the breach occasioned a rush of Turks to the spot and thus time was gained for the arrival of the first body of Hassan Bey's troops.

Djezzar's gratitude enabled Smith to persuade him at last to allow troops to be employed in the gardens of the seraglio, which abutted the city wall. Hitherto only his Albanians were privileged to defend it but only 200 survived out of the original 1,000 and now he finally agreed to replace them with the best of the reinforcements due to land that day.

Most of the reinforcements that were ferried ashore were the usual mixture of Middle Eastern fighting men, as effective in holding a breach as they were ineffective on the open battle-field. But there was an exception, the Chifflick regiment – named after their barracks outside Constantinople – were trained to European standards and, as soon as they disembarked, Smith proposed they make a sortie. It failed and they were driven back but they had forced the French out of their trenches and into range of grapeshot from the naval guns. Consequently, the Chifflicks were rewarded with the honour of defending the garden of the seraglio.

The heavy French artillery began to concentrate its fire on the weak curtain wall beside the Devil's Tower, bringing down the stone facing in sheets. In the late afternoon, Smith sighted French officers gathering on King Richard's Mount, their gold lace catching the sunlight. 'Bonaparte was distinguishable in the centre of the semi-circle,' he noted, 'his gesticulating indicated a renewal of attack.' Then, he continued in his report to St Vincent:

> A little before sunset, a massive column appeared advancing to the breach with solemn step. The Pasha's idea was not to defend the breach this time but rather to let a certain number of the enemy in and then close with them, according to the Turkish mode of war. The column then mounted the breach unmolested and descended from the rampart into the Pasha's garden, where, in a very few minutes, the bravest and most advanced amongst them lay headless corpses, the sabre, with the addition of the dagger in the other hand, proving more than a match for the bayonet ... Much confusion arose in the town from the actual entry of the enemy, it having been impossible, nay impolitic, to give previous information to everybody of the mode of defence adopted, lest the enemy should come to a knowledge of it through their numerous emissaries.

Two French generals had led the assault: one lay dead in the garden of the seraglio and the other managed to stagger back through the breach, streaming with blood. Smith described the trap, mixing his metaphors, 'We keep the bull pinned and compare our breach to a mouse-trap.' The enemy had been driven out after twenty-five hours' fighting, 'both parties being so fatigued as to be unable to move'.

The lull could only be short, for, Smith wrote, 'the breach being perfectly practicable for fifty men abreast ... we feel that it is by this breach that Bonaparte means to march to further conquest'. Seeing crowds of tribesmen who had massed on the distant hills he emphasized the scale of the decision reached in that bloody breach. 'Tis on the issue of this conflict that depends the opinion of the multitude of spectators on the surrounding hills, who wait only to see how it ends to join the victor' and, when that was decided, 'Constantinople, and even Vienna, must feel the shock.'[13]

On the evening of this last assault, Bonaparte walked on the beach out of range of the British guns with General Bourrienne and mused, 'This wretched place has cost me a number of men and wasted much time. But things are too far advanced not to attempt a last effort. If I succeed ... I shall march upon Damascus and Aleppo ... I shall overturn the Turkish Empire and found in the east a new and grand empire that will fix my place in the records of posterity. Perhaps, I shall return to Paris by Adrianople,* or by Vienna after annihilating the House of Austria.'[14]

That same day Smith had written a letter to Bonaparte. The Turkish ships from Rhodes had brought with them several staff officers, including his French royalist friend Major de Frotté; they had told him of the French consul named Beauchamp, whom Napoleon had sent on a mission to Constantinople to negotiate with the Sultan, even offering the possibility of an eventual French withdrawal from Egypt. Beauchamp had been detained and details of his mission forwarded to Smith, who now wrote to Bonaparte in French, enclosing the Turkish leaflet offering a safe passage home to French soldiers who surrendered:

Since your instructions to your emissary Beauchamp contain

---

* The modern Edirne in western Turkey near the border of Greece.

these words, 'If you are asked whether the French would agree to
leave Egypt' along with your reply, 'Why not?', I believe I may
send you the enclosed proclamation of the Ottoman Porte
without your finding it out of place.

I did not want to ask you the question, 'Are the French willing
to leave Syria?' before you had a chance to match your strength
against ours, since you could not be persuaded, as I am, of the
impracticability of your enterprise ... But now ... you can see
that [this city] becomes stronger each day instead of being weakened by two months of siege, I do ask you this, 'Are you willing
to evacuate your troops from the territory of the Ottoman Empire
before the intervention of the great allied army changes the
nature of this question?'

You may believe me, *Monsieur Le Général*, that my only
motive in asking you this is my desire to avoid further
bloodshed.[15]

Smith did not expect Bonaparte to give up and indeed he had
one final plan. Kléber's division, which had had the relatively
easy task of guarding the inland flank was summoned and they
arrived at the camp on 9th May, the day after he read Smith's
letter. There was to be another assault – the eleventh – on the
10th and Bonaparte declared that he would lead it himself.
Sensing this was to be the climax, Smith took his place on the
walls, hatless as usual – 'We do not in general wear hats,' he
noted, 'there being a hundred and fifty marksmen in the French
trenches stationed to pick off the English.'[16] He cut a wild
figure, describing himself as 'almost blind, what with the dust
from shells, hot sun and much writing.'[17]

Kléber's division was to begin the attack, and they filed,
primed with brandy and brimming with confidence, from the
camp to the trenches. Bonaparte was persuaded against leading
the attack and himself told Kléber to remain in the rear, an
order he ignored. It was not only the walls that had to be
stormed, because the Chifflick regiment, anxious to redeem its
initial failure, had made another sortie and captured the
trenches nearest the walls, pressed on to take more and had
pushed a salient into the French lines. So, while one French
assault column, led by General Fouler, would assault the
breach, another, led by General Bon, would attack the
Chifflicks.

The attack began at 3.00 a.m., before the sun rose. Scrambling
over breastwork of sandbags and rotting corpses, the French

rushed forward, cutting through the Chifflicks and bursting through the breach into the Pasha's garden beyond. The defenders' second line of defence buckled and, as the French seemed about to break into the city itself, Arab women on the rooftops wailed their high-pitched ululations of despair. But the final line held and again the French vanguard was killed, trapped, or driven back through the breach. 'Sir Sidney is pretty well occupied,' said his secretary, 'particularly in the smoke, musketry and ditch fight, all of which is becoming a matter of course.'[18] A final assault was to be made early that same afternoon in the heat of the day.

Bonaparte was watching from the forward siege-batteries and his aide-de-camp, Captain Lavalette, described the initial repulse:

'The grenadiers of Kléber returned to the trenches by a vigorous fusillade, demanding with loud shouts a renewal of the assault. Bonaparte hesitated but, urged by these brave men, he gave the signal. It was a grand and terrific spectacle: the grenadiers rushed forward under a shower of balls. Kléber, with the gait of a giant, with his thick head of hair, had taken his post, sword in hand, on the bank of the breach and animated the assailants. The noise of the cannon, the enthusiastic shouts, the rage of the soldiers and the yelling of the Turks mingled themselves with the bursts of his thundering voice ...

All at once the column of the besiegers came to a standstill, Bonaparte threw himself forward from the battery and then perceived that, at the place where the soldiers were stopped, the ditch was vomiting out flames, a thick explosion of the materials with which the mine was charged, came out of the ground and overthrew everyone ... Kléber, in great rage, struck his thigh with his sword; but the General-in-Chief, judging the obstacle to be insurmountable, gave a gesture and ordered a retreat ...[19]

The battlefield gradually calmed and stayed silent, the scene of desolation dominated by smoke rising from the smouldering jumble of barricades and the sickly-sweet stink of death. Smith sensed that this was the end and, next day, sat down to write another letter to Bonaparte that had long been on his mind:

General, I am acquainted with the dispositions that for some days past you have been making to raise the siege; the preparations in hand to carry off your wounded, and to leave none behind you, do you credit.

This last word ought not to escape my mouth – I, who ought not to love you, to say nothing more: but circumstances remind me to wish that you would reflect on the instability of human affairs. In fact, could you have thought that a poor prisoner in a cell of the Temple prison – that an unfortunate for whom you refused, for a single moment, to give yourself any concern, being at the same time able to render him a signal service since you were then all-powerful – could you have thought, I say, that this same man would have become your antagonist and have compelled you in the midst of the sands of Syria to raise the siege of a miserable, almost defenceless town? Such events, you must admit, exceed all human calculations. Believe me, general, adopt sentiments more moderate; that a man will not be your enemy who shall tell you that Asia is not a theatre made for your glory. This letter is a little revenge that I give myself.[20]

The letter stung Bonaparte. Realizing that his staff knew he had received a letter from Smith, he told them that it had challenged him to a duel but that he would only accept such a challenge from a British general of the standing of Marlborough. He could not bring himself to ask any favour of Smith, even for the most pressing humanitarian reasons. At the time, a small squadron of French frigates was off the coast to the south and, under the customs of war, it would have been usual for him to ask Smith to allow them to evacuate his sick and wounded to Egypt, for it would be almost impossible for them to make the journey overland. But he could not bring himself to ask the favour and, on 13th May, when the frigates were reported to Smith, he ordered the *Theseus* in chase. Then unexpected disaster struck the British. On board the 'seventy-four', a seaman, trying to extract a fuse from an unexploded French bomb for re-use, struck it with a hammer, causing a spark that ignited it, setting off a huge explosion of powder barrels and seventy shells stacked below the poop. Twenty-six men were killed – including Captain Miller, the American who had distinguished himself at the Battle of the Nile – and the upperworks of the ship were shattered.

Next day the French guns opened another barrage; they were not concentrating on the walls, this time, but on the city beyond and the motive seemed to be revenge rather than preparation for yet another assault. In the French camp, Bonaparte assembled his generals and staff and asked their opinions of the prospects of continuing the siege. 'General, I liken the town of

Acre to a piece of cloth,' said Kléber, in his down-to-earth way,
'When I go to the merchant to buy it, I ask to feel it; I look at it,
I touch it and if I find it too dear, I leave it.'[21] Acre, he implied,
was too expensive. Indeed, there seemed to be no possibility of
continuing. Already, nearly half the French army had been
killed, wounded or taken sick and, although the plague was not
as rampant as it had been at Jaffa, new cases were still being
reported in the camp and there was always risk of a major
outbreak. There could be no question of continuing the advance
northward and leaving Acre in their rear, but, if they continued
the siege they could not be reinforced by sea, nor from Egypt,
which was already thinly held, while the British and Turks
could ship as many men and as much war material into Acre as
they wished.

Retreat was, therefore, the only option but there were two
particular problems. One was the wounded and sick, who were
unable to face the long overland journey to Egypt. The other
was the need to convince the world that their defeat had been
a victory. The decision to retreat was taken and the artillery
ordered to fire all their remaining ammunition into the city so
that it could at least be claimed that Acre had been destroyed,
if not captured.

Sidney Smith had no such problem. Acre had been held and
the French dreams of conquest ended. He watched from the
deck of his ship as the French prepared to strike camp, hauling
away a few guns and spiking those they could not move, or
dragging them to the shore and rolling them into the sea. On
20th May, they could be seen forming into columns and beginning their long march south. Next day, Smith, too, left Acre,
sailing for Jaffa in the *Tigre*. At sea, he spent hours in his cabin,
drafting a long report to Nelson, which he sent on the 30th by
the *Theseus*, now commanded by Lieutenant Canes, who had
been Captain Miller's first lieutenant.

'My Lord,' he began, 'the providence of Almighty God has
been wonderfully manifested in the defeat and precipitate
retreat of the French army; the means we had of opposing its
gigantic efforts against us being totally inadequate of themselves to the production of such a result ... The plain of Nazareth
has been the boundary of Bonaparte's extraordinary career.'[22]

Nelson was still at Palermo, preparing the attempt to
recapture Naples from the French and the Neapolitan

revolutionaries, unaware of the outcome of Bonaparte's advance through Syria. Captain Troubridge had, however, told him of Smith's arrival off Alexandria and of his proposal to give the French an opportunity to evacuate Egypt. He was still infuriated by what he saw as Smith's high-handed manner and had written to St Vincent, again belittling Smith: 'If Sir Sidney was an object of anger, I would not serve unless he was taken away; but I despise such frippery and nonsense as he is composed of.'[23] At the end of April, he had written again, saying, 'I am very much displeased with this Levant Commodore with a Broad Pendant.'[24] Several days after Smith had written his report from Jaffa, Nelson, still smarting over his having signed the treaty of friendship with the Turks, wrote to Spencer Smith in Constantinople, initially praising the professional qualities of Sir Sidney before continuing:

> Having said this, it may readily be conceived that I do not like to have any *Junior* to some measure placed, if not over my head, at least as taking from my consequence. I did not think it was necessary for any Sea-officer to be joined in signing a treaty ... but, if it was, I shall ever think that Sea-officer should have been *Nelson*.'[25]

So, instead of congratulations, the first messages that reached Smith from his superiors were harsh questions written many weeks before. He was amazed to receive a letter from Lord Spencer demanding he explain reports of his insubordination towards Lord St Vincent, something of which he was unaware. From the old admiral himself there was a reprimand for having 'given orders to ships not put under his command by Lord Nelson'.[26] This referred to the frigate *Charon*, which, although no longer commanded by Lord Camelford, he had assumed to be carrying the ordnance he needed at Acre, but which had, unknown to Smith, taken the military mission to Constantinople under General Koehler. There it had been held by the general, who was outraged that Smith should be fighting a land battle, which he considered his own responsibility, and had lodged complaints. None of his seniors would have received his final despatches from Acre.

Smith had written a vivid account of the siege for his brother to give the Sultan in Constantinople. Spencer Smith also sent a copy to Nelson, who was now in the Bay of Naples; hearing that the city was about to fall to the royalist counter-offensive, he had arrived with his squadron to find that a truce had been declared and that the rebels, holding out in the city's three great castles, had been granted an amnesty; angrily, he had torn up the agreement and handed the republicans over to the vengeful monarch; the insurgents' admiral had been hanged from his own yard-arm and executions had begun ashore. Despite the tensions arising from his own determination to concentrate on the crisis in Naples and that of the new Commander-in-Chief, Lord Keith, to give priority to watching the French fleet in the Mediterranean, he wrote immediately, impulsively and with his characteristic generosity, to Smith on 20th July, 'We had the great pleasure of hearing that your truly meritorious and wonderful exertions were in a fair train for the extirpation of that horde of thieves who went into Egypt with that arch-thief Bonaparte.' He apologized for not being able to send him any more ships but congratulated him and his officers on 'your and their great merit' and ended his letter expressing his 'greatest esteem'.[27]

Meanwhile, ten months after Smith had been given his double assignment by Spencer and Grenville, Nelson finally learned exactly what this had been and that Smith had been acting within his rights. So he wrote a letter of apology and self-justification to Spencer Smith. After congratulating him on Sir Sidney's achievement at Acre, he continued:

> No one admires his gallantry and judgement more than myself. But, if I know myself, as I never have encroached on the command of others, so I will not suffer even my friend Sir Sidney to encroach upon mine. I dare say he thought he was to have a separate command in the Levant. I find upon inquiry that it never was intended to have any one in the Levant separate from me.

It had been a massive failure of communication.

Smith sent his despatch to Nelson by Midshipman James Boxer, who was commanding a gunboat, one of the *Tigre*'s prizes, and reached him at Palermo. When he arrived, Nelson was breakfasting ashore with the Hamiltons and invited Boxer to join them while he read the despatch aloud. Finally, after asking the midshipman to give his own account of the siege, Nelson rose and said, 'Give your name to the secretary's office; they are making out your commission to be lieutenant.' Then, it was reported, he continued: 'Here the young gentleman put on a woeful countenance, stammering out that he had not passed his examination.' Lord Nelson then said, 'Write to me as soon as you have passed and lose no time.'[28]

When Boxer had left, Nelson wrote a fulsome letter to Smith:

The immense fatigue you have had in defending Acre against such a chosen army of French villains, headed by that arch-villain Bonaparte, has never been exceeded and the bravery shown by you and your brave companions is such as to merit every encomium which all the civilised world can bestow. As an individual, and as an Admiral, will you accept my feeble tribute of praise and admiration ... Be assured, my dear Sir Sidney, of my perfect esteem and regard and do not let anyone persuade you to the contrary. But my character is that I will not suffer the smallest title of my command to be taken from me; but with pleasure I give way to my friends, among whom I beg you will allow me to consider you and that I am, with the truest esteem and affection, your faithful, humble servant, Nelson.[29]

Never again would Nelson mock Smith as 'the Swedish Knight' and not only because of their new-found friendship. Nelson himself had just been created Duke of Bronte by King Ferdinand of the Two Sicilies, and given an estate on the slopes of Mount Etna, which had been confiscated from the church and from which the dukedom took its name. Perhaps Nelson had been teased as 'the Sicilian Duke'. Also, the Sultan was to present both Nelson and Smith with the gift of a *chelengk*, a spray of diamonds that was to be worn in the hat, its centre revolving by clockwork.

When the news of Bonaparte's defeat reached London, there was satisfaction rather than the euphoria that had greeted Nelson's victory in Aboukir Bay. But it was realized that they were parallel achievements and both Houses of Parliament passed resolutions of praise for Sir Sidney Smith. Lord Spencer spoke in the House of Lords of:

an exploit which has never been surpassed, and scarcely ever been equalled, in the annals of history – I mean the defence of St. Jean d'Acre by Sir Sidney Smith ... The splendour of such an exploit as defeating a veteran and well-appointed army, commanded by experienced generals, and which had already overrun a great part of Europe, a fine portion of Africa and attempted also the conquest of Asia, eclipsed all former examples ...[30]

Lord Grenville recalled how 'Sir Sidney Smith had been long, with a most cool and cruel inflexibility, confined in a dungeon of the Temple, from which he was only rescued by his own address and intrepidity ... This hero, in the progress of events, was afterwards destined to oppose the enemy in a distant quarter.'[31] In the House of Commons, Henry Dundas, the Secretary of State for War, echoed their sentiments but added:

I have heard that Sir Sidney Smith, who has had his difficulties, has sometimes been lightly spoken of by some persons; whoever they are, they were inconsiderate, and they may now be left to their inward shame if they do not recant. Be that as it may, the House, I am confident, agrees with me that the conduct of Sir Sidney Smith for heroism and intrepidity and active exertion has never been surpassed on any occasion.[32]

Motions of thanks were passed by both Houses and Smith was awarded an annuity of £1,000. The print shops displayed dramatic engravings of him in the breach of Acre and a huge, hastily painted *Great Historical Picture of the Siege of Acre* was exhibited with a printed key describing the British, Turkish and French participants. Popular ballads were published and sold on the streets, one beginning:

> Shall Acre's feeble citadel,
> Victor, thy shattered hosts repel?
> Insulting chief, despair –
> A Briton meets thee there![33]

The *Naval Magazine* joined the chorus with more specific praise:

> See how Sir Sidney grows in fame,
> While over Asia spreads his name:
> His glory is to boast,
> That e'en a seaman has made flee
> The Conqueror of Italy
> With all his vet'ran host.[34]

Smith and Nelson were now the two national heroes. They had something more in common than success in battle, a mixture of dash and ambition, a flair for leadership and a foreign title. Both had been passed over for the highest honours. Nelson had been offended when only awarded a barony after the Battle of the Nile, while Jervis had become an

earl after the far less important victory of Cape St Vincent. Yet,
Sir Sidney Smith was not honoured with any British title after
his own victory, which had finally saved, not only the Ottoman
Empire, but perhaps eastern Europe and India from the French.
He was still a Swedish knight and yet it was he, and not
Nelson, of whom Bonaparte finally said, 'That man made me
miss my destiny.'*[35]

* 'Cet homme m'a fait manquer ma fortune.'

CHAPTER SIX

'You love glory'

CAPTAIN SMITH AND General Bonaparte both set out on journeys when the siege of Acre was raised. The latter was struggling to extricate his half-wrecked army from Syria and, with his genius for manipulating opinion, had tried to hearten his soldiers with a proclamation presenting their defeat as a victory:

> Soldiers, you have crossed the desert which divides Africa from Asia with greater speed than an army of Arabs ... You have dispersed in the plain below Mount Tabor the horde of men from every corner of Asia who had gathered in the hope of looting Egypt ... After maintaining ourselves in the heart of Syria for three months with only a handful of men ... after razing the fortifications of Gaza, Jaffa, Haifa and Acre, we shall return to Egypt. I am obliged to go back there because this is the season when hostile landings may be expected ...
>
> At this point the capture of Acre is not worth wasting even a few days ... Soldiers, there are more hardships and dangers facing us ... You will find in them new opportunities for glory.[1]

The men he harangued knew this was hollow boasting but it set the scene for a triumphant return. Bonaparte sent a message to Cairo announcing that his victorious return in triumph was imminent: 'I shall bring many prisoners and captured flags with me ... I have razed ... the ramparts of Acre and I have bombarded the city in such a manner that not one stone remains in its place.'[2]

The reality was different. One problem was that more than 1,200 wounded and sick men could not be expected to survive the long march back to Egypt. He still could not bring himself to ask Smith to help evacuate them to Alexandria, or even to France, on parole, or in neutral ships. So the wounded would have to accompany the retreat and those suffering from plague were abandoned. What was left of the demoralized army struggled back along the coastal road, until British gunboats pulled close inshore to pepper the vanguard with grapeshot and they were forced to veer on to an inland track. General Bourrienne recorded:

> I saw with my own eyes officers, who had limbs amputated, being thrown out of their litters ... I have seen amputated men, wounded men, plague-stricken men, or people merely suspected of having the plague, being abandoned in the fields. Our march was lit up by torches with which we set fire to the towns, the villages, the hamlets and the rich harvests that covered the land. The entire countryside was on fire.[3]

Bonaparte ordered that nobody who could walk, himself included, was allowed to ride and all horses must be used to carry the wounded.

Finally arriving at Jaffa, they were first met by the stink of thousands of rotting corpses of the Turks they had slaughtered on the beach, and the hospital was still crowded with sick Frenchmen. There were six ships lying off the town and these were loaded with the wounded and ordered to make for Egypt, although short of food and water and without enough seamen to work them. They sailed but, disobeying Bonaparte's orders, immediately gave themselves up to Smith's watching warships 'in full confidence of receiving the succours of humanity', as Smith put it in his report, 'in which they were not disappointed ... Their expressions of gratitude to us were mingled with execrations on the name of their general, who had, as they said, thus exposed them to perish.'[4]

When Bonaparte left Jaffa it was occupied by Ismael Pasha, the Governor of Jerusalem, who sent 2,000 horsemen to harry the French on their way to Egypt. Meanwhile the British put a landing party ashore just in time to stop further massacre of Frenchmen abandoned in the hospital. When Midshipman Janverin landed, he reported, 'I found seven unfortunate Frenchmen in the act of being led from their hospital, where they had been left by the army under plague, to be put to a summary death; and, after a great deal of trouble ... and some little danger from the Turkish soldiers, I rescued them';[5] they were taken out to a ship and sent to Egypt.

Smith spent several days following Bonaparte's journeys to Nazareth and Jerusalem. At Nazareth, after the Battle of Mount Tabor, Bonaparte, who, like his soldiers, had been born a Christian, had shown curiosity and also reverence, rebuking those Frenchmen who did not; the *Te Deum* had been sung to celebrate their victory and their general had shown the same diplomatic courtesy as towards the shrines of Islam. Smith, on the other hand, gave thanks for *his* victory at the cave of the Annunciation. He was welcomed to Jerusalem by both Christians and Moslems as their deliverer 'from the merciless hands of Bonaparte'[6] and allowed to enter the city with his officers armed and in uniform, an exceptional privilege.

The remnant of Bonaparte's army struggled into Egypt. As they took the road to Cairo, the sick and wounded were left at French camps they passed, so that only the healthy should be seen making their triumphant entry into the capital. This had been carefully stage managed and, when the army arrived on 14th June, it marched down streets strewn with palm fronds, each man wearing one in his hat. Captured Turkish flags were paraded in the principal square before French generals, Egyptian dignitaries and vast crowds. However, as one French officer remarked, 'They seemed extremely curious to know how many there were left of us.'[7] The explanation for the small size of the parade was that much of the army had been left on the coast and in the delta to face possible invasion by the Turks, as, indeed, Kléber's division had been. The casualties to which Bonaparte admitted were 2,200 dead and 2,300 wounded and sick, although the actual total would seem to have been much higher. Peyrusse wrote:

> This campaign may be considered very disastrous for our establishment. The losses it occasioned no longer permits us to undertake any further expeditions and we have to mourn great men and the best soldiers. The army is resting today from its labours; already a proclamation by the commander-in-chief announces more battles to come. Good God, when shall we stop fighting?[8]

Smith now sailed to Rhodes, where another Turkish army was assembling for the re-conquest of Egypt. His own position was increasingly unclear. When the British Government had appointed him joint minister to the Sublime

Porte, he had also been given, as a naval officer, whatever
ships in the eastern Mediterranean were commanded by more
junior captains. In the first rôle, the Sultan had verbally given
him command of his army and navy; in the second, both St
Vincent, Lord Keith, who succeeded him that June, and Lord
Nelson had made it clear that, as a naval officer, he was under
the latter's orders and must either correspond with him as a
subordinate captain, or as a joint minister, in which case he
must write jointly with his brother; this was of course, an
impossibility, as he and Spencer were many hundreds of miles
apart. Although Nelson was still plying between Naples and
Palermo, Rhodes was clearly his responsibility, so Smith could
only offer advice to the Turks. He wrote to Nelson at his
customary length, pointing out that his political authority had
been exercised at Acre and that:

> I have now to inform your Lordship, that … in consequence of
> the treaty [with the Ottoman Government] I have not only the
> Turkish fleet … but the Turkish army put under my orders, not
> as captain of the *Tigre*, of course, but as the King of Great Britain's
> minister … I shall not, of course, deviate from the very confined
> line your Lordship has traced me as captain of the *Tigre*,
> commanding the blockade of Alexandria; but, as experience has
> proved the utility of quitting that blockade, while I was ignorant
> of being so confined, I trust your Lordship will see the necessity
> of setting me at liberty to act as was concerted at Constantinople
> with that discretionary power which circumstances on the spot
> can alone dictate …[9]

He knew that Nelson himself had disregarded the letter of
his own instructions when circumstances suggested the use of
initiative and he expected him to agree and allow him the
leeway he expected himself, and was, indeed, exceeding in his
relations with Lord Keith. But, in the light of the stern rebukes
he had received from both admirals – the letters of congratula-
tion not having yet arrived – he could not take control of the
Turkish expedition, which was about to sail from Rhodes for
Egypt. So he could only recommend to Mustapha Bey, who was
in command, that he land in the Nile delta, away from any
French concentration, and make contact with other Ottoman
forces before facing Bonaparte on the battlefield; he left Major
Bromley – alias de Tromelin – as his military adviser and hoped
for the best.

Smith himself was to accompany the second Turkish convoy from Rhodes, with 2,000 men embarked, while the main force of 5,000 under Mustapha Bey went ahead; the latter was off Alexandria in the second week of July. General Marmont, who commanded the garrison, expecting an immediate attack, recalled his forces deployed along the coast, so leaving the delta open to an unopposed Turkish landing. But, despite the advice to make such a landing being repeated by Major Bromley, Mustapha chose to put his men ashore in Aboukir Bay because he was confident that they could easily overwhelm the small fortified town of Aboukir on its point overlooking the scene of Nelson's victory.

It was as easy as he had expected and the defences were stormed, and 300 French defenders slaughtered. When 35 more Frenchmen, who had been holding the keep, surrendered, they were only saved from being killed in cold blood by the intervention of Major Bromley. When Smith arrived five days later, the whole of Mustapha's army was ashore, too excited to complete new defensive works that would include essential wells outside the town, so that their flank lay open on the sands. The Turkish army had grown to 7,000 and it defended a fortified town on a peninsula with a fleet and all necessary ammunition and stores lying offshore, so its position should have been impregnable as Acre had proved to be.

The tireless Bonaparte was, however, already marching from Cairo at the head of 10,000 infantry and 1,000 cavalry, with Kléber's division following. French scouts had reported that the Turkish flank was still open, so Napoleon decided – as Nelson once had in the bay beyond – to go straight into the attack. The Turks had no cavalry, so the French cavalry charged and the flank was turned despite desperate efforts by gunboats from the *Tigre* and *Theseus* to beat them back. There were no British to stiffen the defences ashore, and, when Turkish discipline broke, they turned and fled to the fort on the point. Major Bromley and a British major of marines, went ashore and tried to rally the defenders and they held out for a week, when shortage of water forced them to surrender. Ships' boats were able to save hundreds of Turks but the army itself was destroyed. This victory was exactly what Bonaparte needed and his despatches wildly exaggerated Turkish losses, the first claiming them to be double the actual strength of the Turkish army and the second adding another 5,000 to that figure.*

When it was over, Bromley, who had saved the captured Frenchmen, was sent ashore to negotiate an exchange of prisoners but Bonaparte, who now knew his true identity, refused to deal with a royalist *émigré* and Smith's secretary, John Keith† was sent ashore. He was courteously received and he soon realized that they had heard no recent news from France. So, when a French officer came out to the *Tigre* to conclude exchange arrangements, Smith casually gave him two newspapers – the *Gazette de Francfort* of 6th June and the *Courrier Français de Londres* of the 10th – and he also mentioned that the British had captured a French ship carrying a letter to Bonaparte from the Directory, ordering him to return to France. This news reached Bonaparte in camp as he was preparing for an even more triumphant victory parade through Cairo. He was horrified to read that, in Europe, French armies were being expelled from Italy and Germany, and was convinced that only he could save the republic: this was his hour of destiny.

Out at sea, Smith could make an accurate assumption of Bonaparte's reaction and he wrote to the Admiralty to warn that he expected Bonaparte would try to return to France; therefore every effort should be made to intercept and capture him at sea. He added that Kléber would probably be left in command of *L'Armée d'Egypte* and that it might well be possible to negotiate the French evacuation of Egypt with him.

Having decided to return, Bonaparte indeed wrote to Kléber, summoning him to a conference at Rosetta on the coast of the delta on 24th August, knowing that, by then, he himself would already be at sea. He dictated a brief farewell message to his solders: 'the army will soon have news of me; I can say no more.'[10] He then went aboard the frigate *Muiron*, which he had named after a favourite aide-de-camp, killed in the act of saving his master's life in the Italian campaign. Taking with him several of his most faithful generals – including Berthier, Marmont, Murat and Lannes – he sailed early on 23rd August, the day before Kléber arrived for the proposed conference to be given a letter informing him that he was now in command of

* A Metro station in Paris was to be named 'Aboukir' after this battle.

† later to be drowned when a boat capsized off Rosetta

the army. The voyage was tense and slow, a British sail always expected, and occasionally seen, on the horizon. But the *Tigre* had gone to Cyprus for replenishment and the *Theseus*, which had taken over her coastal patrol, had had to make for Rhodes for the same reason and there had been delayed, so the frigates found a clear run to France, landing Bonaparte at Fréjus on 9th October.

On that day, the *Tigre* was still off Cyprus, Smith having found that the survivors of Mustapha Bey's army had been landed there and were likely to mutiny and massacre the Christian population. Again, he took command, wearing the diamond *chelengk* in his hat to illustrate the authority invested in him by the Sultan. The mutineers were calmed and, in gratitude, the Greek archimandrite presented him with a cross once worn by King Richard Coeur de Lion while he was the Grand Master of the Knights Templar, and proclaimed him Grand Prior of the order in England – as King Richard had been – although it had been extinguished in the Middle Ages. When he heard that Bonaparte had reached France, he was disappointed that he had escaped capture but glad that he could now deal directly with General Kléber.

Smith was well aware that Nelson was wholly opposed to the negotiation of any terms with the French in Egypt and that he had received his written order forbidding him to allow a single Frenchman to return to France under any conditions; they must surrender unconditionally. On the other hand, instructions given him as a minister plenipotentiary by the British Government and agreed by their Turkish allies were diametrically opposite: to achieve the expulsion of the French from Egypt and the Levant by any means. Smith had thrown them back from Acre with loss of few British lives and it now seemed possible that he could achieve their withdrawal from Egypt with the loss of none. Nelson, at that very time, was disregarding Lord Keith's orders to leave Palermo and concentrate his ships at Minorca, which he believed to be threatened. He thought that a vital but vulnerable ally, the Kingdom of the Two Sicilies, was under greater threat and was the more important, whether or not he was influenced by the presence there of his mistress, Emma Hamilton. After disregarding such orders, Nelson had written to Lord Spencer, 'To say that an officer is never, for any object, to alter his orders is what I cannot comprehend. The circumstances of this war so often vary, that an officer has almost every moment to consider – What would my superiors direct, did they know what is passing under my nose?';[11] and later, 'I am fully aware of the act I have committed; but sensible of my loyal intentions, I am prepared for any fate, which may await disobedience.'[12] He and Smith had much in common.

Yet, although Sidney Smith was a senior officer in this particular theatre of war, he was not to know whether circumstances and opinions had changed in London. Nelson had already made his views known to the Government, but it had not contradicted Smith's proposed policy of expelling the French by peaceful means. So he assumed that its views were his own. Smith was worried about the next Turkish attempt, which was to be made by a much larger army, numbering something between 50,000 and 80,000, now slowly making its way overland, south through Syria on its way to Egypt, and which he felt certain would prove no match for Kléber's worn but experienced soldiers. So he again launched a leaflet campaign against the French, repeating the Sultan's offer of a free passage home for those who surrendered.

Smith wrote to Kléber in his fluent French, asking whether he would be interested in discussing terms. From the moment the general had heard of Nelson's destruction of the French fleet in Aboukir Bay, he had known that Bonaparte's grand strategy could not succeed; by now, only a minority of officers, led by General Menou, who had embraced Islam – and an Egyptian wife – disagreed with him. Kléber and Bonaparte had held each other in grudging admiration and personal dislike; their men, however, preferred the former, seeing themselves as betrayed by the latter. Bonaparte had been able to excite and inspire them, but only for a time; it was Kléber, the down-to-earth 'soldier's soldier', with his wide, blunt face and mane of hair, whom they liked and trusted. Kléber regarded Bonaparte's secretive escape to France (and Bonaparte advising him of his intentions and the fact that he was now in command by letter to be read *after* his departure), as typically devious. He at once stopped work on major defence works, and on the grandiose lighthouse that Bonaparte was having built on the site of the ancient Pharos of Alexandria, spending the money on his soldiers' pay and welfare. Despite mutual antipathy, Bonaparte had chosen Kléber as his successor because he was the rival he most feared in his ambition to become dictator of France and this seemed a sure way of prolonging his exile.

Kléber, for his part, knew that Bonaparte had made a tentative approach to the Turks to assess their willingness to negotiate a variety of options to end hostilities, but had received an insulting reply; he was not unduly worried by this as the Turks, on their own, posed no serious military threat and it was obvious that it was the British who would have to be approached. Bonaparte's parting instructions to Kléber had been that 'if, by next May, you have received neither help nor news from France and if, in the coming year, despite all precautions, the plague should kill more than 1,500 men ... you are authorised to make peace with the Ottoman Porte, even if the evacuation of Egypt should be the principal condition.'[13] Kléber chose to disregard all Bonaparte's instructions, if only because he knew that he had no authority, having returned to France without permission. So, instead, he wrote an angry letter to the Directory in Paris, declaring that Bonaparte had returned because 'he saw the fatal crisis approaching',[14] leaving him with an army reduced to half its original strength. He would now make his own policy.

Meanwhile, the main Turkish army was gathering itself for another assault and the first move was to establish a beachhead – as had been attempted at Aboukir – so that it could be ferried across from Syria without a long march through the desert. At the end of October, they landed under covering fire from the *Tigre* on the delta coast farther to the east and drove off a small French detachment. Three days later, General Verdier arrived with 1,000 French troops and was subjected to a wild Turkish charge, which might have succeeded had it been controlled; a French counter-attack routed them. It was not quite the decisive victory it seemed; too many demands had been made on the French soldiers and they mutinied, demanding their overdue pay and threatening to claim the Sultan's offer of a free passage home that Sir Sidney Smith had broadcast so widely. So Kléber wrote to Smith on 30th October, agreeing to send officers to meet him on board the *Tigre*, adding, 'It is time that two nations who may not be able to love each other, but who consider themselves to be the two most civilised nations in Europe, should stop fighting each other.'[15]

Smith knew Nelson would instinctively oppose any peace negotiations with the French; he had already torn up the truce agreement with the Neapolitan rebels, signed by another of his captains, with fearful consequences in terms of human suffering. But he kept him informed, writing on 8th November, after a report on the latest Turkish defeat, that French losses, which could not be replaced, 'must cost them dear in the end – a truth I, of course, endeavour to impress on them in order to induce them to come to terms of evacuation without further effusion of blood.' He admitted, 'I have opened a correspondence with the French Commander-in-Chief on this subject, which bids fair to come to a satisfactory issue as I find I have a liberal, humane man to deal with in General Kléber.'[16]

While arranging to negotiate, Smith decided that the war should be fought vigorously but with diplomacy. The vast Turkish army had now passed Gaza and Colonel Bromley – recently promoted – was sent to tell the Grand Vizier, who was in command, that they must cooperate to capture the fortress of El Arish, which was seen as the strategic key to Egypt. He would also say that a peaceful evacuation by the French would be to Turkish advantage; he did not add that this was partly because just half the original French army could probably defeat the Turks. For his part, Kléber chose two impressive negotiators, General Desaix, who had led the French expeditionary force up the Nile to Aswan, fighting brief but bloody battles and discovering the archaeological marvels of Ancient Egypt, and Poussielgue, the shrewd Controller of Finances. However, it was not easy for them to reach Sir Sidney because surf along the open delta coast, where they were to embark, prevented them from reaching the *Tigre* until 23rd December.

When they came aboard, they at once gave Smith a letter from Kléber, setting out his terms for the French evacuation of Egypt. These were: the ending of the alliance of Britain, Turkey and Russia against France; that France should be granted Malta and the Ionian islands – currently occupied by the Russians – in perpetuity and given ships in which to return to France with their weaponry. He added, understanding Smith's motivation, 'You love glory, General, and it seems to me to attach one's name to such an event would be the greatest glory one could win.'[17] Smith replied that it was out of the question to dissolve the alliance, at least until Egypt had been evacuated, and awaited Kléber's response; meanwhile they immediately agreed to a truce of one month.

In another letter addressed to the Grand Vizier, Kléber had written, 'I offer peace, friendship and the evacuation of Egypt with one hand and I accept battle with the other. Your Excellency in his wisdom will make the choice.'[18] The letter was forwarded, together with news of the truce, to the Grand Vizier but it reached him too late. Smith had asked him to halt his army at Gaza but he had continued to El Arish and when the French garrison mutinied and surrendered, most of them were massacred. Kléber, hearing of this in the first week of 1800, was furious but realized that it was another unintentional failure of communications; yet he was further persuaded that his army had lost heart and that a negotiated return to France was the only practicable option.

When negotiations re-opened after a month, Smith was confident of success. One potential embarrassment had been the intervention of Lord Elgin, who had arrived at Constantinople in November and was now the senior British 'ambassador extraordinary' to the Sublime Porte. But he had written, telling Smith that he was 'fully authorised by his situation to concert with the Grand Vizier any agreement which might be found eligible for rescuing the Turkish Provinces from the French troops', urging him to press ahead urgently with negotiations, adding, 'In this melancholy state of affairs, I feel myself doubly called upon to recommend every possible means that can aid in forcing the French out of Egypt.'[19] This was particularly gratifying because Smith had feared that Elgin's arrival would, at least, complicate his relations with the Ottoman leadership. When the Grand Vizier heard the new ambassador's name he mistook it for an Arabic name for a devil and said, 'Oh, but Elkin is very bad – it is "evil genius" – it is the devil. How could the English Government send us such a person?' Smith explained that it was a Scottish name and the Vizier replied, 'Ah, then I understand that your Government has also got its mountain chiefs to conciliate.'[20]

Confident in his position, Smith made a gesture of good faith by agreeing that the French wounded and the *savants* could return to France at once with passes to allow them through the British blockade; but he did not know that a ship-load of wounded he had allowed to return from Jaffa to France under similar conditions had been stopped by Nelson's ships and sent to Corsica. The negotiations on board the *Tigre* were between Smith and Poussielgue, with whom an easy rapport seemed to have developed, while Desaix acted as military adviser and observer, watching the British officer's mounting excitement with a mordant Gallic eye. He wrote privately to Kléber:

> The Commodore thinks only of negotiating ... The glory that would come to him from his own country, from the Russians and from the Turks has turned his head ... he trembles at not hearing from you, he strikes his foot, he cries, 'General Kléber must answer me; I have dealt honestly with him; I thought him more reasonable than General Bonaparte.'[21]

Smith's enthusiasm had been worthwhile. Early in January, a gale blew and the *Tigre* – with the French delegation on board – had to run before it, up the Levant littoral and past Acre. The time was put to good use and when she had returned to her anchorage off El Arish, provisional terms for an agreement had been reached. Smith saw his own rôle as adviser and broker and that any final agreement should be signed by the Grand Vizier on behalf of the Sublime Porte and not by himself. So they all disembarked on 15th January and made their way to the fortress of El Arish, where the Turkish army was encamped. There, Desaix heard a disturbing report from France and immediately forwarded it to Kléber. He wrote, 'Beware of evacuating Egypt. It is being whispered that there has been a revolution in France and that Bonaparte is at the head of the state.'[22] If that were true, Kléber was too late to achieve that ambition and it would be safer to remain in Egypt and await developments. But when the letter reached him, Kléber disregarded the advice; his mind was set on evacuation.

What Smith called the 'Convention of El Arish' was signed by the Grand Vizier, Poussielgue and Desaix on 24th January and ratified by Kléber four days later. Under the agreement, there would be a truce of three months – longer if necessary – to allow the French army to concentrate at Alexandria, Aboukir and Rosetta with its arms and baggage to await embarkation for France; there was also to be an exchange of prisoners. Smith himself took a particular interest in one French captive, Captain Gabriel Thevenard, whom he dined on board the *Tigre*, the invitation being accompanied by the note:

Sir Sidney takes the liberty to send some clothes, which he supposes a person just escaped from prison may require. The great coat is not of the best; but, excepting naval uniform, it is the only one on board the *Tigre* and the same Sir Sidney wore during his journey from the Temple till he reached the sea. It will have done good service if it again serves a similar purpose by restoring another son to the arms of his aged father, dying with chagrin.[23]

He also arranged a passage for Captain Thevenard to Rhodes, gave him money and introductions to those who might help his onward journey from Constantinople.

On 30th January, the day on which the ratifications were exchanged, Smith wrote to Nelson, explaining the background to the agreement, which he himself had engineered but not signed: 'The great object of our operations in this quarter being the recovery of Egypt for our ally and the security of British possessions in India, advantages not to be compared to trifling sacrifices, I doubt not that your Lordship will agree with me that the utmost has been obtained by negotiation that could have been acquired by victory ...'[24] Just as Nelson had sent an officer to India with news of his victory in Aboukir Bay, so Smith sent Janverin – now a lieutenant – there to report the signing of the Convention; first calling at the French headquarters, he set out on his adventurous journey to the Red Sea and thence by ship with his sabre, a pair of pistols and an Arab girl given him by a French general in Cairo.

Although Smith knew Nelson's policy was one of unconditional surrender, or annihilation, he expected his support because the British Government had been kept fully informed of his own evolving policy and he assumed he still had the support of Lord Elgin. However, views in London had changed. Not only were Nelson's views accepted and supported by Lord St Vincent, who had now returned to London, but they seemed to be validated by an intercepted letter from Poussielgue to the Directory, in which he presented a pessimistic view of the condition of the French army in Egypt. The aim of this had been to persuade them to send reinforcements but the British Government took it at its face value and assumed that it would now be easy for the Turks to defeat the French in battle. In February, Bonaparte had established himself as First Consul and dictator of France and was taking

the offensive against the allies, so the British – and, even more
so, the Austrians and Russians – were appalled at the prospect
of some 18,000 seasoned French troops returning to fight in
Europe. So, on 15th December, Lord Spencer had sent strongly
worded instructions to Lord Keith to prevent any such agreement being reached, or, if it had, to consider it invalid and
resume hostilities.

The first Smith knew of this was on 20th February, when he
called at Cyprus for stores and received a letter from Lord
Keith, a stern Scottish disciplinarian, who disliked dealing with
a subordinate naval officer who was also a senior diplomat.
This told him bluntly that if an agreement had been reached
with the French, its terms were invalid and would be disregarded. Smith immediately informed Poussielgue, who,
realizing that the letter had been written before the signing of
the Convention, immediately wrote a letter of explanation to
Kléber, adding, 'Smith seems sincerely distressed. He told me
that he risked his life in not following the orders he had
received but that he would rather lose it a thousand times than
not to try every means without exception to facilitate the
complete execution of the agreement.'[25] When he received it,
Kléber, a realist, assumed that this was another example of a
muddle due to slow communications that could now be
put to rights.

But Smith was filled with foreboding and replied to Lord
Keith at length:

> I own, in my office as mediator in this business, it never entered
> into my ideas that *we* could put any obstacle in the way of an
> arrangement so very beneficial to us in a *general* view ... As to
> disarming them and persuading them to surrender as *prisoners* ...
> I assure your Lordship it was perfectly out of the question. If the
> business is allowed to go on in the way it is now settled, the
> gigantic and favourite projects of Bonaparte are rendered
> abortive and, surely, it is no bad general mode of reasoning ... to
> say that whatever the wishes of the *enemy* may be, we ought to
> cross *them*; *he* wishes this army to remain in this country, far from
> himself, whom they both despise and detest for all his conduct
> here and his ultimate desertion of them ...

He went on to explain that Kléber was Bonaparte's rival and
it was in the allies' interest to allow him to return with his
army:

Believe me, my dear Lord, there is no way of finishing this long contest ... but by putting our opponents one against the other ... I speak from the experience that I gained at Paris when I say France can only be set to rights by Frenchmen and, until she is set to rights in the internal springs of her government, we never can have peace.[26]

He asked Poussielgue, whom he liked as a gentlemanly Frenchman amongst so many egalitarian republicans, to act as his courier, first taking this letter to the admiral and then continuing to London to explain the situation to the British Government.

He also wrote urgently to the Grand Vizier, urging him to observe the peace terms and not to move his army and sent it by Lieutenant Wright, as courier, to the Turkish camp. He wrote to Lord Elgin, asking that the transports that were about to start evacuating the French from Egypt be allowed free passage, adding, 'The great national object is attained if we can get the French army *out of the country*, even if they took the Pyramids with them.'[27] Smith could have kept Lord Keith's letter to himself but he trusted Poussielgue and if they did not know that the agreement might be disregarded by Keith and the Turks they might be taken by surprise if attacked either in Egypt, or at sea. So he wrote to Lord Spencer, 'However true it may be that the French army, with which we still have to contend, would now be a set of skeletons bleaching on the sand, if I had led them step by step to perdition as was certainly and evidently in my power, I pity the man that can wish it at the expense of our national honour.'[28]

Enclosed with Lord Keith's letter had been another to General Kléber and this he also ordered Wright to show to the Grand Vizier and then to take it to Cairo, where he could explain the circumstances of the confusion. There was little time because the Vizier had disregarded Smith's request and left El Arish at the head of 40,000 men on his way to Cairo. Although Smith did not know it, Lord Elgin, too, had changed his mind. He had already asserted himself by removing all but one of the Smith brothers' staff in Constantinople, so alienating them and showing himself as dominant to the Ottoman court, which understood such blunt realities of power. Some of the beys transferred their attentions to the thirty-six-year-old peer, who was more experienced in the study of classical art than

oriental intrigue, and with lordly self-confidence, disdained the
Smith brothers' advice. The beys had suggested what Elgin was
to call 'a stratagem of war',[29] which was to allow the French to
start withdrawing from their defences in Egypt and then attack
them.

Nelson had made his own uncompromising views clear,
writing to Elgin:

> I hope your recommendation for the Vizier's pushing on in Egypt
> will be attended to and I have no doubt that the campaign will
> end in the destruction of the French ... I own my hope yet is that
> the Sublime Porte will never permit a single Frenchman to quit
> Egypt; and I own myself wicked enough to wish them all to die
> in that country they chose to invade. We have scoundrels of
> French enough in Europe without them.[30]

So the ambassador had sent an officer from the military
mission, Captain Lacy, to the Grand Vizier – without Smith's
knowledge – to urge an attack on the French. He also passed to
Lord Grenville in London the beys' complaints that Smith was
meddling in Turkish affairs and had exceeded his authority,
particularly by putting down the mutiny in Cyprus.

By the time the French heard of the Turkish advance, they
had already begun to act on the terms of the Convention, withdrawing the garrisons of distant forts, dismounting the guns in
the Citadel at Cairo and columns of French troops were on the
march for the coast; so urgent orders to concentrate at Cairo
were sent out by troopers of the *Régiment de Dromedaires*. Kléber
also wrote to Smith inviting him both to Cairo for a conference
and to join him at a meeting outside the capital with the Grand
Vizier. But Smith had been ordered to remain at sea because, it
was rumoured, reinforcements from France were trying to run
his blockade. So the Franco–Turkish meeting was held in the
desert outside the city and, without Smith's influence, the
Grand Vizier rejected Kléber's proposal that they observe a
truce for another month and decided to seize Cairo.

It was now that Lieutenant Wright arrived with Lord Keith's
letter. Kléber was enraged by its tone and content:

> Sir, I inform you that I have received positive orders from His
> Majesty not to consent to any capitulation with the French troops,
> which you command in Egypt and Syria, at least unless they lay
> down their arms, surrender themselves prisoners of war and

deliver up all the ships and stores of the port of Alexandria to the allied powers ... I think it equally necessary to inform you that all vessels having French troops on board with passports from others than authorised to grant them will be forced by the officers of the ships, which I command, to remain in Alexandria: in short, that ships which shall be met returning to Europe with passports granted in consequence of a particular capitulation with one of the allied powers will be retained as prizes and all individuals on board considered as prisoners of war.[31]

Kléber's reaction was so angry, said one who was with him when he read the letter, that he 'roared like an infuriated camel'[32] and issued an order of the day to the army: 'Soldiers! We know how to reply to such insolence – by victories. Prepare for battle!'[33] On 19th March, he reviewed his veterans, drawn up across cornfields near Heliopolis and shouted to them from horseback, 'You possess nothing in Egypt but the ground you stand upon! Retreat one step and you are lost.'[34] They formed their usual, impregnable squares early next morning but when the Turkish cavalry charged they did not ride towards the bristling bayonets but thundered past, out of musket-range, into Cairo. While his horsemen gloried in their triumph and celebrated it by slaughtering Coptic Christians in the city, the Grand Vizier brought his massed infantry – outnumbering the French by more than three to one – up to the squares and summoned Kléber to surrender. His reply was volleys of musketry and the fire of sixty field-guns and then the French advanced with the bayonet. Again the Turks turned and ran into the desert, the Grand Vizier being rescued from his tent by Captain Lacy.

The Convention of El Arish lay in ashes. Due to the slowness of communications, minds had been changed, orders had become contradictory and, because of poor briefing of senior officers, there had been professional jealousy and touchiness, all leading to confusion. The French, regarding themselves betrayed by the British and Turks were not going to evacuate Egypt; the Turks had been finally defeated by the French and were in no position to take further military action; the British were regarded, at best, as uncoordinated incompetents; and Sir Sidney Smith was, once again, widely regarded as a vainglorious meddler who had usurped the responsibilities of his superiors and produced a military and political disaster.

When the British Government heard about the signing of the Convention they were aghast but, on reflection, realized that Smith had acted within his rights and according to his duty as he had seen it and repeatedly explained it to his political superiors. Therefore, to repudiate it – as Lord Keith already had – would be tantamount to a breach of international good faith; they were not to know that the Turks were already guilty of that. They therefore sent an urgent message to Keith, ordering him to reverse his policy. So, on 25th April, the commander-in-chief wrote grudgingly to Poussielgue, claiming that he had given no orders against the observance of the Convention as he had received no orders from London to do so:

> I was of the opinion that His Majesty should take no part in it, but since the treaty has been concluded, His Majesty, being desirous of showing his respect for his allies, I have received instructions to allow a passage to the French troops and have lost not a moment in sending to Egypt orders to permit them to return to France without molestation.[35]

Smith himself was then gratified to be cleared by a letter written on 30th March by Lord Spencer:

> Though I cannot say that I think the termination of the Egyptian expedition is, in all points, such as I could have wished, I cannot avoid writing … to congratulate you on … the most indefatigable and spirited exertions, which for so long a continuance, and with such a scarcity of means, have never before been displayed.

But then he continued, 'Had you known what we do here, when you were treating with the French General, I am willing to believe that you would have seen the subject in a light a little different from that in which you appear at the time to have seen it …'[36] He went on to suggest that Kléber's only motive in negotiating had been to gain time in the hope of reinforcements being sent from France.

There was no question of negotiating with Kléber now for he distrusted both the British and the Turks and was determined to stay in Egypt. Having pursued the remnants of the Turkish infantry he returned to find their cavalry still occupying Cairo, enjoying the support of the Moslem population. It took him several weeks of hard street-fighting to recover the city. There was never to be another chance of negotiating with Kléber because on 14th June, while walking in the garden of his headquarters, a young Syrian approached, as if seeking some favour, and stabbed him to death. The assassin confessed to acting on behalf of Turkish officers and, at his trial, the French court blamed the Grand Vizier; in any case, the revenge was misguided because Kléber's original desire had been to evacuate Egypt. The aftermath was ghastly: Kléber's funeral was combined with the beheading of three sheikhs believed to have been implicated and the ceremonial punishment of his assassin by the roasting of his right hand, then execution by impalement. The command of the French army now devolved on General Menou, who had converted to Islam and had no wish to leave Egypt. 'I must ever regret Kléber, almost as much as if we had been friends instead of opponents,' mourned Sidney Smith, 'We had fought long enough to respect and understand each other.'[37]

When the British Government assessed the political and military situation in the Middle East, they found it bleak. The basic problem was in Europe, for the alliance opposed to France was cracking and crumbling: Bonaparte had defeated the Austrians at Marengo and signed a truce, while the Russian armies had been withdrawn and there was a risk that Bonaparte might establish an alliance with the Tsar. If this forced peace upon Europe, the French army would remain in Egypt, where it could be reinforced and would present a permanent threat to the British in India. The Convention of El Arish would have removed this probability but the chance had been lost and the time for a negotiated evacuation was past. There was only one viable option, military action against the French; but the Turks had shown themselves incapable, except when controlled and stiffened by the British.

With sombre inevitability, it became obvious that the only way of dislodging the French from Egypt was by use of the British Army. More by chance than contingency planning, an expeditionary force was available. It had originally been formed for an assault on Belleisle, which had been cancelled, as had others planned against the Spanish ports of Ferrol and Cadiz. The British Army had known nothing but failure in the seven years since war had broken out with Revolutionary France, but this army was the best that could be assembled. It numbered some 14,000 and was commanded by Sir Ralph Abercromby, a tough, kindly Lowland laird aged 66, liked for his direct and down-to-earth manner, described by one of his officers as 'a noble chieftain: mild in manner, resolute in mind, frank, unassuming, just, inflexible in what he deemed to be right, valiant as the Cid, liberal and loyal as the proudest of Black Edward's knights.'[38] This force, it was decided, was to be increased to 15,000 for the invasion of Egypt, where they would be joined by a second force of more than 7,500, shipped from India.

Inevitably, there were delays in mounting the operation but this was to prove an advantage. Lord Keith showed that he had recognized Smith's worth by asking his advice on choosing a base on the Turkish coast from which to launch the invasion, writing to him that because of the 'long experience that you have had, the local information which you have acquired and the extensive knowledge you must possess of the nature of the country, as well as the character and disposition of the people with whom we are to deal' could he suggest a safe haven with water and local farm produce for 'a fleet of at least eighty, or ninety sail'.[39] He chose the almost land-locked natural harbour at Marmaris, which became the assembly-point for nearly 16,000 British infantry, artillery and cavalry. It was also a sheltered training area for amphibious warfare, and the red-coated and kilted infantry spent days clambering in and out of flat-boats, scrambling up beaches and forming squares.

Smith was to be part of this but only as a captain commanding his own ship and the naval landing parties, for he had finally been removed from the command of naval forces in the Levant, so losing the temporary rank of commodore. This particularly pleased Lord Elgin, who was becoming increasingly hostile and wrote to Lord Keith:

I am induced ... to express the satisfaction which every person acquainted with the affairs of this neighbourhood, and anxious for our success, must feel on your appointing a senior officer to Sir S. Smith to come for a time to these seas. Sir S. has by no means the steadiness for the situation he has held. And unless the plain conduct of the English navy is substituted for the indescribable line of proceedings, which has been going on here, I can answer for nothing.[40]

The triumph of Smith's enemies was hollow for he had become the unrivalled authority on the Levant and on good terms with all the Ottoman leaders, except the Constantinople beys; nobody else could advise General Abercromby, or, indeed, Admiral Keith. As if to illustrate this, 'Smit Bey', as he was called by the Turks, took to exchanging his naval uniform for Turkish robes and a turban and grew a luxuriant moustache and side-whiskers.* This was to demonstrate to the British the ease with which he moved amongst Turks and Arabs, to whom it was a gesture of courtesy. Abercromby saw to it that this did not become a fashion: when one of his officers returned to Marmaris from a mission to Constantinople, he cut a theatrical figure in similar robes and half-grown moustachios, until the general saw him and remarked, 'Why, my good friend, I had no notion that you meant to be a character.'[41]

General Abercromby relied on Smith for every aspect of planning for the invasion of Egypt. On 20th January, Sir Sidney attended a conference of all senior naval and military officers on board Lord Keith's flagship, the *Foudroyant*, at Marmaris and, supported by Captain Ben Hallowell, one of Nelson's 'Band of Brothers' at the Battle of the Nile, explained that a land attack on Alexandria could be mounted from a beach-head in Aboukir Bay. He and Lieutenant Wright had themselves reconnoitred the coast east of Alexandria the year before so could confirm that it would be possible to land reinforcements and supplies over the beaches all along the line of advance to the city.

Although Lord Grenville had told Elgin that 'the powers and commission with which Sir Sidney was furnished have long ceased ... he is now charged with no function which can in any manner interfere with the duties of your Lordship's embassy',[42] the latter had patronizingly congratulated him on being given command of the expedition's gunboats. Smith still had much to offer; in particular, he was negotiating with Murad Bey, the Mameluke, who had conducted a fighting retreat up the Nile before the advance of General Desaix but who had been won over to their cause; the French, with characteristic pragmatism, had made him governor of Upper Egypt. It was important to persuade him to change sides again so that the British expedition from India could be landed safely on the Red Sea coast of

---

* He was to be emulated during the First World War by Col. T.E. Lawrence – 'Lawrence of Arabia' – for much the same reasons.

Egypt. It was a measure of Smith's influence that Murad was to reply, 'I thank you, my excellent friend for thinking of me in my present situation, for writing to me as a friend ... The ships you mentioned have been seen on the coast; I have sent camels to meet and aid them; I shall do all I can, all you desire ...'[43]

Although he now had no diplomatic authority, Smith was used as a liaison officer with the Turks at Marmaris and, until the landings began, he had little naval responsibility beyond the command of the *Tigre*. Rear-Admiral Sir Richard Bickerton had taken over as second-in-command to Lord Keith from Nelson, who had made a leisurely progress across Europe with the Hamiltons on his way to London; the officer commanding the seaborne assault was to be Captain Sir Alexander Cochrane. The army – the red-coated line regiments, the Coldstream Guards, the kilted Highland regiments, Welsh and Irish battalions and six regiments of dragoons, the flower of the British Army – had reached a peak of training in making an opposed landing. On 20th February 1801 – as, far distant, Nelson, who had now parted from his wife and fathered Emma Hamilton's twin daughters, prepared to sail for the Baltic as second-in-command to Admiral Hyde Parker – they finally embarked. Two days later they sailed for Egypt, arriving in Aboukir Bay on 1st March in a stiff breeze and a swell that broke in boiling surf, making a landing impossible.

It was a week before the assault could be launched but by then the empty dunes and scattered groves of palms above the beach had become busy with the French deploying infantry, siting guns and patrolling with cavalry. Even though surprise had been lost, a rocket arched through the sky above Aboukir Bay in the chill darkness at midnight on 7th March; it was the signal for the attack to begin and the waiting troops began to clamber down the sides of the transports into the boats pitching and slewing below. At 3.00 a.m., a second rocket went up and the boats' crews hauled at their oars, pulling towards the beach, five miles to the south. At first light, the rowing stopped and the long, bobbing lines of boats could be seen, lying beyond a range of shore batteries, while small warships and gunboats slowly moved into position on either flank. There were 5,500 soldiers packed into the boats, which were now spread in three parallel lines. The exercises at Marmaris now showed their value, as each coxswain looked to the flapping

Knight of the Sword in title and performance: Captain Sir Sidney Smith on the walls of Acre, painted in 1802 by John Eckstein.
(National Portrait Gallery)

The lieutenant: Sidney Smith, aged about nineteen, painted by Daniel Gardner.
(Spink and Son)

The diplomat: Spencer Smith aged thirty-two, on his return from Constantinople.
(National Portrait Gallery)

The destruction of Toulon in 1793; an engraving after the painting by Thomas Whitcombe. (National Maritime Museum)

The prisoner in the Temple, sketched in November 1796, by Hennequin and engraved by Maria Cosway the following year. (British Museum)

'Scenery entirely new, but whether tragedy or comedy I cannot yet pronounce': Sir Sidney Smith exercising in the courtyard of the Temple prison; an illustration from the *Naval Chronicle*.

Arrival at the Sublime Porte in 1799. Captain Smith reaches Constantinople in the
Tigre, as seen from the Tophana, and engraved from a drawing
owned by Spencer Smith.
(Grosvenor Gallery)

Acre under siege as seen from the sea in an engraving after a drawing by
F. B. Spilsbury, surgeon in the *Tigre*. (National Maritime Museum)

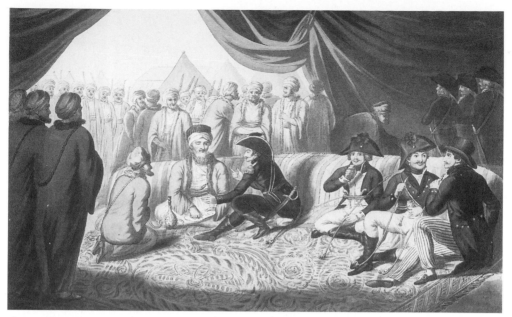

In an Ottoman tent: Captain Sir Sidney Smith confers with Djezzar Pasha at Acre, while similarly moustached British naval officers smoke. Another engraving by Surgeon Spilsbury. (Parker Gallery)

On the ramparts: Captain Sir Sidney Smith striking a heroic attitude during the siege. (Grosvenor Gallery)

The national hero: Lord Nelson at the height of his fame, painted by James Northcote. (Private collection)

The aspiring hero: Sir Sidney Smith sketched by Thomas Stothard. (British Museum)

Naval officer and secret agent: Captain John Wright in an illustration from the *National Chronicle*.

Smuggler, spy and inventor: Captain Tom Johnson drawn by Harry Hunter. (Author's collection)

Death of the CORSICAN FOX: a caricature from 1803 showing a Napoleonic fox being thrown to hounds whose collars bear the names of British admirals, including Nelson, St Vincent and Smith. (British Museum)

The passage of the Dardanelles: a glorified version of Admiral Duckworth's fleet entering the narrows on 19th February 1807, painted by Thomas Whitcombe. (National Maritime Museum)

THE BOMBARDMENT OF ALGIERS: the final reckoning in 1816, inspired by Sir Sidney Smith and carried out by Lord Exmouth; painted by P. H. Rogers. (National Maritime Museum)

Remembered in London: the statue of Sir Sidney Smith by Thomas Kirk outside the National Maritime Museum, Greenwich.

Remembered in Paris: the tomb of Admiral Sir Sidney and Lady Smith in the cemetery of Père Lachaise

colours marking the boat of the officer commanding their particular wave of assault. Captain Smith commanded the third wave, carrying the artillery, which was ready for landing, the guns mounted on their carriages and planks rigged as ramps from bows to beach. The soldiers, cramped and chilled after six or more hours in the boats, looked across at the tossing panorama and the silent beach ahead and a Highlander of the 92nd Regiment – the Gordon Highlanders – was to recall, 'I contemplated the scene with an anxious, aching heart.'[44] General Abercromby, watching from the deck of a bomb-ketch, waiting to bombard, only said, 'This is really taking the bull by the horns'[45] and gave the order for the assault.*

As the ships' guns and mortars opened fire with billows of smoke shot with flame, the long lines of boats were pulled desperately for the beach. Then in the cloud of smoke and dust along the dunes more stabs of flame came from the French guns as they came into range. The soldiers cheered as the sea spouted with falling shot; boats shattered, spilling their men into the surf, and a howitzer shell burst in one packed with straight-backed guardsmen of the Coldstream. The boat carrying Captain Cochrane was the first to run ashore and soon soldiers were tumbling into the bloody water and charging ashore.

On the dunes, General Friant, commanding the 2,000 French defenders, had counted on his guns and musketry slaughtering the British as they reached the shore, where the survivors would be cut down by his cavalry. But, before he could react, the British were ashore, colours were planted in the sand as rallying-points, companies formed, bayonets were fixed and they charged the French positions in the dunes. As Smith's boats ground on to the beach, the field-guns were wheeled down the ramps and fired while still dripping sea-water, then 300 seamen dragged them up the dunes to enfilade the French defences. Training and discipline told and, before the French could recover from the shock of the assault, Abercromby's army had landed and was advancing towards Alexandria, with the reserve, commanded by Major-General John Moore, following. The cost had been high

* This was the first major beach-landing since 1762, when Vice-Admiral Sir George Pocock had landed 12,000 British troops in a surprise attack on Havana.

but not as high as expected, the Navy's casualties amounting to about 100 and the Army's to 625, of whom 135 were killed, or missing. Smith had established liaison both with the ships out at sea and the Egyptians in the desert, while showing his men how to make themselves as comfortable as possible. He demonstrated how to dig for water near date palms, how to minimize the risk of dysentery and warned them of 'The Minor Plagues of Egypt': rats, flies ('numerous beyond credibility'), fleas, lice, mosquitoes ('in no other country are they so numerous as in Egypt'), centipedes and scorpions.[46]

The town and fort of Aboukir were quickly taken, some fierce skirmishes fought and, although the British lacked the cavalry for a quick dash to seize Alexandria, Abercromby moved steadily westward between the sea and a chain of great shallow, brackish lakes. On 20th March, a Bedouin reached the British lines with a letter for Smith from a friendly sheikh, warning him that General Menou was advancing from Cairo with his main army to launch a night attack. By this time the British had been reduced by battle casualties and fever to about 13,000, whereas the French could muster a total of some 30,000 in Egypt, including locally recruited auxiliaries and 800 reinforcements, who had been slipped through the blockade in frigates. Abercromby doubted the report because he expected Menou to wait behind defences close to his reserves and supplies rather than choose to fight in the open, but took Smith's advice and put his army on full alert that night.

General 'Abdallah Bey' Menou had with him about 12,000 men, but this included effective cavalry, which the British lacked for want of suitable horses. Then, long before dawn on 21st March, an officer from a British cavalry picket came galloping up to Abercromby's tent to report masses of French infantry advancing; his message was confirmed by the distant crackle of muskets. The British front of about two miles rested its right flank on a jumbled mass of Roman ruins close to the beach and it was there that the French concentrated their attack. To the thunder of side-drums and shouts of, 'En avant! Vive la République!', the tread of the French phalanxes could be heard by the waiting British. The artillery opened fire, the gun crews labouring by lamplight and then the French cavalry charged, cutting through the British line, re-forming and charging again; this time they were held. The sun rose on the two armies struggling in battle. So confused was the fighting that the 28th Regiment fought back to back.*

General Abercromby himself was caught up in a French charge and, thrown from his horse, was ridden down by a French dragoon, who was himself shot dead in the act of slashing at him with his sabre. The first officer to gallop up to the general was Sidney Smith, who had been slightly wounded in the right shoulder and whose sword had been broken; so Abercromby, staggering to his feet, gave him the sabre of the French dragoon, who had so nearly killed him. Then, seeing a staff officer, a Major Hall, who had lost his horse, Smith turned to his own mounted orderly to tell him to give his horse to the officer; at that instant, the orderly's head was smashed by a cannon-shot. 'This is destiny,' said Smith, with cool theatricality. 'The horse, Major Hall, is yours.'[47] Later, Smith escaped being shot by British troops when he had to ride a horse taken from a French dragoon and branded with the large identification number that marked it out as such; he was wearing a blue undress uniform coat and, having been taken for an escaping French officer, he was the target for several ragged volleys. Later, he joked that he would have been hit if they had *not* been aiming at him.

Nobody noticed, however, when Abercromby was hit by a musket ball in the thigh but he limped along the British lines, giving his orders, without complaint. By 9.00 p.m. both armies were exhausted and the ground between them covered with the bodies of men and horses. Both had expended most of their ammunition and the explosion of two French ammuntion wagons seemed to announce the end. Menou re-formed his divisions and began to withdraw covered by field-guns. The British were left in possession of the battlefield but they lacked sufficient cavalry to pursue. By 10.00 a.m. that morning the guns were silent.

In what came to be known as the Battle of Alexandria, the British Army had at last triumphed over the French. British casualties had amounted to about 1,500, of whom about 250 had been killed, but French losses were more than double that. Abercromby himself did not survive to receive his laurels;

* This won them the privilege, as the Gloucestershire Regiment, to wear badges with a sphinx insignia on both the front and back of their caps.

taken out to Lord Keith's flagship, the *Foudroyant*, he seemed to recover but the musket-ball had worked its way into the hip joint, the wound turned septic and, a week after he had been hit, he suffered a relapse and died on 28th March. Abercromby was universally mourned. One story told was that, when wounded, he had been told to lie down, and when he had asked what was being used as a pillow he was told it was only a soldier's blanket. He replied, 'Only a soldier's blanket! A soldier's blanket is a thing of great consequence. You must send me the name of the man to whom it belongs, that it may be restored to him.'[48]

While Abercromby lay wounded in the *Foudroyant*, Smith approached the French lines under a flag of truce to present a letter from the general and Lord Keith offering terms. If the French surrendered, they would not be regarded as prisoners of war and would be repatriated to France, although they would have to leave their weapons and shipping to the victors. The offer was indignantly refused. He also established good relations with the local Egyptians, insisting that food was not plundered by the British but purchased, sending Lieutenant Wright to supervise this and, it was reported, he 'insisted on paying liberally, having Sir Sidney's directions for that purpose.'[49] Admiringly, his fellow-officers watched as desert sheikhs came to visit him, one recording, 'Eleven Arab Chiefs came to Sir Sidney Smith; they were all very intelligent men with uncommonly fine physiognomies ... It was impossible to regard these Chiefs without thinking of the Wise Men of the East.'[50]

Abercromby was succeeded by Major-General the Honourable John Hely-Hutchinson, a forty-four-year-old Anglo-Irishman, known for his caution and his lack of both leadership and charm. He was, therefore, unlikely to appreciate Captain Smith, which proved to be the case. He did, however, allow himself to be persuaded by Smith, who was commanding a flotilla of gunboats on the Nile, to advance on Cairo with cavalry riding along either bank of the river. However, Hely-Hutchinson was ill at ease with so imaginative and volatile a subordinate and listened to complaints from the Grand Vizier that Smith had been meddling in Turkish affairs. The interference that now rankled with the Turks was that Smith had warned Kléber that the Convention of El Arish was about to be broken by them and the French attacked in the 'stratagem of war'. The general took this as an excuse to relieve Smith of his military duties ashore and send him back to his ship. Lord Keith now rejoined the persecution, ordering that his three French royalist officers, de Tromelin (still known as Colonel Bromley), de Frotté and Le Grand, leave the ship as unwanted foreigners, although there were some 500 foreigners serving with the army ashore.

Then Smith heard that he had been censured by the Government in Parliament for concluding the Convention of El Arish without authority. He at once wrote to Lord Elgin:

> I find myself under implied censure, from which I trust you to relieve me, for the word 'unauthorised' never can remain applied to me, if your Lordship has the goodness to transmit copies of what passed originally on the subject, wherein I was not only authorised but required and urged *by you* to bring matters to a conclusion in Egypt ... It would be most proper for your Lordship to be the person to correct this error in the minds of the ministers.[51]

As he might have expected, Elgin replied vaguely that 'The only possibility of proceeding with fairness and consistency' would be 'to refer every circumstance of whatever nature to the proper authority';[52] clearly, he had no intention of taking any action whatsoever to clear Smith's name.

Smith's final action was an attempt to avert a massacre of Christians and Mamelukes by the Turks when they took control of Egypt after the British finally withdrew. As he was now confined to his ship, he acted through intermediaries, amongst them an Austrian interpreter, whom he had engaged for the campaign. The interpreter had, however, written letters criticizing Abercromby's successor for being unduly influenced by the Grand Vizier, for dismissing Smith, and for his lack of grip on the country, which was allowing the Turks to commit the atrocities Smith had feared. These letters were intercepted and sent to Hely-Hutchinson, who was furious and forwarded them to Lord Elgin, who, in turn, sent them to Lord Grenville, claiming that they 'display a regular system of espionage'. He added, 'It is very painful indeed, my Lord, that a discovery too important to be withheld from His Majesty should implicate a British officer, especially one of so high a spirit, so able and so enterprising as Sir Sidney Smith.'[53]

At the beginning of July, General Belliard, who commanded the French garrison of Cairo, finally realized that no relief would be possible and capitulated on condition his men could be evacuated to France. On the 6th they marched out of the city bearing with them the body of Kléber in a black-draped coffin to the beat of muffled drums. A month later they sailed for France, but Menou, who had never wanted to leave, held out in Alexandria. He tried, however, to send the *savants* home by sea but they were intercepted by Lord Keith and returned to port. During the summer British reinforcements reached Egypt and the siege of Alexandria was intensified so that on 2nd September 1801, General Menou finally surrendered. He did so, as had Belliard, on broadly the same terms as had been offered and accepted under the Convention of El Arish. Had Smith's initiative been honoured by the British and Turkish governments, the British expedition would have been unnecessary and some 700 British lives, nearly 5,000 French lives – together with those who would not survive wounds or disease; the 160 British soldiers and innumerable Frenchmen blinded by ophthalmia, for example – and countless thousands of Turkish and Egyptian lives would have been saved together with a vast expenditure by the British Government in mounting the invasion.

Perhaps because Lord Keith knew this in his heart, he granted Sir Sidney Smith's request to have the honour of carrying his despatches announcing the final victory to London. If Smith was unpopular with his superiors, he was popular amongst those who had fought in the campaign ashore and afloat, as one of them, Major Robert Wilson, wrote in his *History of the British Expedition to Egypt*, which he was drafting and which would be published in London two years later:

Sir Sidney was endeared to officers and men by his conduct, courage and affability. With pride they beheld the hero of Acre; with admiration they reflected on the Convention of El Arish; they had witnessed his exertions and calculated on his enterprise. The Arabs regarded him as a superior being. To be a friend of Smith was the highest honour they coveted and his word the only pledge they required ... It is true that, as a seaman, he could not complain on being ordered to resume command of his ship; but the high power he had been invested with, the ability he had displayed as a soldier and statesman entitled him to a superior situation in this expedition and the interest of the service seemed to require that the connexion he had formed with the Mamelukes should, through him, be maintained. The army, therefore, saw Sir Sidney leave them with regret but he carried with him their best wishes and gratitude.[54]

CHAPTER SEVEN

'An amorous situation'

SIR SIDNEY SMITH boarded a frigate, *El Carmen*, captured from the Spanish, for his passage home, looking half a British officer and half a Turkish warrior. He was, noted Midshipman George Parsons, 'of middling stature, good-looking, with tremendous moustachioes, a pair of penetrating black eyes, an intelligent countenance with a gentlemanly air, expressive of good nature and kindness of heart'.[1] He was carrying Lord Keith's despatches to the Government and, indeed, the admiral seemed to have relaxed his stiff front of opposition to Smith's activities, writing in his covering letter to the Admiralty, 'Captain Sir Sidney Smith, having served with such distinguished reputation in this country, having applied to be the bearer of the despatches announcing the expulsion of the enemy, I have complied with his request.'[2] General Hely-Hutchinson's despatches were being carried by Colonel Abercromby, the son of his dead predecessor, and duplicate despatches were to be sent a fortnight later by a sloop.

Eager to be home with the glorious news – and his own vindication – as soon as possible, Captain Smith addressed Captain Selby, who commanded the frigate, thus: 'Captain Selby, if you will do me the honour to be guided by my advice, we will make a passage that shall astonish the world.' It was not, in fact, his own advice but Lord St Vincent's, which he had remembered from a conversation about Mediterranean navigation. This was to sail, on a west-bound passage, as close as possible to the African coast to catch the onshore wind by day and the offshore breeze at night; in the event, the wind dropped at night, so that they were becalmed, and was so strong during the day that it nearly blew them ashore at

Derna. Midshipman Parsons was on deck during this crisis and recorded:

Behold this Spanish tub (age unknown), under close-reefed topsails and reefed courses, going one foot ahead and two feet to leeward – a thick haze – no observation for two days previous – wind blowing dead on shore – a sneezer and no mistake – first lieutenant fidgety – and with the gunner securing guns with hammocks, hawsers and cleats; for the heaviness of the sea made her roll gunnel-to and great apprehensions were entertained of the bolts drawing and setting our eighteen-pounders free, the consequence of which would be instant destruction.

Sir Sidney's good-humoured countenance acquired a more sedate cast and Captain Selby gazed eagerly to leeward and evinced great anxiety, which by our dead reckoning was sufficiently near the horrible coast of Barbary to justify more apprehension than was openly displayed.

'Get a cast of the deep-sea lead, Mr. Mowbray,' said the captain, addressing Old Soundings, the master.

'Ay, ay, sir.'

'Men in the weather chains, pass the line along; all ready, forward from the weather cathead; heave without shortening sail, Mr. Mowbray, for fear we have no room to spare; look at her wake.'

'She falls to leeward like a sand-barge, fifty fathoms up and down', called the master, 'It has not struck bottom, Sir Sidney. I believe it is a bold shore and an iron-bound coast' ...

'But hold on, lads,' shouted the master, 'for here comes a topper.'

The frigate, from having little way, had fallen off in the trough of the sea and a mountainous wave, rolling on the beam, seemed determined to swamp us; onward it came in its resistless might, breaking over the frigate and sweeping away the boats and spare spars.

'Hold on, good sticks [masts]', said Sir Sidney ...

'Land three points on the lee bow,' called the catheadman. 'Wear the ship, Captain Selby', advised Sir Sidney. [Go about on the opposite tack]

'It is Cape Dern,' said Sir Sidney, 'and I fear we are embayed. All hands wear ship, ahoy.'

After a shrill whistle from the boatswain and his mates and 'Tumble up, there – tumble up' sounded through the decks of *El Carmen*, 'Take the mainsail in, Mr. Langdon, weather clue first'; but although our first luff proceeded to shorten sail in a seaman-

like manner, the mainsail blew to ribbons as she came to the wind
on the other tack; and, fortunately, for the old frigate, it so
happened, for we were taken flat aback in a heavy squall and,
had the mainsail still remained set, we most certainly should
have gathered stern way and foundered.

'There's a sweet little cherub that sits up aloft,
To look out a good berth for poor Jack.[3]

The weather moderated and then east of Gibraltar, Parsons
continued:

We one night fell in with a frigate and, taking her for an enemy
from not answering our signals, prepared for action, when Sir
Sidney appeared on deck in the costume of Robinson Crusoe, a
rifle on each shoulder and countless pistols.

'I will head your boarders, Captain Selby, and only advise one
broadside with the muzzle of your guns touching the
Frenchman's.'

The frigate proved to be Algerian and, after Smith had given
her captain a friendly letter for the Bey of Derna, the voyage
continued. Midshipman Parsons observed Captain Smith with
an amused eye and noted his views on diet:

Sir Sidney, among many peculiar eccentricities, asserted that rats
fed cleaner and were better eating than pigs or ducks; and, agree-
ably to his wish, a dish of these beautiful vermin were caught
daily with fish hooks, well baited, in the provision hold, for the
ship was infested with them, and served up at the captain's table;
the sight of them alone took off the keen edge of my appetite.[4]

Passing Gibraltar, the frigate steered north and in the Bay of
Biscay struck another storm. Parsons wrote:

It blew so hard, with such a sea, as was conceived dangerous for
the old tub to scud in. Accordingly she was made snug by getting
the top-gallant masts on deck and we hove-to under a close-
reefed topsail. I only saw Sir Sidney once during the gale, when
he jocosely remarked that he was only a passenger and therefore
should return to his cot, which he deemed the most comfortable
place in the ship.[5]

Next morning they sighted a large ship labouring in the
heavy swell, flying her American colours, reversed as a distress
signal. According to Parsons, the American captain called
across:

'I am in a sinking state and I calculate I shall only be able to keep
her up two hours or so. The people are frightened and I am in a
bit of a shake. Therefore, Britisher, I will take it as a compliment
if you will send your boat – mine are washed away – and save us
from being drowned like rats in this tarnation leaky hooker.'

'I will stay by you,' said Captain Selby, 'but no boat will live in
this sea.'

Upon this declaration, Jonathan Corncob spat twice as fast as
ever and observed, 'You might oblige us with a boat, captain?'

... Sir Sidney's kind heart was touched by this scene.

'Captain Selby, if you will risk your lee-quarter cutter, I will
save, by the help of heaven, those despairing creatures.' Parsons
was relieved that he did not catch Smith's eye and that 'his choice
fell on the first lieutenant (there is no accounting for taste) ... for
I fully concurred with my captain that no boat could live.

Sir Sidney was the first man to spring into the lee-cutter.
Captain Selby, having remonstrated against his risking so valuable a life, was answered gaily by the gallant hero calling to our
first luff, 'Mr. Langdon, if your tackle-falls give way, you will be
drowned for your carelessness.' He continued with a stream of
orders – as Parsons recorded in detail and at length years later –
then ordering, 'Watch her roll, men, when I give the word – for
on your attention and skill depend the lives of the cutter's crew
– your first luff – to say nothing of my own and Chips, the
carpenter, whom, with your leave, Captain Selby, I will take on
board Jonathan, who I suspect is not as bad as stated but rather
lost in his reckoning.' In extravagant prose Parsons described the
'cool magnanimity of Sir Sidney as he steered alongside the wall-
sided monster of a Yankee, who rolled awfully as he sprang on
board.

'I guess you are the captain of that there Britisher,' said
Jonathan Corncob, addressing the hero of Acre, 'and I take your
conduct as most particularly civil.'

'I am only a passenger in yon frigate and am called Sir Sidney
Smith. But let your carpenter show me where he thinks the leak
is and I shall be glad to look at your chart.'

'You shall see it Sidney Smith (we do not acknowledge titles in
our free country)' and Jonathan unrolled a very greasy chart
before Sir Sidney.

'I do not see any track pricked off. What was your longitude at
noon yesterday? And what do you think your drift has been since
that time?'

'Why, to tell you the truth, Sidney Smith, I 'aven't begun to
reckon yet; but mate and I was about it when the gale came on. I

think we are about here.' And Jonathan Corncob covered many degrees with the broad palm of his hand. 'Mate thinks we are more to the eastward.' This convinced Sir Sidney that he rightly guessed that the man was lost ... The carpenter, by this time, had diminished the leak; and Sir Sidney, giving Captain Corncob the bearings and distance of Brest ... offered to take him and his crew on board the *El Carmen*, leaving the boat's crew to run the tarnation leaky hooker into Brest and claiming half her value as salvage. But Jonathan gravely demurred and, calling to the mate, 'Reverse our stripes and place our stars uppermost again, where they should be', while he kindly slapped Sir Sidney on the shoulder, calling him an honest fellow from the old country: and in the fullness of his gratitude offered him a quid of tobacco and a glass of brandy.[6]

On 9th November, 1801, *El Carmen* finally reached Portsmouth to be greeted by the news that the sloop carrying the duplicate despatches had not only sailed a fortnight after her but arrived a fortnight before. News of the victory in Egypt was now stale and had, in any case, been overtaken by the signing of a preliminary peace agreement with France. It also meant that Captain Selby was denied the knighthood and handsome purse that he might have expected and it was unlikely that Sir Sidney Smith would receive any special honour.

On the day Smith came ashore, Lord Nelson was being cheered through the streets of London. He and Sir William Hamilton were guests at the inauguration of the new Lord Mayor and joined his procession through the City. Their coach was mobbed by excited crowds, who unharnessed the horses and themselves hauled it to the Guildhall. It was mortifying for Smith when he was not even recognized as the bearer of victorious despatches, although, with customary showmanship, he did what he could to catch the public eye. On 11th November, *The Times* reported:

Yesterday morning at eight o'clock Sir Sidney Smith arrived at the Admiralty from Portsmouth. The vessel, in which he came home, having been charged with duplicates of the despatches, which have already been published, Sir Sidney brings no news: he has, however, brought with him a great number of letters from our countrymen in Egypt, which will no doubt prove highly acceptable to their relatives. Sir Sidney was attired in the Turkish dress, turban, robe, shawl and girdle round his waist with a brace of pistols, and appeared in good health and spirits.

Despite the display, Smith was conscious of being snubbed. Lord Keith had not praised him in his despatches, so there was no special mention of his part in the campaign when Parliament passed a vote of thanks to the victors. He was, however, received by William Pitt, the Prime Minister, who confessed that he had been unaware of the scope of the double naval and diplomatic responsibility Smith had been given by Spencer and Grenville and that it had not been made clear that the latter had come to an end with the arrival of Lord Elgin. Smith then explained the sequence of events leading to the Convention of El Arish and the muddles and delays that had led to the misunderstandings, adding that he had not signed the agreement himself, to which the signatories had been the Turkish and French commanders-in-chief, who were, of course, fully entitled to do so. The interview ended amiably with Pitt congratulating Smith on his 'skill, exertions and bravery'.[7]

Some in power were even having second thoughts about the tendency to dismiss Smith's achievements and Lord Grenville suggested in a speech, reported in *The Times*, that it would have been in British interests to have taken advantage of the Convention of El Arish and:

> negotiated a Peace when a Capitulation was made by Sir Sidney Smith with General Kléber; by which the nation would have saved the burthen of so large a national debt contracted since that period? The intrigues of France with Russia and other Northern Courts would have been avoided besides the loss of many thousand lives ... What advantages have we since gained to compensate for these evils?[8]

The siege of Acre had not been forgotten. Had he been an admiral, his feat would doubtless have won him an earldom and a handsome financial reward, but there were a hundred captains senior to him in the *Navy List*. However, the King allowed him to add some commemorative flourishes to his armorial bearings, and the House of Commons did pass a vote of thanks and awarded him an annuity of £1,000. A week after Nelson's visit to the Guildhall, Smith was there being awarded the freedom of the City of London and was given an engraved presentation sword at a ceremony in the Guildhall, involving an exchange of flowery compliments. Describing the defence of Acre in high-flown language, the City Chamberlain continued:

I cannot help exulting, on this happy occasion, at the vast acquisition of national reputation acquired by your conduct at the head of a handful of Britons in repulsing him who has been justly styled the Alexander of the day ... till then deemed invincible. By this splendid achievement you frustrated the designs of our foe on our East Indian territory, prevented the overthrow of the Ottoman power in Asia, the downfall of its throne in Europe and prepared the way for that treaty of peace, which, it is devoutly to be wished, may long preserve the tranquillity of the universe ...

He concluded that an historian, writing about the feats of King Richard I at Acre, had, lost in admiration, asked, 'Am I writing history or romance?' There was no doubt which they were now celebrating and these 'actions, no less extraordinary than those performed by the gallant Coeur de Lion, have been achieved by Sir Sidney Smith.'[9] Smith replied with becoming modesty, accepting a presentation sword 'as the most honourable award that could have been conferred on me'.[10]

More importantly, he was, in May, invited by the Parliamentary constituency of Rochester to stand for election as their Member of Parliament and he happily accepted, making it clear that he would be no party hack: 'My political creed is the English constitution, my party the nation. Highly as I prize the honour of becoming your representative, I will not purchase even that, or any other distinction, by renouncing an atom of my independence.'[11]* In London, the Convention of El Arish, and the question of whether Abercromby's invasion of Egypt had been tragically unnecessary, was a principal talking point among the sophisticated, and factions were ranged for and against Sir Sidney Smith. But he was a popular figure amongst newspaper readers and he was duly elected by the freeholders of Rochester.

The political scene had changed in 1801. First William Pitt's administration had resigned in March because of King George's veto of his plan for Catholic emancipation in Ireland. He had been succeeded by Henry Addington as Prime Minister, Lord Hawkesbury as Foreign Secretary and Lord St Vincent as First Lord of the Admiralty. Under their direction, peace

---

* Nelson made his own political creed clear to Pitt three years later: 'I gave some specimen of a sailor's politics by frankly telling him that ... I ... must not be expected to range myself under the political banners of any man in or out of place. That England's welfare was the sole object of my pursuit.'

negotiations with France had begun and been concluded in March 1802, by the signing of the Treaty of Amiens. The terms, under which Britain surrendered all her conquests including Malta and the Cape of Good Hope, but excepting Ceylon and Trinidad, were widely condemned. During the negotiations in the preceding October, St Vincent had risen in the House of Lords to defend the Government, stressing the important achievement of keeping Ceylon and Trinidad, and Nelson, who had just taken his seat in the Lords, was asked to support him. Realizing that the Hero of the Nile was politically naïve, the politicians had persuaded him that it was his duty to support the Government, to which he owed his rank and position, by declaring that the losses of Malta and the Cape were of no strategic consequence. He did not believe this but obeyed, declaring that it did not matter who occupied Malta, so long as it was not the French, and now that fast, copper-bottomed ships did not need to stop at Cape Town to replenish, it was no more than an expensive tavern on the way to India. 'How can Ministers allow such a fool to speak in their defence?'[12] asked William Huskisson, the former under-secretary of state for war, and even Nelson's friend, Captain Hardy, grumbled, 'I see almost by every paper that Lord Nelson has been speaking in the House. I am sorry for it and I am fully convinced that sailors should not talk too much.'[13] Nelson himself was ashamed, excusing himself by saying, 'You will see my maiden speech – bad enough but well meant – anything better than ingratitude.'[14]

In early summer, Smith and Nelson were to meet for the first time since they returned from the Mediterranean. The latter had in the meantime fought and won the bloody Battle of Copenhagen, which had not been a popular victory. He had also become a scandalous figure and his affair with Emma Hamilton had made him the butt of caricaturists, notably Gillray, who drew him as ludicrously mock-heroic, her as a fat voluptuary, and her husband, Sir William, as a desiccated cuckold. Ostracized by the Court and polite aristocratic society, he had taken his friends from other, often more interesting, strata of society: a newspaper editor, a painter, a Jewish financier, his own prize agent and, of course, his many naval friends. In public he was careful to cut a dignified figure and his speeches tended to concentrate on patriotic themes.

However, he was an instantly recognizable, commanding figure; one, who saw him at this time, describing him as 'very brown in the face (tanned greatly); his countenance had a firm expression... He held himself well erect – like a man accustomed to command and who would be first everywhere.'[15]

Since he had come to understand the background to Smith's behaviour in the Mediterranean, Nelson had gone out of his way to be friendly. In the autumn of 1801, while he was still commanding the counter-invasion forces in the North Sea and Channel and was based at Deal, he had taken the Hamiltons to visit Smith's father at Dover. On 19th September, the *English Chronicle* reported that they had called at:

> his neat and curious house near Dover, called the *Cave*. The visit was of a friendly and not of a formal nature. His Lordship, taking the venerable gentleman by the hand, said that he was happy in the opportunity, which his temporary residence on the coast afforded him, of paying his personal respects to the father of his worthy and much-esteemed companion in arms. The Noble Admiral and his suite, after being elegantly entertained, returned the same evening to Deal.

The Sicilian duke and the Swedish knight, who had jointly thwarted Bonaparte's advance on India, were guests of honour at a subscription dinner to raise money for the Naval Asylum, a naval orphanage. It was held on 2nd June at the London Tavern in Bishopsgate Street Within, which had a banqueting hall able to seat 355 and tanks of live turtles in the cellars to provide their soup. Two hundred contributed to hear the two heroes and Admiral Sir Hyde Parker, Nelson's elderly superior at Copenhagen, who was not himself seen as a hero because he had, apparently, tried to order his doughty second-in-command to break off the action.

Nelson's health was drunk to and he responded briefly, as the *Naval Chronicle* reported, 'thanking them for their attention to the orphans of those brave men, who had died in the service of their Country; it was an Institution that could not fail, for it must be grateful to the Deity, who would bless and prosper so charitable an undertaking.' Such polite but prissy sentiments were not for Sidney Smith, who responded to his own toast and 'the warmest applause' by echoing Nelson's concern for the orphans of brave men. The report continued:

Unfortunately for him, too many were in the list of his dearest friends. (Here Sir Sidney's feelings were too great for utterance – his head sunk – the big tear rolled down the hero's cheek). A solemn silence prevailed for several minutes and soft sympathy filled many a manly bosom, until Sir Sidney was roused by the thunder of applause which followed.

He then declared that he would hand the Government 'a list of those sufferers' and he began to list them, describing their glorious deaths in the service of their country. There was Captain Miller of the *Theseus*, who had left two children. There was Major Oldfield, also a father, whose dying body had been fought over by British and French outside the walls of Acre, this described in vivid detail. There was Lieutenant Canes, his first lieutenant in the *Tigre*, who had succeeded Captain Miller in his command but, although 'he had not lost his life in the *numerous actions* in which he was engaged, but in carrying despatches to the Mediterranean of the Preliminaries of Peace, he perished at sea with his ship and crew'; he, too, had 'left young orphans, who want support', together with 'many others who have so nobly fought and died in their King and Country's service'.

As he sat down to more applause, an orphans' choir sang 'Rule Britannia' and 'God save the King' 'with high glee' and one of the little boys recited a poem, ending:

> Ah! not in vain, *their* gallant blood they shed,
> Since British bounty shrinks not from the dead,
> But nobly shields, against the ills of life,
> The brave men's orphans in his Country's strife.[16]

The occasion raised £1,537.10s. for the Naval Asylum. Realizing that he had been upstaged by Smith, Nelson was not put out but, with characteristic generosity, warmed to him and suggested he visit Merton Place, the country house in Surrey, which he was sharing with the Hamiltons. They had more than popularity, a flair for leadership, originality as naval commanders, ambition and vanity in common. Nelson, while unpopular with social grandees, was loved by the mass of the people, who admired his courage and watched with enthusiastic prurience his affair with his friend's wife, which seemed to show that he was human, after all. Sidney Smith had also strayed from the straight path of moral righteousness and he upstaged Nelson in that, too.

Smith had been staying at Maze Hill on the edge of
Blackheath to the south-east of London with his friend Colonel
Sir John Douglas of the marines, who had fought with him at
Acre. While there, Sir John and Lady Douglas had taken him to
dine with an exciting neighbour at Montague House, a mansion
facing Blackheath and backing on to Greenwich Park, close to
the Ranger's House. This was the estranged Princess of Wales.
She, the former Princess Caroline of Brunswick, had married
the dissolute heir to the throne in 1795 and, although she had
borne him a daughter, they had parted within a few weeks; he,
returning to his libidinous routine (and making Nelson neurot-
ically jealous when he cast an approving eye towards Emma
Hamilton); she, to a succession of lovers. Princess Caroline was
a coarse, gregarious but lively minded woman and held court
at Blackheath to those who found her amusing, or her company
socially flattering. Florid and highly charged sexually, there
was indeed something of Emma Hamilton about her.

'Sir Sidney Smith's conversation, his account of the various
and extraordinary events and heroic achievements in which he
had been concerned amused and interested me,'[17] the Princess
was to confess. He caught her imagination and she proposed to
decorate a room in Arab style. Sir Sidney, she was to recall,
'furnished me with a pattern ... in a drawing of the tent of
Murad Bey, which he had brought over with him from Egypt
and he taught me how to draw Egyptian arabesques, which
were necessary for the ornament of the ceiling.'[18] Soon it was
apparent to the Princess's circle that a love affair was imminent
and the Duke of Gloucester noted 'how very free she permitted
Sir Sidney Smith to be' and warned, 'as Sir Sidney was a lively,
thoughtless man, and had not been accustomed to the society
of ladies of her rank, he might forget himself and she would
then have herself to blame.'[19] But the Princess was delighted by
her suitor, although by no means turning away other candi-
dates and telling Lady Douglas that if one of them heard about
her current interest, 'I will cheat him and throw dust in his eyes
and make him believe Sir Sidney comes here to see you.'[20]

Early in 1802 it was universally believed that Sir Sidney and
Princess Caroline became lovers, although there was little
direct evidence. The Earl of Minto, who had watched the development of Nelson's affair with Emma Hamilton with a
mordant eye, wrote to his wife in March that the Princess was

'at present entirely wrapped up in Sir Sidney Smith, who is just the sort of thing that suits her'.[21] A page, William Cole, later reported that when taking sandwiches to the Princess in her drawing-room he 'found the gentleman and lady sitting close together in so familiar a posture as to alarm him very much and after supper, when the ladies have retired, about eleven o'clock, he has known Sir Sidney remain alone with the Princess an hour or two afterwards.' A housemaid, Mary Wilson, declared that she had surprised the couple in the Princess's bedroom 'in such an indecent situation that she immediately left the room and was so shocked that she fainted away at the door'. There seem to have been late-night visits, via a side entrance to the house, and Cole further reported that 'one night, about twelve o'clock, he saw a person wrapped in a great coat go across the park into the gate at the green house and verily believes it was Sir Sidney'. Later that year, the domestic staff at Montague House maintained that 'the Princess certainly was with child'.[22]*

The child was not necessarily Smith's, however, for he was far from alone; others involved with Princess Caroline at this time included George Canning, the politician, Thomas Lawrence, the painter, and Captain Thomas Manby, Royal Navy. It was the latter who supplanted Smith in the Princess's affections. At one of Princess Caroline's dinner parties, Smith 'observed her see Captain Manby's foot under the table and, when she had succeeded, put her foot upon Captain Manby's and sat in that manner the whole evening, dealing out equal attention and politeness above board to them both';[23] later he saw Manby kiss her on the lips and he walked out of the house, swearing never to return. The rift was acrimonious. The Princess also quarrelled with the Douglases, sending anonymous letters to Sir John – traced to her, nevertheless – illustrated with obscene drawings of 'Sir Sidney Smith doing Lady Douglas your amiable wife'.[24] Smith was quick to deny any such impropriety and Lady Douglas herself recorded:

Sir Sidney Smith gave Sir John his hand, as his old friend and companion, and assured him in the most solemn manner, as an

---

* A family named Smith living in Prince Edward Island, Canada, is descended from John Dubois Smith, who was claimed to be the illegitimate son of Sir Sidney Smith and 'a member of the Royal Family'.

officer and a gentleman, that the whole was a most audacious
and wicked calumny ... Sir Sidney added, 'I never said a word to
your wife but what you might have heard; and had I been so base
as to attempt anything of the kind under your roof, I should
deserve you to shoot me like a mad dog.'[25]

The three of them tried to confront Princess Caroline but she
refused to see them and the affair was brought to an end by the
Duke of Kent pleading that it would upset the King, who was
already overwhelmed by family problems.

Smith had been elected to represent Rochester in time for the
opening of the new parliamentary session by the King on 23rd
November 1802; his brother Spencer taking his seat as Member
for Dover at the same time. It was a tense time because, a week
before, a plot to overthrow the Government and assassinate the
King had been uncovered and the conspirators arrested. The
King was to be murdered on his way to open Parliament by
secretly loading a large Turkish cannon, brought home from the
Egyptian campaign as a trophy of war and parked on the Horse
Guards Parade, and firing it at the royal coach as it passed.
Even more extraordinary, the ringleader of the plot had been a
former friend of Lord Nelson's, Colonel Edward Despard, a
disaffected Franco-Irish officer from Honduras; he and Nelson
had served together in the Nicaraguan campaign of 1780.* This
news increased the tension, which was mounting as the fragile
peace was strained by French aggression in Piedmont and
against Switzerland, together with warlike preparations on the
Dutch coast and the British refusal to evacuate Malta.

The debate on the Navy Estimates on 2nd December gave
Smith the chance to deliver his maiden speech, which, for him,
was remarkably short. Unlike Nelson, he had no dutiful
instincts towards the Government because his friends, Spencer
and Grenville, were now in opposition. He had admired the
present First Lord of the Admiralty, but St Vincent had been
harsh and, he thought, unfair towards him in the
Mediterranean. The old admiral was now supporting his
Government's lowering of the Navy's state of readiness for

* Nelson spoke bravely and warmly of Despard's former character at his trial
in February 1803; Despard and other conspirators were sentenced to death
but the sentence was commuted – probably due to Nelson's intervention –
from hanging, drawing, while alive, and quartering, to hanging followed by
decapitation.

renewed war, despite the Prime Minister, Henry Addington, telling the House that the Royal Navy currently manned 192 ships of the line – 60 more than the combined force of France, Spain and Holland – and 209 frigates; Smith felt that, even so, cuts ashore and afloat had reached dangerous levels. So, it was reported in the parliamentary records, he 'expressed considerable regret at the great reductions which were suddenly made, both in the King's dockyards and in the Navy in general. A prodigious number of men had been thus reduced to the utmost poverty and distress; and it might be apprehended that they would be obliged to seek employment from foreign states ...' He warned that the former enemy should not be trusted, alluding obliquely to Bonaparte's recent exploits:

> he himself had been present at some of the changes which had taken place in France; they resembled more the changes of scenery at a theatre than anything else. Everything was done for stage effect and, whether it was the death of Caesar, the fall of Byzantine, or the march of Alexander, it seemed to Frenchmen almost equally indifferent.
>
> If the invasion of Britain was to be produced, it might have stage effect enough to draw 400,000 volunteers to join in the procession.[26]

This showed the importance of maintaining a strong Navy, he concluded, ready to frustrate any such attempt. There was an immediate response from Captain John Markham, who served with St Vincent on the Admiralty Board, defending its conduct 'in contradiction of the instances adduced by Sir Sidney Smith'.[27] Whether Smith's apprehensions were exaggerated or not, he had – unlike Nelson a year earlier – shown himself to be concerned at the nation's apparent lack of preparedness for war.

Smith's apprehensions were well founded, for relations with France deteriorated sharply and on 17th May 1803, hostilities were renewed. During more than a year of peace, many well-to-do British travellers had taken the opportunity to visit France and some were taken by surprise by the outbreak of war. Amongst these was Lord Elgin, who had purchased the Parthenon marbles in Athens on his return journey from Constantinople, and who was arrested in Paris, denied diplomatic immunity and interned.*

* He was not released until 1806.

When the treaty had been signed, Bonaparte granted an amnesty to royalist émigrés, and numbers of them returned, including: Colonel Bromley, who, becoming de Tromelin again, settled on his family's estate in Brittany; Major Le Grand; Captain Boisgirard, who had also played his part in Smith's escape from the Temple seven years before, and was still dancing at the Opera in Paris. But Charles de Frotté did not return, since his half-brother General Louis de Frotté, the royalist commander in Normandy, had been shot on Bonaparte's orders. One who dared to return to Paris was John Wright, the naval intelligence officer, who had been imprisoned with Smith in the Temple. He was warned to stay away by the British Embassy and, finally, by a French friend, who told him that he was to be arrested, so enabling him to escape to England.

In 1802, while in the Mediterranean, Wright had been promoted to commander and given command of the sloop *Cynthia*, in which he returned to England. After his brief and dangerous visit to Paris, he was promoted to captain and given command of the sloop *Favorite* but, as she was in dock and there was urgent need of his services, he was appointed to the brig *Vincejo*, an old Spanish prize. Again, his task was to put secret agents and subversives ashore in France and to maintain contact with the royalist guerrillas in Normandy and Britanny. Many of these agents had been trained at a camp near Romsey by Georges Cadoudal, a tough, red-headed Breton, whose main ambition was to assassinate Bonaparte. When one attempt to blow up the First Consul's carriage as he left the Tuileries palace in Paris failed, Cadoudal decided to make the next one himself. So in August 1803, he and four other royalists travelled to the Sussex fishing port of Hastings, boarded the *Vincejo* and set sail for France. On the night of the 20th, Captain Wright took his ship to the enemy's coast and sent the five men ashore in a small boat to land on the long, desolate beach at Biville south of Cap de la Hague on the north-west of the Cherbourg peninsula. During the coming weeks, the ship made two more crossings, landing more agents, including General Charles Pichegru, who had been arrested by the Directory in 1797 for trying to restore the monarchy and exiled to French Guiana, and who still had useful friends among officers in the republican army. On each night, those landed disappeared into the darkness on the next stage of their journey to Paris. Sidney Smith, too, was implicated, vaguely and mysteriously. His brother, Spencer Smith, was now British minister at Stuttgart, where he was well placed for dealings with a claimant to the throne of France, the young Duc d'Enghien, who was living at Ettelheim, also in Germany. The Smith brothers' first cousin, the rakish Lord Camelford, had, meanwhile, become involved with French émigré plotting and was even said to have made the bomb (he was an ingenious amateur chemist) that had nearly killed Bonaparte.

Smith himself had, on 12th March 1803, been appointed to command the *Antelope* of fifty guns. While shadowy skirmishes were fought between secret agents, the *Grande Armée* had returned to the Channel coast and transports were being collected at ports from Texel to Brest. His orders, again from Lord Keith, who now had command of the North Sea station and was thus primarily responsible for defence against invasion, ran, 'As the enemy have made, and are still making, extensive preparations at the port of Flushing and in the River Scheldt for the invasion of this country, it has become highly necessary that their operations should be watchfully attended to...'[28] and he was given command of a squadron of eight small warships – six sloops and two cutters, one named the *Lord Nelson* – based on Sheerness. With the temporary rank of commodore, once again, his task would be to patrol and blockade.

This was not a role suited to Smith's intense activity particularly when, in December, Lord Keith had told him that the French invasion forces were moving south from the Scheldt estuary to concentrate between Ostend and Boulogne, where 1,000 transports and gunboats had been assembled, although Dutch troops, who were to join the invasion, would remain. Smith opened the year 1804 with a brisk cutting-out expedition, bringing three small merchant ships out of a little Dutch port, only to be rebuked by Lord Keith that 'you should not hazard your men and boats on such frivolous enterprises'.[29] But he did make another such attack with his boats when a French frigate and other enemy ships were sighted anchored off shore: the frigate took shelter beneath shore batteries, one small transport loaded with fascines* was captured but a large gunboat was

* wattle fencing for shoring the sides of trenches

boarded, captured but then run aground so it could neither be taken away nor burned because of the number of enemy wounded on board; the British loss was four killed and fourteen wounded. Not all the stories about Smith's dash involved chases and cutting-out expeditions. Once, when the *Antelope* was in danger of being blown on to sandbanks off the enemy coast and all seemed lost, he summoned his officers and asked their advice. When all declared there was nothing they could do but pray, Commodore Smith said that they were agreed that their situation was unenviable and ordered the cook to send up coffee.

Just as Nelson's command of the counter-invasion forces at sea before the Peace of Amiens had been partly to allay public anxiety by appointing the most celebrated naval hero to this task, so Smith – the other public hero of the campaign against Bonaparte in the Middle East – was also reassuring as alarming stories of impending invasion and imaginings of the guillotine being set up outside St James's Palace took hold. In July, the *Bath Journal* published a long patriotic poem, equating Smith's achievement with Nelson's, which ended:

> For hark! the thunder of the Navy roars –
> Strong beats the pulse for War – loud sounds the drum,
> And our brave Sons invite the Foe to come;
> For they remember *Acre's* famous fight,
> When Britons put the vaunting Gaul to flight;
> Remember, too, the Battle of the Nile,
> And at the threats of rash invasion smile.[30]

Commodore Smith and his little squadron were patrolling the flat, desolate shores between Flushing and Ostend at the beginning of May, while his friend John Wright – now aged thirty-five – in the *Vincejo*, accompanied by the cutter *Fox*, was off the rocky coast of Brittany surveying the coast for future landings and supporting what remained of the royalist counter-revolutionaries ashore. Wright had just boarded a Spanish brig and taken from her some American newspapers, in one of which was a verse addressed to the British, which ended with the words, 'Return victorious, or return no more' words he took to repeating this to himself as he paced his quarterdeck 'in a kind of reverie',[31] it was noted by his officers.

On the evening of the 7th, Captain Wright was ashore on the

island of Houat in Quiberon Bay and had difficulty regaining his ship, first because of fog and then because of a sudden gale. Back on board, he steered towards Port Navalo but the wind dropped and dawn found the *Vincejo* becalmed. She lay in sight of the harbour and soon activity ashore was sighted and then seventeen large French gunboats emerged under oars. Wright, who had again been heard muttering, 'Return victorious, or return no more', broke out of his reflective mood and briskly ordered his own boats to tow his ship. They began to make way towards the open sea when the tide turned and the flood carried her inshore again. There was nothing for it but to fight and Wright spurned his officers' suggestion that he himself – a valuable prize to the French – should escape in the cutter before she pulled away under oars and then caught a light gust of wind that carried her to safety. The British fought their short-range, eighteen-pounder carronades to little effect, while the French could stand off and fire their long twenty-four-pounders with accuracy. After four hours, the *Vincejo* was shattered and clearly doomed. As the ship's surgeon, John Lawmont, put it:

Our firing almost ceased, three of the guns being dismounted, and the rest encumbered with lumber from the falling of the booms, their supporters having been shot away; the men falling fast, the foremast nearly shot away and the vessel nearly sinking, Captain Wright was forced to hail that he had struck just in time to save the lives of the few that could keep the deck, as the gunboats were rowing up alongside with numerous troops to board. He himself was wounded in the thigh early in the action by grapeshot but never left the deck.[32]

The French towed their prize into the archipelago of rocks and islands at the mouth of the River Vilaine and took the prisoners by boat up to Auray, where they were put ashore, the officers held in private houses under guard and the men kept in the prison. A few days later the prisoners were marched to Vannes, Wright in a small cart with an escort from the *Garde Nationale* commanded by a Swiss officer. There, Wright was lodged at an inn and interviewed by the departmental governor, General Julien, who had been wounded and captured in Egypt and, by an extraordinary coincidence, had been taken out to the *Tigre*, where Wright had given him his cabin. Julien immediately recognized him and, next morning, had him arrested at the inn with orders that 'for his comfort' he was to be sent to Paris under escort. With the gendarme, Julien sent a letter to the Minister of Police, Joseph Fouché, explaining that, on hearing that prisoners taken from a captured British ship were passing through Vannes, he had checked to see if they included 'any traitors like those who had lately been vomited on the coasts; but what was his surprise when, in the commander, he recognised the celebrated Captain Wright, who had landed Pichegru, etc., and whom he had formerly known in Egypt'. He was sending Wright, together with his young nephew, who had been on board, and his servant to Paris. 'Captain Wright is a most artful and dangerous adventurer', he continued, 'who thought himself destined to act some high part – that he set all interrogatories at defiance as he acted on the orders of his Government and was accountable only to it – but if he is properly questioned he will make revelations of much importance to the Republic.'[33]

Wright, unaware of this chilling introduction, boarded a guarded coach that stopped outside the gates of Vannes, where survivors of his ship's company were drawn up. 'Captain Wright there took an affectionate leave of them, many of whom shed tears', it was reported. 'He said as he passed before them, that in whatever situation he might be placed, he should never forget that he was a British officer.'[34] Then he boarded the coach again and was driven off towards Bonaparte's Paris.

A few days after Wright's capture, Smith was in action in the North Sea, trying to stop the junction of fifty-nine small French ships lying off Flushing with twenty-two at Ostend. It was a fierce fight but a failure, the French making use of the sandbanks to cover their passage, so that most of the Flushing ships reached Ostend, although one was captured and several driven ashore. On Smith's ships thirteen had been killed and thirty-two wounded. This sort of warfare in the North Sea was not to Smith's liking. After his years in the Mediterranean sun he hated the cold and damp and his health began to suffer. So after this final action off Ostend, he requested and was granted sick leave, being relieved as commodore by Sir Home Popham.

Smith had just heard of Wright's capture but there had been more bad news. Both General Pichegru and Georges Cadoudal, whom Wright had put ashore in France, had been arrested, and

Fouché's police were extracting information under torture from more captured royalists about the whereabouts of other leaders; one confession implicated Spencer Smith, now the British minister in Stuttgart, in the plotting. Lord Camelford, who had been so deeply involved in planning an attempt on Bonaparte's life and was rumoured to be about to return to Paris via Holland, had been safely in London but the same newspapers that announced the arrests in France reported that he had fought a duel to settle a quarrel over a woman and had been seriously wounded; he lingered for a few days, but on 10th March he died. But speculation began that the quarrel over a shared mistress might not be the full story. It was odd that his opponent, a Captain Best, was considered the best shot in England, the only one more deadly than Camelford himself. So had the quarrel and the challenge been engineered by Fouché's agents?

On the day Camelford died, Bonaparte and two other consuls, the Grand Judge of the Republic, Fouché, and Talleyrand, met in Paris to decide on further counter-measures against royalist conspiracies. They agreed that their purpose was to kill the First Consul and replace him with a monarch, and that the most likely candidate would be the thirty-one-year-old Duc d'Enghien. It was decided that he should be kidnapped on German territory and brought to Paris. This was done on the night of 14th March, when 300 French dragoons – their horses' hoofs muffled with sacking – and three detachments of gendarmerie surrounded his house at Ettelheim, woke the duke and rushed him over the border into France. He was taken to the fortress of Vincennes outside Paris and interrogated, tried by a military court of seven colonels and sentenced to death. Before dawn on 21st March he faced a firing squad in the moat of the fortress, himself holding a lantern to illuminate his chest. A fortnight later, General Pichegru was found strangled in his cell at the Temple prison in Paris. In another cell in the same prison – indeed, in the same cell that had held him nearly a decade before – Captain Wright awaited his fate.

Smith did what he could to help. His own pleading to the French would be useless because he was as deeply implicated in royalist subversion as his friend. There was now no chance of planning a successful escape since most of the royalists he knew in France had been arrested and these now included de

Tromelin, who had been taken from Brittany to join the others in Parisian prisons. On arrival in Paris, Wright was taken again to the Temple and locked in a room in one of the upper turrets. Recognizing this as the same he had occupied ten years before, he remembered hiding tools for cutting through iron bars, including a file and a hacksaw, under a brick in the floor. He found the brick, lifted it and found the tools still in place. Yet he was in no condition to contemplate escape, for the bullet wound in his thigh was painful and he was limping.

Wright was interrogated but refused to answer questions. He refused again on 2nd June when he was taken from prison to the court where Georges Cadoudal and other captured royalist leaders were on trial for their lives. The defendants pretended they did not recognize him but he was recognized by the gaoler of the Temple, who reported that the *Moniteur*, 'saw him there when he was a prisoner ... with Sir Sidney Smith'. Then de Tromelin was brought into court and taken unawares, so that 'he was also recognised ... by one Tromelin, now under arrest, who had been taken with Sir Sidney Smith and put with him in the Temple, where he passed for Sir Sidney's servant, by the name of John. Being sent out of France, he returned soon after in disguise, and contributed to Smith's escape. All these facts he confessed.' But Wright still refused to say more than that 'being a prisoner of war, he could not depose of anything and that being an Englishman and faithful subject he would not answer any question'.[35] After repeated questions met with the same response, the crowd in the gallery began to applaud and, to avoid further demonstrations of sympathy and because it was obvious that he was weak and in pain, Wright was 'allowed to withdraw, which he did, bowing to the spectators, who again applauded him'. His fourteen-year-old nephew was then brought into court to be questioned but he, too, 'answered with a coolness and firmness that again excited the applause of the spectators'.[36]

Wright and his nephew were then allowed to share a room at the Temple and the other officers of the *Vincejo*, who had been in solitary confinement on a diet of bread and water for a month while undergoing interrogation, were also brought to the Temple, where they were able to meet Wright before being moved to join other prisoners-of-war in fortress-prisons. Shaking hands with Mr Lawmont, the surgeon, he said,

'Whatever happens to me in my present position, I will behave, believe me ... like a Christian and a British officer.'[37] Soon afterwards, he wrote a letter to Lieutenant James Wallis, his first lieutenant, thanking him for the news that had reached him in prison that he had been confirmed as a post-captain so that he would now move automatically up the *Navy List* and, if he survived, become an admiral. He also asked Wallis to look after the midshipmen 'as a sort of foster-father to my little admirals in embryo'. Now he had, he said, just the company of 'a little amiable cat that has just taken the caprice of laying her whole length on my paper and purrs to me'.[38] Soon afterwards, he heard that Georges Cadoudal and twelve other royalists had been executed. Jacques-Jean de Tromelin and Captain Wright were kept in prison.

Smith struck his broad pendant in May 1804, and at the same time was given the courtesy rank of colonel of the Royal Marines – as the corps were named in that year – an honour also accorded to Nelson, which meant an increase in pay. On leave, he occupied his time considering ways to overcome the dangers of the shallow coastal waters in the North Sea. Sometimes, at low tide, it had been impossible to put landing parties ashore even in ships' boats and he remembered the difficulties he had had with these when trying to land field guns from them in Aboukir Bay. So he sketched a new design of landing-craft based on the twin-hulled canoes of the South Seas, which had been described by officers who returned from Captain Cook's voyage of exploration. He visualized pairs of larger craft, the size of wherries, to be joined by a deck twenty feet square, on which troops, or guns, could be ferried ashore, or to assault coastal fortifications. He developed his sketches into a model and a prototype was built on the Thames. This was rowed up to Chelsea by six men and, off Greenwich, was rigged with four sails.

Finally, the Admiralty approved the building of two prototype catamarans at Dover and, in September, Sir Sidney arrived to direct their trials. They were named the *Cancer* – because it seemed to approach a beach crab-wise – and the *Gemini*. The former was a galley forty-eight feet in length, cut in two from stem to stern, the halves joined by beams supporting a platform on which stood a field gun, its wheels in grooves extending on to a ramp, which could be lowered on to the beach when the craft grounded. She could also carry fifty soldiers, while a mast on either beam carried sails, and there were eight oars on each side. She was lined with cork to prevent foundering in the surf. The other craft was double the size and constructed of two complete galleys, each with sixteen long sweeps on the outside of the pair and sixteen paddles on the inside. When fully loaded, both catamarans drew only eighteen inches of water.

On a sunny afternoon in early September, the trials began, watched by crowds ashore. According to a contemporary report:

> Both the piers were crowded with company to witness this interesting spectacle. A number of officers and their wives and, in short, all the *élégantes* of the town, were assembled to behold the brave Sir Sidney; while the oldest inhabitants of this his native place* hailed him as the ornament and honour of their town; many remembered him as a little boy and he recognised his old friends as he passed through them with the greatest kindness and affection.

Twenty gunners from the Royal Artillery boarded the catamarans to man the guns and, escorted by other craft, the two strange vessels put to sea. The report continued:

> All this added to a most beautiful day and a distinct view of the French coast, the *coup d'oeil* made the scene enchanting. After trying those boats in every way which they could possibly be managed ... the artillery ... were put on board them and several shots were fired in different directions ... They were then run on shore ... near to the cottage occupied by Sir Sidney's aunt. The cannon were landed in a moment of time with the greatest ease and several shot being fired by the way of experiment, they were again, in an instant, shipped with the most apparent ease and expedition Sir Sidney and his party retired to regale themselves on shore.[39]

Since war had broken out again in May 1803, it had escalated quickly. Vice-Admiral Viscount Nelson, as he now was, had been appointed commander-in-chief in the Mediterranean and by July he was off Toulon, watching the French fleet. The most direct threat was, however, to England and that summer,

---

* His father had latterly lived in a little castellated house near the harbour, nicknamed Smith's Folly.

Bonaparte himself again took command of the Army of England on the Channel coast. This was to expand to about 170,000 men with 10,000 horses, while 2,300 invasion craft were assembled from Ostend to Boulogne manned by 17,000 sailors. The core of this array was Boulogne, where, at any one time, there were about 1,000 ships in the harbour and semi-circular basin, while Bonaparte himself lived a few miles inland in the little chateau at Pont-de-Briques. His presence at ceremonial parades and his promise of the looting of London kept anticipation keen. Round their camp fires his soldiers sang songs such as one mocked Nelson's failed attack on Boulogne in 1801:

> Devant Boulogne,
> Nelson faisait un feu d'enfer!
> Mais ce jour-là, plus d'un ivrogne
> Au lieu de vin, but l'eau de mere
> Devant Boulogne!*

To meet this threat, the British Isles were defended by some 200,000 regular troops and militia and 400,000 volunteers but only the regulars could hope to stand against the *Grand Armée*, which could choose its landing-point if the French fleet could command the sea for a few days. So the prerequisite for an invasion was either to defeat the main British fleets, or lure them away from the narrow seas between France and England.

At the beginning of December, Bonaparte crowned himself the Emperor Napoleon I in the cathedral of Notre Dame and the stage seemed set for the *grande finale*; a few days later, Spain declared war on England and the necessary naval supremacy seemed attainable. The grand strategy was sweeping and almost global: if the French fleet could break out of Toulon and then out of the Mediterranean, luring Nelson's fleet in hot pursuit, they would cross the Atlantic as if to attack Jamaica and the other rich, British Caribbean islands, there joining with French and Spanish squadrons from the Atlantic ports. While Nelson searched for them, they would head straight back to Europe and then be strong enough to command the English Channel while the *Grande Armée* crossed. In April 1805, the French fleet, under Admiral Villeneuve, broke out of Toulon and the first stages of the strategy unfolded. Nelson followed to

* Off Boulogne, / Nelson poured hell-fire! / But on that day, many a toper/ Instead of wine, drank salt water, / Off Boulogne!

the West Indies and then, realizing he had been tricked, followed them back. But, although the Spanish Admiral Gravina had sailed from Cadiz and kept his rendezvous with Villeneuve, Admiral Ganteaume, had been unable to break through the British blockade of Brest. So, when the combined fleet headed eastward again with Nelson in pursuit, they were met by a British squadron off Finisterre, fought a brief, indecisive action, and then, losing heart, decided to make for port rather than the Channel. On 20th August, the combined French and Spanish fleets reached the huge, almost landlocked, harbour of Cadiz.

The British prepared to defend themselves. Apart from building defences, such as the Martello towers along the south coast, and recruiting and drilling volunteers, morale was kept up by patriotic songs and caricatures of a burly John Bull on the cliffs of Dover mocking the caperings of a dwarfish Napoleon on the far shore. Mock-playbills were circulated, one for 'Harlequin's Invasion, or the Disappointed Banditti' included the scenes:

> Harlequin's Flat-Bottom Boats Warmly Engaged
> by the Wooden Walls of Old England

and:

THE REPULSE
Or, Britons Triumphant
The parts of John Bull, Paddy Whack, Sawney MacSnaish and
Shone-ap-Morgan by Messrs. NELSON, MOIRA, St Vincent,
GARDNER,
HUTCHINSON, WARREN, PELLEW, S. SMITH, etc.
The Chorus of 'Hearts of Oak' by the JOLLY TARS and
ARMY OF OLD ENGLAND

During these months the vortex of the war was the narrow stretch of water between Dover and Calais. Smith knew that his temporary successor, Home Popham, had various schemes for pre-emptive attacks on Boulogne in the hope of succeeding where Nelson had failed in 1801. Now, as then, the port was defended by a line of small but heavily gunned warships, which would emerge to moor in line abreast to keep attacking British ships out of range of the harbour itself. The French ships had heavy netting rigged between gunwales and yard-arms to prevent boarding and – in the event that boarding was

achieved – they were moored by chains that axes could not
sever. Nelson had attacked with boats and boarding parties;
Home Popham had used fire-ships and secret explosive
weapons that looked like odd-shaped casks – known to the
Royal Navy as 'infernals' – in his attack on 3rd October 1804,
but that too had failed; the infernals had exploded at the wrong
time or not at all. In December, he had used them again in an
attempt to demolish Fort Rouge, built on piles in the sea off
Calais, and that, too, had failed.

Although few knew exactly what they were, the secret
weapons, and the exaggerated claims made of their success,
had become a joke and one comic song about them included the
lines:

> Your project new, Jack mutters, Avast! 'Tis very stale:
> 'Tis catching birds, land-lubbers, by salt upon the tail.
> So fireships, casks and coffers blazing, now bring Vauxhall to
>   mind:
> As if ten thousand galas were in one gala joined.
> There in that blaze go fifty! And there go fifty more!
> A hundred in disorder, there run upon the shore!
> From them the joyful tidings, soon flew to London town:
> By hundreds and by thousands, they burn, sink, kill and
>   drown.'[40]

After the failure at Fort Rouge, Popham expected and was
given another appointment, that of senior naval officer of an
expedition to South America. Smith resumed command of the
squadron in the Channel, by now privy to the secrets of the new
weapons. On 15th October, soon after the failure of Popham's
attack on Boulogne, he had been invited to attend trials in
Walmer Road within sight of the residence of William Pitt, who
had returned to office as Prime Minister, and, in the largely
ceremonial appointment of Warden of the Cinque Ports, had
the use of Walmer Castle. Pitt's brother-in-law, Lord Stanhope,
who was a scientist as well as a politician, had been urging the
Government to assess some of the extraordinary new weapons
that had been devised by a young American inventor.

Most of the senior politicians – including the Prime Minister
and Lord Castlereagh, the Minister for War – accompanied by
senior naval and military officers, including Smith and Popham
– to meet 'a man of grave and mysterious carriage of body ...
under the name of *Francis*. It was *whispered* that he was a *Yankey*

American of some consequence, whose real name was *Fulton*.'[41] Robert Fulton had come over from the York Hotel at Dover, where he had been staying under his *nom de guerre*, at the suggestion of Lord Stanhope, to arrange a demonstration of an invention that had been discussed with a mixture of fascination and apprehension in Whitehall for several years. Fulton was the pioneer of undersea warfare by submarines, torpedoes and mines.

Experiments with submersibles had been tried since the American War of Independence when an unsuccessful attempt had been made to sink a British ship of the line at anchor off the coast of Connecticut. Fulton had continued to nurture the idea of building such a vessel, but actually to do so was such an expensive proposition so that only a nation at war was likely to become his patron. This was to be America's old ally, France, and he arrived in Paris before Bonaparte's expedition had sailed for Egypt. He explained his ideas to the Directory, telling Barras that, if his plans could be put in to practice, 'warships destroyed by means so new, so secret and so incalculable, the confidence of the sailors is destroyed and the fleet rendered worthless ... In this state of things the English republicans will rise to facilitate the descent of the French, to change their government themselves.'[42] His plans 'for placing the Submarine Bomb, or *Torpedo*, under a vessel' ran into technical difficulties and he wrote to his friend Gaspard Monge, who had led the *savants* into Egypt, 'I have by reflection and Experiment found a certain and very simple method for fixing the Torpedoes to a ship and sending them under her bottom whether she be at anchor, or under sail.'[43] Monge had the ear of Bonaparte and, with his support, Fulton built his first submarine, the *Nautilus*, of iron and copper, twenty-one feet in length and with a beam of seven feet. Designed to cruise at a depth of about twenty-five feet and stay submerged for five hours, she successfully underwent trials in the Seine and then at sea off Le Havre. Off Brest, she sank a target-ship and tried unsuccessfully to attack a passing British frigate.

Fulton also designed submarine bombs, or mines, which he called 'carcasses', which would either explode by contact with a ship's hull, or by a clockwork timing device. But he dealt with the French in what seemed to them a high-handed manner, demanding financial guarantees and an officer's commission as insurance that he would be treated as a prisoner of war if captured by the British. However, the French did not like the idea of his *bateau-poisson*, one admiral telling him, 'Go, sir, your invention is good for the Algerians, or Corsairs, but learn that France has not yet abandoned the ocean.' Bonaparte himself dismissed the idea, telling his secretary, 'Bah, these projectors are all either intriguers, or visionaries. Don't trouble me about the business,' adding, 'Don't mention him again.'[44]

The British had been aware of his experiments and Lord Stanhope had warned the House of Lords of their dangers in 1802. In the following year, a British agent named 'Mr. Smith' – there was no evidence that it was Spencer Smith, or his brother, or that the name was anything more than a coincidence – approached Fulton in Paris to suggest he transfer his experiments to England. Accordingly, in 1804, Fulton arrived in London soon after William Pitt had again become Prime Minister, and an encouraging group of enthusiasts for unconventional warfare were in place. It was only then that Bonaparte realized the full implications of other plans being offered by Fulton, who had also been working on designs for steam-ships. These, if mass-produced, could enable him to send his soldiers across the Channel when the British fleet was becalmed. But it was too late; the inventor was already in London and Bonaparte sadly mused that steam-ships 'could change the face of the world'.[45]

Fulton had now concentrated on mines and torpedoes. These were not self-propelled but were fixed to a ship's hull, or were fastened together by a length of rope and launched upstream of an anchored ship, either side of her mooring cable so that the current carried them down each side of the hull. They had been tried by Popham at Boulogne but had been swept away by strong tides, exploded prematurely, or failed to ignite. The trials at Walmer, a fortnight after the attack on Boulogne, were Fulton's attempt to demonstrate the potential of his inventions.

William Pitt had been recalled to London before the trials could begin but most of the senior executive were present, watching from the ramparts of Walmer Castle on 15th October 1805. A brig, the *Dorothea*, had been anchored offshore as the target and several naval officers were so sceptical that they offered to remain on board throughout the trials, one joking that even if he were seated at dinner on board 'he should feel no concern for the consequence'.[46] He was wrong. The boats pulled out to the brig and two linked mines – each set to explode in fifteen minutes – were attached to her mooring cable. The power of the explosion blew the brig in two. In his report to Castlereagh Smith described how:

> the masts ... fell over and crossed each other; in short, in less time than you have taken to read these six lines, they were, as it were, as two felled trees would appear on the axe cutting the last fibre that held them upright, and the hull appeared a misshapen black mass floating on the surface with the casks that were in her hold going astern. This news will, of course, get over to Boulogne and deter them from lying in the outer road, which is what we want for our ultimate operation.[47]

Not all the British were as euphoric and Lord St Vincent told Fulton that 'Pitt was the greatest fool that ever existed to encourage a mode of war, which they who commanded the seas did not want, and which, if successful, would deprive them of it'.[48] Lord Keith, too, was dismissive, describing Smith's plan as 'nonsense' and that the only way to destroy the invasion flotilla at Boulogne was by 'a large military force and a well-digested plan, or by a dash in a dark night by a few determined *seamen*, well prepared to set fire and return instantly to their boats'.[49] Yet Castlereagh was excited and readily gave Sir Sidney Smith permission to include Fulton's weapons in any future operations, particularly against Boulogne. Smith was already ahead of him, planning to combine attacks from underwater by mine and from the air by Colonel Congreve's new rockets.* Seamen were always terrified by the risk of fire, so, while the French were watching the fiery rockets descend from the sky on to their combustible ships, Mr Fulton's mines could be exploded under their hulls. The possibilities of such weapons, he realised, extended far beyond the immediate prospect of attacking the invasion flotilla.

In mid-November, Smith made a trial night attack on Boulogne. It, too, was a failure. French guardships swarmed out of the harbour, the sea was rough and, as Smith reported to Castlereagh, 'Rain and wind are bad concomitants for fire-

---

* The son of Sir William Congreve, controller of the Royal Laboratory at Woolwich and the first baronet. Colonel William Congreve was an officer in the Royal Artillery and author of *A Concise Account of the Origin and Progress of the Rocket System*.

works on shore, but worse afloat ... The launches *rolled* so much from the ground-swell ... that the rockets went out of the frame into the water', and could be seen flaring and bursting beneath. Eight boats towing carcasses set out to attack the ships anchored before the harbour mouth but were swamped and never reached the mooring cables. Optimistically, he concluded, 'By next summer, we shall have practice enough to try Boulogne in fine weather.'[50]

The failure prompted the admirals to discourage any further such attempts, which would, Lord Barham, the First Lord of the Admiralty, who had expressed confidence in Smith a few days earlier, now wrote, 'release us from the anxiety of seeing our bravest men cut to pieces in fruitless attempts'. Then, returning to the old distrust of Smith, he continued, 'There seems to me such a want of judgement in our friend Sir Sidney, that it is much safer to employ him under command than in command.'[51] That was exactly what the Admiralty had in mind. During the summer, when Nelson had returned from his abortive chase of the French fleet to the West Indies and back, the two had had several meetings and past differences had been discarded. Five years earlier, Sir William Hamilton had recognized that this was coming and had written to Smith's uncle, General Edward Smith. 'Be assured that Lord Nelson now understands Sir Sidney well and really loves and esteems him; and I will venture to say, will give him every proof of it, if ever they should meet on service together, as I hope. They are certainly the two greatest heroes of the age.'[52] This was now about to happen. The two men had met at Lord Castlereagh's office in Downing Street, at Greenwich and, one Sunday in September, at Merton Place, and Nelson clearly realized that they had much in common: originality, dash and the willingness to take the initiative in defiance of out-dated orders. So, before returning to take command of the Mediterranean Fleet, Nelson asked for Smith to command one of his squadrons. Writing to William Windham, Smith announced that he had been 'called upon by Lord Nelson (in consequence, he told me, of his suggestion to Mr. Pitt, in which he agreed) and offer'd the command of his inshore squadron in the Mediterranean, with full powers to act as circumstances might render practicable in attacking the enemy ...'[53] This was the final vindication.

Nelson sailed in his flagship, the *Victory*, to take command of his main fleet from his second in command, Vice-Admiral Sir Cuthbert Collingwood, on 14th September. Meanwhile, there was the immediate task at Boulogne and, despite their new-found friendship, it would be gratifying to succeed there when Nelson had failed. Smith was also pleased that Pitt and Castlereagh were taking so keen an interest in the plans that he could deal directly with them rather than submit all ideas to the stern eye of Lord Keith, who regarded rockets and torpedoes as warlike toys and no substitute for a battle fleet.

As the Boulogne operation was discussed a more ambitious plan emerged. The rocket and torpedo attack was not only to be followed by an immediate naval attack on the line of French ships off the harbour mouth but by a landing on the beaches by British troops and an assault on the port itself. This was to be commanded by Major-General Sir John Moore, who had been the most effective commander ashore in Egypt; he was a man of few, but pertinent, words and he and Smith were opposites in temperament. Smith had taken Moore across to Boulogne in the *Antelope* on a close reconnaissance at the end of September, when, on their approach, thirty-two French ships had come out of the port to anchor in a defensive line. He was excited by his view of the shipping packed in the great basin and told Lord Keith in a letter that the transports were 'in such close contact with each other as to ensure the rapid spreading of flames, if once fire was communicated to any part of the ... forest-like assemblage of masts.'[54] General Moore did not share Smith's enthusiasm, writing to the Duke of York, Commander-in-Chief of the Army, that he had himself seen between 5,000 and 6,000 French troops drawn up along the shore so that only a large assault force could land, defeat the enemy, burn the ships in the harbour and safely withdraw.* Smith hated any such cool caution and himself wrote to Castlereagh that 'General Moore ... would do his utmost to realise any plan laid down for him ... but he is too wary to undertake such a task voluntarily, though, of course, foremost when ordered to go to work.'[55]

Smith visualized Congreve's rockets being launched from catamarans, such as he had had built at Dover, as these would prove steadier platforms than round-bottomed boats. He

* Plans for this attack on Boulogne were remarkably similar to those for the disastrous attack on Dieppe in 1942.

visualized a dozen catamarans, each firing 48 rockets at the shipping in the basin from a maximum range of 2,500 yards. Meanwhile, 19 boats under oars would tow the 'carcass' mines towards the anchored guard-ships, set their timers and attempt to attach them to their mooring cables. Under cover of this double attack, Moore's soldiers could storm the beaches. The approach to Boulogne was to be guided by an experienced Channel pilot, Captain Tom Johnson, or Johnstone, a former smuggler, whom Castlereagh introduced to Smith by letter, saying that he had been 'employed, during the late war, in various services of a confidential nature by Government, wherein he proved himself of much utility by his dexterity and boldness and by his knowledge of the coasts of the enemy'.[56] Johnson had asked that the Admiralty purchase a lugger named the *Nile*, which he could man with other smugglers for this purpose.

Just as the plans were being completed, a report reached Sir Sidney that French troops were being withdrawn from the coast around Boulogne and he took this as an encouragement to attack. It was, however, the first sign of a fundamental change in Napoleon's strategy: the invasion of England was to be postponed again while he turned on the Austrians and the *Grande Armée* began its march east. Neither Smith nor Moore had realized that the French troops they had counted on the bluffs above Boulogne were parading to conceal this fact and that Napoleon himself had left Boulogne at the end of September.

There was, however, another possibility. Smith expected to be joining Lord Nelson, either blockading the combined Franco–Spanish fleet in Cadiz, or in the Mediterranean, and his aerial and submarine weaponry might well be useful there. Specifically, he could possibly pre-empt any great battle that Nelson might fight off Cadiz by destroying the enemy fleet in that harbour with Colonel Congreve's rockets and Mr Fulton's torpedoes. Even Lord Barham was enthusiastic, writing to Castlereagh that:

> the subject has already taken wind; and, if you do not *immediately* send Sir Sidney off to Cadiz, without thinking of Boulogne, that part of the project that bids the fairest will be lost. The combined squadrons now lie in a disorderly state at Cadiz. If the rockets can be of use, a better opportunity cannot be desired. Nothing here

depends upon Johnson, nor reconnoitring boats. Compared with this, the burning of boats is not worth a thought. In attempting the former, the professional people will go with you, but they are unanimous in condemning the latter.[57]

Castlereagh at once wrote to Nelson, giving him the latest news of 'Mr. Francis's' inventions – Fulton's underwater weapons and Congreve's rockets. He replied on 3rd October from the *Victory* off Cadiz that a dozen enemy ships of the line were in the outer anchorage, so:

> if gun- and guard-boats do not prevent them, the way in is open to Mr. Francis. But I have little faith; however, that is for His Majesty's Ministers: he shall have every assistance from me. The rockets, if the account of them is true, must annoy their fleet very much; but I depend more upon hunger for driving them out and upon the gallant officers and men under my command for their destruction, than any other invention.[58]

On 21st October, Castlereagh again wrote to Smith urging him to make another attack on Boulogne before moving on to Cadiz and asking him to suggest a date. This was because of delays with assembling the necessary spare parts and ammunition to accompany Smith's unconventional mission to Cadiz. Five days later, Castlereagh again wrote to Nelson that:

> With respect to the enemy's fleet in Cadiz, I hope your Lordship will either have the glory of destroying it at sea, or that we shall find the means, sooner or later, of getting at them in port. I have not thought it desirable to send either Mr. Congreve or Mr. Francis to your Lordship till they have provided themselves with all the necessary means of giving effect to the respective modes of attack. Since your Lordship sailed, the power of Mr. Francis's instrument has been satisfactorily ascertained by an experiment upon a large vessel purchased for that purpose and which was approached in the usual manner and the carcass thrown across the cable.

He then explained the technicalities and how cork had been used to give the torpedo the necessary buoyancy. All had then gone according to plan and 'the explosion taking place at the moment to which the lock was adjusted, it blew the ship into fragments ... I have thought it right to say thus much in confidence that you may be able to estimate the power of the weapon.'[59]

Commodore Smith's mind was now focused on Cadiz and

his new method of warfare snatching the laurels of victory from Lord Nelson. Then, early on the morning of 6th November, news reached London that he was too late: the French and Spanish fleets had sailed from Cadiz and, on 21st October, Lord Nelson had brought them to battle. The enemy had been destroyed off Cape Trafalgar, but, in the hour of victory, Nelson had been mortally wounded and had died that same day. When the news reached Smith he was at sea, preparing an attack on Boulogne, and in a letter to Castlereagh on 8th November about his latest plans, he wrote, 'Alas, poor Nelson! I grieve on every account.'[60] Next day, deciding that the enemy might not know of their defeat, and must be told, he sent a boat into Boulogne under a flag of truce with a copy of the *Gazette Extraordinary* from London giving the news. On that same day Sir Sidney Smith was promoted to flag rank as Rear-Admiral of the Blue Squadron; in London a silver medallion was struck in commemoration bearing his profile on one side and his motto, 'Coeur de Lion' on the other. It joined the outpouring of medallions, prints, busts and ceramics being mass-produced to commemorate Lord Nelson as the martyred saviour of his country. But Sir Sidney Smith was now the living hero.

But this promotion was shadowed by terrible news from France. Captain John Wright had been kept in his Paris prison despite efforts to secure his release. It had been suggested to the French that he be exchanged with a captured French officer of similar rank but, as in Smith's case nearly a decade earlier, this had been contemptuously refused. Then on 24th October it had been reported to Napoleon, who had arrived at Munich, that Wright's cell in the Temple had been searched and under a brick in the floor, files, ropes, a hook and money had been discovered – the cache he had hidden in 1796, and which he had himself found on his return. Concluding that a new escape was being planned, Napoleon replied angrily, 'Have the prisoner Wright put in solitary confinement, this miserable assassin who wished to escape from the Temple.'[61] On 28th October, the day after this order was received by Fouché, Captain Wright was found dead in his cell, lying on his bed with his throat cut. The French announced that he had committed suicide, the *Gazette de France* reporting simply: 'Captain Wright of the English navy, a prisoner in the Temple, who had debarked on the French coast Georges [Cadoudal] and his accomplices, has put an end to his existence in his prison after having read in the *Moniteur* an account of the destruction of the Austrian army.'[62] This reason seemed improbable not only because of Wright's resolute character but because the same newspaper carried a report that the combined French and Spanish fleets were leaving Cadiz and he would have known that an action was imminent and would have had no doubt as to the outcome. Also, earlier in the night on which he died, he had been heard playing his flute and softly singing snatches of a satirical song about Napoleon and Nelson.

It seemed clear to the British that he had been murdered, but why, and on whose orders? The Duc d'Enghien had been shot on Napoleon's orders and he was known to have ordered other atrocities, notably the slaughter of Turkish prisoners at Jaffa. Royalists, such as General de Frotté, had been lured into captivity and executed, or like General Pichegru, murdered in prison; indeed it was said that the suspected assassin of the latter had been seen in the Temple at the time of Wright's death. So had Napoleon himself ordered the killing, perhaps in a coded message from Munich? 'If Wright was put to death, it must have been by my authority,' he was to say. 'If he was put to death in prison, I ordered it. Fouché, even if so inclined, never would have dared to do it.' He insisted that Wright had killed himself for fear of[63] compromising others in the assassination plot. The Battle of Trafalgar had been fought the day after the action at Ulm, so could the first news of it to reach Paris have prompted his murder in revenge? Yet there are no reports of it having reached the capital before 30th October. Wherever the responsibility lay, Captain Wright had died because he was an intelligence officer in the same web that covered England and France and stretched across the Mediterranean to Istanbul and Levant; the very web that his friend Sidney Smith had helped to spin.

CHAPTER EIGHT

'This brave man's foibles'

THE DEATH OF Nelson at the age of forty-seven was followed three months later by that of William Pitt, at forty-six. Pitt was succeeded as Prime Minister by Smith's friend Lord Grenville in the coalition 'Ministry of All the Talents', with Charles James Fox as Foreign Secretary and Windham back at the War and Colonial Office. Smith's name had not appeared amongst those of naval officers attending Nelson's magnificently grand and sombre funeral at St Paul's Cathedral on 9th January because he had been so busy getting his new flagship, the seventy-four-gun *Pompée* – like the *Tigre*, a French prize – ready for sea at Plymouth. He was anxious to know whether Windham was as enthusiastic about unconventional weapons as Castlereagh had been and wrote to enquire on 12th February as he prepared to sail for the Mediterranean to join Nelson's friend and successor, Vice-Admiral Lord Collingwood.

Reminding Windham that Nelson himself had requested his appointment to command the inshore squadron in his fleet 'with full powers to act as circumstances might render practicable in attacking the enemy in their own harbours and in their coast *communications* both by *sea* and *land*'. He continued:

Mr. Congreve's rockets and Mr. Francis's submarine exploding carcasses ... were annexed to my command for this sort of amphibious service ... All this is in train and can be set in motion through the fiat of government through Lord Collingwood, my present commander-in-chief, to whom I was directed to explain all that had passed in Downing Street, when Lord Nelson, Mr. Francis, Mr. Congreve and myself attended at Lord Castlereagh's office and met Mr. Pitt.

He listed not only the 'infernals' but also the landing-craft he had designed – 'double galleys like the South Seas canoes, calculated for rowing, sailing and landing field-pieces and infantry in a surf' – together with the *Atalanta*, 'a laboratory store vessel', and the pilot lugger, the *Nile*, 'commanded by Mr. Johnson, the crew to be selected by him from the smugglers on the coast, who are allowed additional pay to induce them to relinquish their trade, which is so injurious to the revenue'. He urged that the new weapons be used offensively, adding, 'Surely Lord Nelson's death ought not to operate so disadvantageously to us as to change our system into a simple and passive one of defence.'

Finally, Smith warned that Napoleon might attempt another eastward lunge:

Knowing Bonaparte as I know him, I can easily imagine his thirst to realise a *spéculation manqué* on Constantinople and the route to India. He cannot fail to find it increase on being nearer to the capital of the eastern Empire than he is to his own. He will be surrounded by *Polish* adventurers and *Venetian* navigators of the Black Sea, who will suggest plans ... These he will propose in dictatorial style to the Porte ... he will send ... his army to garrison Byzantium and the Dardanelles, while his Venetian flotilla creeps along the coast of the Morea [Greece] and carries sailors to man the Turkish fleet by way of balancing his loss at Trafalgar. All this he can do if not counteracted ... I dare say I shall be looked to for the Herculean labour when the difficulties of it are found; but I trust, after the manner in which my brother and I have been flouted and thwarted that I shall not be expected to volunteer my services under the direction of any person totally ignorant of Turkey, or any one that may have acquired the knowledge they may have by travelling the road explored and beaten flat for them by our labour.'[1]

This was a reference to Lord Elgin.

Since Trafalgar, there had been no enemy battle fleet to escort a troop convoy back to Egypt and Collingwood commanded the Mediterranean. But the re-conquest could be attempted, as Smith had suggested, by the French crossing from southern Italy to Greece and thence into Turkey and the Levant. Even if this were blocked by the recapture of Italy, it might still be achieved through the mountainous country along the eastern shore of the Adriatic and thence through Greece to Turkey. Any such plans would have to be countered by Smith's inshore squadron; looking even farther ahead, he had his eye on a command in the Indian Ocean, where the climactic battle might be fought and where there should be limitless opportunities for distinction.

Smith joined Lord Collingwood off Cadiz at the end of March and found him to be someone in total contrast to Nelson. A tall, grey-haired man, looking more than his fifty-five years, he was solemn and introspective. Those who knew him well found a man of delicate wit and sensitivity, while those who did not sometimes saw 'an old bear'. Smith found him courteous but realized that, as Captain William Hoste, one of Collingwood's captains and Nelson's former protégé, put it, 'Old Collingwood likes *quiet people*',[2] and that did not augur well for their future relationship. More immediately, Collingwood distrusted the idea of unconventional weapons, writing to the new First Lord of the Admiralty, the Honourable Charles Grey, reporting a conversation with Smith 'in which I endeavoured to impress on him the inefficacy of that mode of war which is carried on by explosion-vessels and sky-rockets. I know no instance of a favourable result from them. They serve merely to exasperate, to harass our own people ... As a general mode of warfare they are unworthy of the English.' Like St Vincent, he realized that such weapons could prove most damaging to the British, adding that if the enemy were 'goaded into retaliation, with very little activity on their part, Gibraltar Bay would not be a safe place to lie in for one night'.[3] So, orders to ship the rockets and 'infernals' from England for an attack on Cadiz were cancelled.*

But Collingwood did confirm Nelson's appointment of Smith to command the inshore squadron, with which he was to concentrate on the defence of Sicily. Both saw – as Nelson had seen – the Kingdom of the Two Sicilies as the strategic key to the Mediterranean. It was for this reason that Nelson refused to obey Lord Keith's orders to withdraw from Neapolitan or Sicilian waters and join the main fleet. Southern Italy and the island of Sicily not only dominated both basins of the inland sea but offered ports for repair and replenishment, unlimited

---

* The rockets were, however, used to effect during the second attack on Copenhagen in September 1807.

stocks of munitions, materials for repairing ships, provisions and manpower. The same Spanish Bourbon sovereign, King Ferdinand IV, whom Nelson had not only rescued from his rebellious subjects but replaced on his throne in Naples, still ruled with his forceful, neurotic Queen Maria Carolina, the sister of the executed Queen Marie Antoinette of France. In supporting them, Smith would again be carrying on Nelson's duties, as she was to constantly remind him. Problems lay ahead: Napoleon's defeat of Austria at Ulm and Austerlitz had opened the way into Italy again and, on 15th February, French troops had entered Naples, the royal family once more taking refuge in Palermo. On 30th March Napoleon had proclaimed his brother Joseph King of the Two Sicilies – he was to be known simply as the King of Naples.

When Smith arrived at Palermo on 20th April, he found King Ferdinand dejected. His British and Russian allies had both provided troops for the defence of the mainland but they had been withdrawn and a British force numbering some 7,500 – including Sicilian and Corsican battalions – had been landed at Messina under the command of Major-General Sir John Stuart – an officer of panache, but touchy and prone to professional jealousy – in the hope of keeping the French out of Sicily. As the French swarmed through the mountains south from Naples, only the fortress of Gaeta – on a peninsula, like Acre – 30 miles north of the city, remained in royalist Neapolitan hands under the command of the Prince of Hesse. So, this was to be the first operation for his inshore squadron of the *Pompée*, another 'seventy-four', Collingwood's old ship, the *Excellent*, two 'sixty-fours', the *Intrepid* and *Athénien*, two British frigates and one Neapolitan.

Smith's priority was the relief of Gaeta, where 6,000 defenders faced up to 12,000 besiegers. Without permission from his superiors – British or Sicilian – he collected all the arms, ammunition and stores he thought he might need from the arsenal at Palermo, and set sail. His appearance off the fortress put heart in the defenders. Sixty Neapolitan soldiers were ferried out to the squadron in fishing boats and, on the night of 12th May, they, together with marines, landed from British boats in the rear of the forward French battery, spiked the guns and re-embarked without loss. Three days later, the garrison made a sortie supported by Smith's gunboats, and news of it reached

Napoleon himself, who wrote to his brother in Naples, 'From all I hear about Gaeta, it appears the Neapolitans have ... succeeded in their sortie and killed many of your French troops. I desire that you will not demoralise my troops by allowing them to be defeated by Neapolitans. The sally from Gaeta is a real defeat ...'[4] Smith had also landed ordnance and supplies for the garrison and, confident that they could hold out, sailed for the Bay of Naples and the heart of the French occupation of Italy. There they were joined by a third 'seventy-four', the *Eagle*, commanded by the dashing Captain Sir Charles Rowley.

The waterfront of Naples was festooned with lights and the Palazzo Reale illuminated with flares for the coronation of King Joseph. Smith was tempted to cruise past the palace and blow in its windows with broadsides but, realizing that he would probably kill more Neapolitans than French, he desisted and sought another objective. He had not far to look: the wide sweep of the bay from the Sorrento peninsula, past Vesuvius, past the city itself and to the island of Ischia to the north, was dominated by the dragonback silhouette of Capri, 17 miles out to sea. The island – nearly 4 miles long and 2 miles wide – rose to almost 2,000 feet at the summit of Monte Solaro; its two little towns, seemingly impregnable above cliffs, sometimes dropping 1,500 feet, sheer into deep, clear water. It was garrisoned by an under-strength French regiment without artillery and, although it offered no harbour worth the name, nor even a secure anchorage, its strategic position and its theatricality gave it value both as a vantage point and as a symbol of dominance. It would be worth capturing.

The island would not be easy to attack. The main town with its church and campanile, lay on the saddle between the heights crowned with the ruins of the Emperor Tiberius's villa and the cliffs rising to Monte Solaro; above it stood the little Castiglione fortress, below to the east the fishing port of Marina Grande and, on the far side, the Piccola Marina, where fishermen hauled their boats on to the shingle. The second town, Anacapri, lay much higher, and could only be reached by a flight of stone steps built by the Phoenicians across the face of a precipice and, it was said, by a goat-track known only to islanders.

According to the courteous customs of war Smith liked to

observe, he sent an officer ashore on 11th May with a summons to surrender, warning the French commander that, if he did not, he would force him to accept less favourable terms. Captain Chervet of the 101st Regiment replied that 'a true soldier does not surrender until he has tried his force with that which attacks him. You are, sir, too good and brave a soldier to blame me if I do not accept your polite invitation.'[5] Smith therefore decided to bombard and then assault the Marina Grande. Accordingly, early next morning, the *Eagle* moved within point-blank range of the little harbour and opened fire from both decks of guns. She bombarded for an hour, lying so close that French musketry killed a seaman and wounded her first lieutenant. Then marines and seamen from the 'seventy-fours' boarded boats and were pulled ashore, ran across the stone-flagged quays and, led by Captain Bunce of the Royal Marines, raced up the narrow, twisting steps to the town above. Meanwhile, the *Athénien* had landed her marines at the Piccola Marina to be led by Captain Stannus up the steep path to the Castiglione, where the French were preparing a last stand, and there Stannus himself shot and killed Captain Chervet; one British marine also died. With that, the French surrendered with honourable terms and were immediately shipped across to Naples, while Captain Chervet was buried at the parish church of Santo Stefano. The Castiglione was renamed Castle Hill, Smith drafted ashore a provisional garrison of 200 marines, who set up their headquarters in a large house, the Palazzo Inglese, and the British occupation of Capri began. Hearing the news from King Joseph, Napoleon replied, 'I could have told you what would happen to you at Capri. When dealing with an isolated island there is only one principle to follow: either put a lot of troops there, or none at all.'[6]

Well pleased with his cruise, Sir Sidney Smith returned to Palermo. There, he followed Nelson into the private *saloni* of the King and Queen of the Two Sicilies. Ferdinand and Maria Carolina, both in their mid fifties, had markedly aged since their second flight from Naples at the beginning of the year. His long, lugubrious face was more deeply lined and her haughty Habsburg looks and long, elegant neck were tense with frustration. The King was moderately content with his hunting park outside the city, where he could entertain at the oriental pastiche, the Palazzina Cinese, in elegant rooms hung with

English prints given to them by Nelson. Maria Carolina, however, was obsessed with the urgency of recapturing their lost lands and capital and was still burning with the desire to revenge the killing of her sister. 'The Queen is generally called clever', noted a shrewd British officer. 'She is active, meddling and intriguing. She has assumed so much of the character of a man as to make her unamiable as a woman [he then crossed out the last word and wrote "bitch"]. The late Empress Catharine of Russia is perhaps her model. But the truth is she is not clever but in intrigue. She is a violent, wicked woman.'[7] The influence of Emma Hamilton had once combined with strategic necessity to bind Nelson to their cause as a decisive ally and now she was delighted to find in Sidney Smith a man of her own volatile temperament: at best, brave, impulsive, imaginative and talkative. For his part, he was, like Nelson before him, flattered at the attentions he received from royalty in these lofty, fresco'ed rooms, hung with great dark paintings in gilded frames, where the strong Sicilian sun was filtered through gauzy curtains and heavy drapes to lend drama and significance to discourse within.

There was an essential difference between the strategic views of the Queen and the British diplomats and generals: she saw landings and warfare ashore in southern Italy as the key not only to reconquest but to the security of Sicily; they wanted to concentrate all available forces on the island, which could also be defended by the Mediterranean Fleet. She described to Smith the means they and Nelson had employed to recover southern Italy in 1799; how their military prelate, Cardinal Ruffo, had raised the *massi*, the fierce mountain men of Calabria, and how they had, in the name of the King and the Cross, seized Naples before Nelson had arrived with his ships to seal their victory. This, she suggested, could be achieved again. More cautious was the advice of the King's Prime Minister, Sir John Acton, an expatriate Englishman of handsome Latin appearance, who had also known Nelson and who was now 70; he realized that, 7 years earlier, the *massi* had not had to face trained French troops, nor the committed will of Napoleon Bonaparte. Now, the Emperor's brother was pretender to their throne in Naples, supported by a French army said to number 50,000. Acton's position had, however, been weakened by Smith's arrival because he brought with him a letter of introduction to his principal rival, Count Circello, from Lord Grenville, who had taken the leadership of the British Government since writing it. He and a group of Sicilian aristocrats and French royalist émigrés now sought urgent offensive action, encouraged by Smith's success at Gaeta and Capri. For his part, Smith had told the Queen how his greatest success – in the Levant and at Acre – had been achieved because he had had a dual rôle as naval commander and diplomat. The idea took root and King Ferdinand appointed Smith to be Viceroy of Calabria and soon he was signing relevant orders as 'Commander-in-Chief on behalf of King Ferdinand', just as he had on behalf of Sultan Selim.

Smith's strategy was to raise the Calabrese against the French, who would then be forced to concentrate, so enabling him to put British regular troops ashore to attack them. His opinions were not shared by the senior Army officers, who distrusted unconventional land warfare just as Collingwood and St Vincent had shied away from unconventional warfare at sea. These officers had seen in Egypt and Syria how trained European troops could, even when vastly outnumbered, destroy undisciplined Turkish armies. Consequently, they put their trust in tactical drill and controlled fire-power. Smith, on the other hand, had seen at Acre what brave, if undisciplined, foreign troops could do when commanded by British officers and stiffened by British rank and file. His critics saw him as the puppet of the Queen and her extravagant ideas. One such critic, Lieutenant-Colonel Henry Bunbury, wrote:

> Sir Sidney Smith entered at once into her wild schemes of raising the Calabrese; and, without the slightest communication with Sir John Stuart, our naval commander was invested with unlimited authority on the land (the southern provinces of Naples) as well as on the sea.
>
> Sir Sidney was an enthusiast, always panting for distinction; restlessly active but desultory in his views; extravagantly vain; daring, quick-sighted and fertile in those resources which befit a partisan leader; but he possessed no great depth of judgement, nor any fixity of purpose, save that of persuading mankind, as he was fully persuaded himself, that Sidney Smith was the most brilliant of chevaliers.

But to that he added a footnote: 'Let me not in exposing this brave man's foibles omit to add that he was kind tempered, generous and as agreeable as a man can be supposed to be who is always talking of himself.' Yet even Bunbury had to admit that:

The coming of the Admiral, and the energy of his first proceedings soon produced a wide effect; arms and ammunition were conveyed into the mountains of Calabria; the smaller detachments of the enemy were driven from the shores; and some of the strongest points were armed and occupied by the insurgents and parties of English marines and seamen ... and the insurrection soon kindled throughout ... the two Calabrias.[8]

Smith and the Queen were trying to persuade General Stuart to take the offensive on the Italian mainland but were faced with the opposition of Sir William Hamilton's successor as British minister, Hugh Elliot, the brother of Nelson's friend, the first Earl of Minto. Agreeing with the cautious policy of Sir John Acton, Elliot held that the defence of Sicily must have priority, while Smith followed Nelson's theory that attack was the best means of defence; however, the minister gave Smith substantial financial backing for intelligence-gathering on the mainland. So when the admiral and the Queen finally convinced Stuart that he could pre-empt a French assault across the strait of Messina by attacking their bases on the far shore, they told him that Elliot should not be informed.

In May, Smith arrived at Messina from a cruise off Gaeta and sent ashore plans of the French entrenchments before the fortress, which he wished to have copied. General Stuart gave them to a Captain Charles Boothby, who had some training as an engineer, saying, 'When you have finished the plan, Boothby, you will like an opportunity to meet with the hero of Acre. You will admire him of all things, but be sure, when you see him, he will take you to Acre.' Sure enough, Boothby took the copied plans on board the flagship and gave them to Smith, who:

good-humouredly said, 'So, sir, you are the young officer who has had the goodness to copy this for me. Well, now, sir, just look here. They pretend to tell me that this place is indefensible – *me*, who knows pretty well what determined hearts can do behind very simple barriers – who has seen a handful of men behind the angle of a wall bid defiance to the bravest troops led by the finest general in the world – I mean Mr. Bonaparte at Acre. Tally-ho! said I.'

Boothby then recalled, 'I was really in pain lest a smile should be detected on my features ... and that anxiety gave me an air of deeper attention to the inferences of strength and capability of Gaeta, which he drew from the defence of Acre.'[9]

In June, nearly 5,000 British troops – about half the garrison of Sicily – and some Corsican irregulars – were embarked on his ships, which sailed up the west coast of Calabria, while others were ordered eastward to confuse the enemy. Reports that more than 5,000 French troops – all that could be spared from counter-partisan operations in the mountains – were marching south down the western coast under General Reynier, and had reached the valley of the shallow little River Lamato, led Smith to anchor in the Gulf of Santa Eufemia on the evening of 30th June. That night his force was landed in the summer heat radiating from the scorched earth and rocks, to the trilling of cicadas and the scent of rosemary and pine. At first light, they advanced inland through the olive groves and scrubby woodland covering the hillsides. The landing of guns and ammunition continued unhindered for two days, when it was learned that the French had deployed beneath the hilltop village of San Pietro di Maida, overlooking the valley from the south. Both sides found difficulty in establishing the whereabouts of the other, the opposing generals cantering through the olive groves, narrowly missing each other. The enemy was shielded at the back by thick woods and to the front commanded a wide field of fire downhill to the river; the position seemed almost impregnable.

The battle began on the morning of 4th July. The British planned an assault but it seemed a forlorn hope. Indeed, so confident were the French of repulsing any attack that Napoleon himself, writing from Paris on hearing the battle was imminent – but, of course, long after it had been fought – declared, 'Nothing could be more fortunate than the landing of the English ... It is difficult to conceive the fatality that has urged them on.'[10] But, at this point, Smith's expectations were realized. The thickets to the rear of the French swarmed with Calabrese snipers, protected by the undergrowth against a cavalry sweep. As Reynier's men began to drop, shot in the back, he realized he had to move and could only advance. So, with drums beating the *pas de charge*, his infantry began to tramp downhill in solid columns against what appeared to be scattered companies of red-coated British beyond the riverbed.

As the heat of the sun increased, the French cavalry suddenly appeared, charged and wheeled in feint attacks, then finally galloped away. When the dust cleared, the British saw a mass of French infantry – three battalions, led by General Compère – bearing down. Colonel Bunbury reported:

> A crashing fire of musketry soon opened on both sides, but it was too hot to last so short a distance and the fire of the English was so deadly that General Compère spurred to the front of his men, and, shouting, *'En avant, en avant!'*, he led them to the charge with the bayonet. As they drew nigh, their ranks disordered by the fatal fire of the British, the British counter-attacked. They had, however, come too close to escape; it was a headlong rout.[11]

The concentrated fire of extended British lines upon phalanxes of infantry had been decisive. The French cavalry charged again and was caught from the flank by unexpected volleys, so their whole line shivered and broke, leaving the battlefield strewn with some 700 dead and 1,000 wounded. 'The action, though sharp, had not been of long duration,' wrote Colonel Bunbury. 'By mid-day, our soldiers were resting on their arms, gasping with heat and thirst, and watching through the dusk, with disappointed eyes, the rapid retreat of the French column.' General Stuart was delighted, riding up and down, exclaiming, 'Begad, I never saw anything so glorious as this! There was nothing in Egypt to equal it! It's the finest thing I ever witnessed.'[12] But he only followed them three miles to the head of the valley, then abandoned the pursuit – he had not enough men or resources to conduct a land campaign – and withdrew to his beach-head. The Battle of Maida had been a victory; after Aboukir, five years before, the second won by the British Army against the French.*

On the beach, the victorious British were reassured to see Smith's ships lying close off-shore and stripped off their uniforms to plunge into the cooling sea. Then, as the naked soldiers splashed in the shallows, a staff officer galloped along the beach shouting that French cavalry were upon them. At

---

* The battle convinced the future Duke of Wellington that British tactics could defeat the French and gave its name to the new London suburb of Maida Vale.

this, Bunbury reported, 'In a moment, the troops sprang to their arms and formed; and Cole's brawny brigade, rushing out of the sea and throwing their belts over their shoulders, grasped their muskets and drew up in line without attempting to assume an article of clothing.'[13] The alarm had been caused by the sudden stampede of a herd of buffaloes.

Although Smith and Stuart did not like each other, the admiral invited the general on board his flagship. There, he confided that he had expected a different outcome and had planned to run a frigate close inshore to give covering fire to the retreating British. Then, as Bunbury remembered:

> he treated us, as was his usual custom, to the whole history of the siege of Acre, not omitting the remarkable circumstance that when there happened a short intermission of fire during several weeks, everybody jumped up in consternation, exclaiming, 'What can be the matter?' Smith and Stuart might not have much to say to each other, but, Bunbury noted, 'Sir Sidney closed the evening by taking one of the many shawls, with which his cabin was hung, and instructing Sir John in the art of wreathing it and putting on the turban after the fashion of the most refined Turkish ladies.'[14]

While the defeat of the French by the combination of regular and irregular forces seemed to vindicate Smith, it reacted against him politically. Hugh Elliot was outraged that he had not been kept informed and that money he had given Smith for intelligence-gathering had been used to arm the *massi*. He wrote a long letter of complaint to the Foreign Secretary, Charles James Fox, charging that General Stuart's successful strategy had been disrupted by 'Sir Sidney Smith, who had assumed to himself the exercise of all civil and military power in the Kingdom of Naples'.[15] He also refused further financial support to Smith, who thereupon borrowed a further £4,500 against his own personal credit. Elliot was at first pleased by the arrival in Palermo of Lieutenant-General the Honourable Henry Fox, the brother of the Foreign Secretary but far less intelligent, who was to succeed Stuart in command, and he poured forth his complaints against Smith to him. However, it then appeared that Fox had been sent out not only to relieve Stuart but also Elliot himself, who thereupon returned to London, where he had difficulty in explaining his opposition to Smith's strategy that had led to the victory at Maida.

General Fox's second-in-command was to be Major-General Sir John Moore, a tall, good-looking man of forty-four, the beau ideal of a relaxed, confident English gentleman-soldier. One of the most brilliant British soldiers of the time, he, putting his trust in British military expertise, had distrusted Smith's unorthodox ideas for an attack on Boulogne. He had now arrived in Sicily with a reinforcement of four battalions. His first act was to tour the theatre of war from southern Calabria to the Bay of Naples, where Capri was now reinforced with a more substantial British garrison. After the triumph of Maida, the campaign on the Italian mainland faltered. On 18th July, Gaeta finally fell to the French and some blamed it on Smith's lack of immediate action to relieve the fortress again after the Battle of Maida. Amongst these was Bunbury, who noted:

> If our Admiral and our General, instead of talking on the evening of 4th July of the siege of Acre and Turkish ladies and Greek girls, had concerted and acted on a vigorous plan of operations, the results might have marked our victory at Maida a feat productive of an important change in the great war of European nations.[16]

The same might have been said about General Moore. On his tour of inspection immediately after Maida, he had visited Capri, where the garrison was mostly composed of ten companies of the Royal Regiment of Malta and ten of the Royal Corsican Rangers, under the command of Lieutenant-Colonel Hudson Lowe,* and supported by some heavy naval guns sent ashore by Smith. Moore spent several hours ashore but had not time to climb the steep steps to Anacapri and pronounced the defences adequate. Two infantry battalions, which had been sent to Capri after Maida, were still in their ships, lying offshore, and Moore, taking a different view from Napoleon on the defence of the island, decided them unnecessary and ordered them to Messina.

Moore, accompanied by Colonel Bunbury, went in search of Smith, who had been cruising on the west coast in the *Pompée*. He had been well pleased with his naval dispositions and, in particular, with Captain Hoste of the *Amphion*, who had cleared the French from the Calabrian littoral east of Messina, capturing the towns of Cotrone and Catanzaro. Moore and

---

* Lowe was to be Napoleon's gaoler in his exile on St Helena.

Bunbury found his flagship at anchor in the bay of Policastro south of the Sorrento peninsula, and were amazed to see the ship 'crippled and torn by shot'. As the cynical Bunbury put it:

> These shot had been received the day before from an old watch tower, on which one gun was mounted. The story told by the officers of the *Pompée* was this: Sir Sidney, coasting along, as was his wont, having the *Hydra* and another frigate in company, and looking out for brigands to receive his muskets and orders, espied a French flag on this tower of ancient days. He simply gave orders that the ships should run in and drive the enemy out of their little fortress by cannon shot; and ... the Admiral went quietly to his cabin to write his letters. The *Pompée* drew near and opened her fire; the one gun then responded; the broadsides of the man-of-war were returned for half an hour by this solitary but unerring gun; at length, the Captain found it necessary to interrupt the Admiral's correspondence by informing him that Lieut. Slessor and a midshipman and several men were killed, many more wounded and the ship seriously damaged. Sir Sidney looked surprised but gave orders that the boats should be lowered and the marines sent ashore to reduce these obstinate Frenchmen. As soon as the boats touched the beach, some thirty Corsicans ran from the tower to meet them, waving a white handkerchief and telling the officer that they had been longing to desert to the British but, as the ship fired at them instead of inviting them to surrender, they had no choice but to use their gun to the best of their ability.[17]

This became yet another story against Smith to be repeated by his enemies. An essentially different story emerged from the *Pompée's* log: of a fort flying the French flag opening fire on her and two accompanying frigates at long range and continuing to do so when they drew nearer, killing seven, including the officer, and wounding thirty-two; hitting the *Pompée's* hull with four shot, the upper works with more and almost severing the mizzen-mast. So marines from all three ships were put ashore and captured the fort, withdrawing when what appeared to be a strong force of French infantry suddenly appeared and seemed likely to cut them off from their boats.

One enemy was General Moore. An intelligent pragmatist, he put his faith in the discipline of regular British soldiers to implement a well-defined strategy. He wrote disparagingly about Smith in his diary that he seemed to be floating aimlessly

off the Italian coast looking for adventures and he was appalled
to see him apparently attacking on all fronts, arming the brig-
andish partisans, who, once they had left their own villages to
fight the French, lived by plundering others. After visiting him
on board his flagship, Moore noted, 'I had a long conversation
with him. He spoke like a man who was directing a formidable
force under distinguished leaders and that nothing but want of
money and arms, which were denied him, had prevented his
driving the French from lower Italy and placing Ferdinand
upon the throne of Naples.'[18]

Moore himself disregarded as immaterial the passionate
hope of the theatrical King and Queen to re-conquer Naples,
which they regarded as their capital and, together with their
vast palace at Caserta, as infinitely more desirable than the
barren hills of Sicily. Their plan was a bold one: now that the
new French commander in Italy, Marshal Masséna, was in
Calabria, they hoped to persuade the British to land 12,000
troops together with 15,000 Sicilians in the Bay of Naples to
recapture the city; then, as Masséna headed north to meet them,
more British would land in Calabria and attack his rear; Smith
was thought to be encouraging the plan. Sicily was, however, of
far more importance than Naples to a strategically minded
general; indeed, he suggested a British occupation of Sicily as a
central Mediterranean bastion against the French even if it
involved deposing the monarch. 'Though the recovery of the
Neapolitan throne was a favourite object with the Court of
Palermo, it was possible to conceive that England might have
views beyond it in establishing themselves militarily in
Sicily,'[19] he reflected later. Smith he saw as being in the Queen's
pocket, writing that 'his intrigues with the Queen and the court
of Palermo were obvious to everyone ... he was sent to
command the squadron ... not to intrigue with the Sicilian
court'.[20] The state of affairs had worsened, as he saw it, since
the dismissal of Sir John Acton as chief minister and his
replacement by the Marquis Circello, whom Moore thought 'a
very contemptible, foolish fellow, a mere tool in the hands of
the Queen and Sir Sidney Smith ... I am not obliged to account
for the motives of such a man. From experience, I know that
nothing is too absurd for his folly, nothing too mean or too
wicked where his vanity or his interest is concerned.'[21]

As Smith saw it, he was trying to implement Nelson's

Mediterranean strategy by making the maximum use of allies. Nelson himself had seen the Kingdom of the Two Sicilies as 'a country of fiddlers and poets, whores and scoundrels'[22] but he had also stressed the positive qualities of the royal couple and the value of their subjects and territories to the British. Like Nelson, Smith was flattered by the attentions of royalty, to which he had become accustomed in the company of King Gustavus and Sultan Selim, and, in Palermo, it was easy to slip into the louche life of the court, as Nelson had seven years before. His vision of the Calabrese partisans may have been over-optimistic, for, as Colonel Bunbury put it:

> Sir Sidney may perhaps have painted in his imagination a people brave and hardy, intelligent and capable of defending their mountains against an enemy. But they must be animated and united by some common sentiment that is praiseworthy. They must not be the dastardly dregs of the Calabrese, led by assassins to plunder and murder every person who is decent and respectable in the country.[23]*

The crux of Smith's problems with his peers and superiors was that he had here, as in the Levant, played triple rôles as naval and military commander and politician. In Constantinople, his ministerial appointment from London had led to the Sultan giving him nominal command of Turkish land and sea forces. Here, the King had called him his viceroy and commander-in-chief without Smith having asked permission to accept the title from any of his naval, or political, masters. After General Fox had paid a visit, he described to Moore the Court of Palermo, where he witnessed:

> more childishness, wickedness and folly than is to be met with in any other part of the world. Sir Sidney Smith is there intriguing and encouraging all their extravagances. Sometimes he is to be Viceroy of Calabria; at others to have the island of Lampedusa to hold as a fief from the King of Naples with the title of Duke and to go to Jerusalem and make instant war on Bonaparte in the King of Naples' name!!!'[24]

Even Admiral Collingwood wrote to his wife from his flagship off Cadiz that he had heard that Smith was, like Nelson, to be rewarded by 'their Sicilian Majesties [who were]

---

* A sentiment that will find echoes amongst some who have worked with guerrilla movements in enemy-occupied countries.

creating him a Sicilian Duke and giving him an estate. If they offer me a Dukedom, I tell you beforehand how I will shew them what my estimation of it is.' He then came as near as he ever did to criticizing his dead friend by declaring that he would receive no such honours from any sovereign other than his own and then he continued to criticize the Bourbon monarchy: 'If they had ability to govern a state, they would not be in the wretched condition they are: but if Mount Etna were made of gold, they would still be poor; for they have not discretion to manage their finances.'[25]

Smith had told Collingwood something of his position at Palermo and the admiral replied with oblique displeasure, 'You mention that the King of the Sicilies has vested certain powers in you', politely adding that 'no officer is better qualified than you' to judge a political situation. However, it was for ambassadors to:

> treat with the Court and to settle with the Government what measures should be pursued. When the plans of operation are to be executed, the Naval and Military Commanders are then to decide upon the manner of performing their respective branches of that service. This I conceive to be the proper course to be pursued and every deviation from it will necessarily produce uneasiness somewhere, which is detrimental to the service[26]

But he dropped all tact when writing privately to his brother, 'I am sadly off with this Sir S. Smith at Sicily; the man's head is full of strange vapours and I am convinced Lord Barham sent him here to be clear of a tormentor, but he annoys me more than the French or Spanish fleet.'[27]

Amongst British officers in Sicily there was amiable banter about Smith's new title, Boothby recording that the phrase ran, 'How nicely Sir Sidney has got himself made viceroy.' Casting a sharp eye at the royal couple – the King swearing his favourite oath, 'Body of Bacchus!' and the Queen, an 'elegant ruin' – the young officer added, 'I can easily believe, remembering their worship of Nelson, that it was a much easier thing for the King and Queen to give such a commission to a renowned naval officer, whom they might view as Nelson's successor, than to a British general.' Certainly, General Stuart did not seem to be put out, particularly after Smith had disarmingly, if, perhaps, a little disingenuously, told him, 'This appointment would have been more suitable for you but I made no difficulty about it, thinking it a great object that *one* of us should have it and the whole powers of the commission are quite as much at your disposal as if your name had been placed in it instead of mine.'[28] Yet Smith was exultant, telling the Queen, 'The advantage of the concentration of authority is already manifest. He who can speak as Supreme Commander can accomplish master-strokes. It is this unity of plan and action that gives Bonaparte his success. Now this unity of power is vested in me. Let it remain in me and I will dare to do more than he will dare to imagine.'[29]

The view amongst British commanders and diplomats from the Atlantic to the Levant was generally that, once again, Sir Sidney Smith had got out of hand. Indeed, one at least refused to obey the orders of the Bourbons' Supreme Commander. When Smith asked General Fox to send at least 1,000 infantry, artillery and money to the mainland because the fate of Sicily would be decided there, he was refused on the grounds that no available land forces could hope to hold a major French offensive. News of the problem reached London; at the British Embassy Elliot had been replaced by William Drummond, who had been moved to Palermo from Constantinople, and now allied himself with the generals. Writing to the British Government, as Moore reported, 'respecting the conduct of Sir Sidney Smith, representing the impossibility of acting with a man who, from a strange perversity of head, seems to have forgotten the honourable status of a British Admiral and is dwindled into that of a Neapolitan courtier.'[30] But since Smith again bestrode the naval, military, diplomatic and political scenes in the central Mediterranean, it was felt that he could only be disciplined by ministers in London.

Happily for Smith, however, responsibility for this would be shared between two friends of his, the Prime Minister, Lord Grenville, and the Secretary of State for War and the Colonies, William Windham. The former wrote to the latter in September 1806, that both of them would share 'the wish of making the censure on Sir Sidney Smith as mild as possible' but they should express 'a decided, tho' mild, disapprobation' of his having accepted a Sicilian commission without permission from his superiors; of having inspired and directed an insurrection in Calabria, which should have been the responsibility of a British general; and having circulated a proclamation by King Ferdinand relating to this. However, Grenville added that 'the censure may certainly be so worded as to attach only on the facts *supposing them to be such as they now appear*.'[31] Their displeasure was derived largely from a letter from Hugh Elliot, who had brought his dislike of Smith back to England with him, and another from General Fox, who, reported Moore, had 'written home representing strongly the facts with respect to Sir Sidney, stating the impossibility of acting in concert with him. He is now at Palermo with his ships in all directions, but not two of them in a state to meet the enemy.'[32] Indeed, all the criticism upon which the censure was based, came from officers and diplomats who resented, or misunderstood, Smith, or, despite his record of success, were intolerant of his undoubted weaknesses and vanity; Collingwood, like St Vincent before him, was a thousand miles away and without first-hand experience of the problems involved. So, just as Nelson had been recalled for much the same reasons, Smith's future prospects in the Mediterranean seemed bleak.

The outcome of the campaign on the Italian coasts was hotly debated. Smith's critics charged that not only had he undermined British policy by supporting the Queen's strategy of holding the French as far away from Sicily as possible with an eye to recapturing Naples but that, by stirring the Calabrese into revolt, he had brought much suffering upon them to no avail. He maintained that his policy would have succeeded but for the generals' lack of support. Yet Smith's policy had succeeded: first with the long defence of Gaeta, which had cost the enemy dear; then with the landing of the army to win the Battle of Maida, which was rightly seen as a perfect example of amphibious warfare. Guerrilla fighting in Calabria had been as horrible as might have been expected but it did have the desired effect of wearing down the French army with casualties from fighting and disease; in the past year, total French losses were estimated as nearly 12,000. With a British army in Sicily and British ships to land it on the coast of the mainland, Napoleon could only hope to conquer the central Mediterranean by employing huge forces, which were needed elsewhere.

Elsewhere, Napoleon was achieving success that could be exploited. In the autumn, Prussia declared war on France and was promptly defeated in battle, and French troops marched into Berlin. Reviving his ambitions in the Middle East, Napoleon had instigated war between Turkey and Russia and, towards the end of the year, had declared the 'Continental System,' to close Continental ports to British trade. This was all compounded by the death in September of the Foreign Secretary, Charles James Fox. The gathering gloom was emphasized by an accidental disaster in the Mediterranean when the *Athenian* – as the seventy-four-gun *Athénien* was generally known – struck a rock at night while on passage from Gibraltar to join Smith's squadron, and sank with the loss of most of her crew.

Finally, the pressure to expel Smith from Palermo was such that Collingwood was happy to implement instructions from the Admiralty for Smith to return to Plymouth in the *Pompée* for further duties in British waters. He had made his farewells to the King and Queen when new orders arrived; he was not to sail west but east. The British Government, alarmed at the possibility of a new alliance between France and Turkey to open the way for another Napoleonic drive into the Levant, ordered a fleet to Constantinople, where it could threaten the Sublime Porte, and, if necessary, destroy its fleet in an attempt to keep the French out of Asia. This might have seemed to be the ideal task for Smith, who knew Turkish waters, understood the Turks and was a friend of Sultan Selim, but the command was given to Vice-Admiral Sir John Duckworth, a bluff sailor with no experience of diplomacy, or the Middle East, with Rear-Admiral Sir Thomas Louis as his second-in-command; Smith was to command the rear division of the fleet.

Even when the imminence of his departure was known, the hostility continued. In an atmosphere of panic and distrust, bedeviled by slow communications, wild rumours circulated. William Drummond reported to London that the Queen was not only negotiating for a large Russian army to be sent to Sicily for the re-conquest of Naples but that she was secretly negotiating with Napoleon through Madrid to buy Naples back with the neutrality of the Kingdom of the Two Sicilies. Recording this in his diary, Moore added:

I believe him to be so unprincipled that he is capable, for any advantage to himself, or gratification to his vanity, first to betray us and then the Queen. His head is a most perverted one and his nature false without bounds. He is a good riddance from Palermo and it is to be hoped that Sir John Duckworth will trust him no further than he sees him.[33]

The orders that reached Duckworth from the Admiralty were a product of panic compounded by diplomatic failure. Napoleon had at last opened a land route to the East by taking control of the eastern shore of the Adriatic with Marshal Marmont's Army of Dalmatia.[34]* He was therefore making overtures to the Sublime Porte in the hope of securing a route through Turkey to the Levant, Egypt and on to India. However, in place of the quick-witted Smith brothers, the British Government was represented in Constantinople by Charles Arbuthnot, who had no more knowledge of the Middle East than Lord Elgin had had. Like the Russian ambassador, he was fearful of the apparent diplomatic success of the French emissary, General Sebastiani, but chose to recommend threats, rather than trying to persuade the Sultan to re-activate the treaty of friendship the Smith brothers had negotiated eight years before.

Had Admiral Smith been sent on a diplomatic mission to Constantinople – perhaps wearing the Sultan's diamond *chelengk* in his hat – he might have recalled the great days at Acre and Aboukir and swung Turkish opinion against the French. Some were aware of this, and a contemporary of Smith's was to write, 'There was one, indeed, not five days' sail from the mouth of the Dardanelles, whose ability and firmness had never been doubted and whose local experience and well-known influence with the Porte eminently fitted him for such an enterprise.'[35] Aburthnot seemed to expect Smith's employment there because he kept him informed of the crisis in long, worried letters. But so much poison had been poured into the ears of his distant superiors that he remained in command of the fleet's rear division.

Orders reached Duckworth at the end of 1806 to take his fleet up to Constantinople, supported by a Russian squadron, and there, in conjunction with Arbuthnot, to demand the expulsion

* One of its officers was Major de Tromelin, who had taken advantage of an amnesty to keep his property in France but had been refused promotion to colonel by the Emperor himself on the grounds that it would be 'too rapid for Sidney Smith's aide-de-camp'.

of the French emissary and the surrender of the Turkish fleet;
failure to comply would unleash British broadsides on to the
domes and minarets of the capital. Collingwood's written
orders, which detailed circumstances under which Duckworth
should take 'measures of hostility against the town',[36] made no
mention of Admiral Smith. Other naval opinion differed, and
the influential *Naval Chronicle* in London was to express amaze-
ment that 'palpably absurd as it must appear', Smith had been
'taken from the active station of Sicily, where he commanded,
and placed, not *first*, not *second*, but *third* in command of an
expedition, of which he alone was competent to be the
Commander-in-Chief.'

Even so, Smith expected his special knowledge to be valued
and, on 12th February, he drafted a personal letter to the
Sultan, recalling their past friendship in flowery diplomatic
prose, urging him to resist French blandishments, and hinting
at the treachery he knew was simmering within the Ottoman
hierarchy:

> Shall it be said that Bonaparte, who could not succeed by force ...
> has succeeded in obtaining the dominion of the entire Ottoman
> territory by arts of another kind, by fallacious reasoning and by
> bribing your Imperial Majesty's servants to desert, and betray,
> their master, as he did his? No! let it be rather recorded that
> Sultan Selim the Third proved himself worthy of his ancestors ...
> by placing your interests in the keeping ... of an ally, whom your
> Imperial Majesty knows to be just and merciful ... and to be most
> faithfully attached to your Imperial Majesty.[37]

He sent copies to Duckworth and Arbuthnot, who had joined
the flagship, suggesting it be sent to Constantinople. But when
a letter was sent, it was not Smith's.

From all aspects – navigational, diplomatic and warlike – it
was to be a risky operation, for which neither Duckworth nor
Louis, were prepared. Nor were these the only risks, for a
reminder of the inherent dangers of the sea came as the fleet
was assembling off the mouth of the Dardanelles: one night the
seventy-four-gun *Ajax* caught fire from an unknown cause, the
flames roared up the main hatchway, touched her magazine
and she exploded, killing at least 250 of her ship's company.

On 19th February 1807, after his ominous beginning, the
fleet entered the Dardanelles, the thirty-eight miles of narrows,

at places less than a mile wide, between the Aegean and the Sea of Marmara. As might have been expected, Turkish shore batteries and warships opened fire and a small Turkish squadron appeared. Smith was thereupon ordered to take his three ships of the line and a frigate and destroy or capture the approaching ships. This he did, in half an hour driving a sixty-four gun ship, two frigates and various smaller ships ashore, capturing two others and, after a chase, he burned another frigate. Landing parties were then put ashore to storm the batteries and spike their guns and burn the beached ships. This smart little action disposed of one Turkish ship of the line, four frigates, three corvettes, one brig and two gunboats for a British loss of four killed and twenty-six wounded. While it was in progress, the main British fleet had entered the narrows and, late that evening, had passed through, entering the Sea of Marmara.

When Duckworth's force – eight ships of the line, two frigates and two bomb-ketches – sailed into open water, Smith's division was bringing up the rear and still passing Turkish shore batteries. So he was not available to remind the navigating master in the flagship of the powerful current that swept from the Black Sea, through the Bosphorus and across the centre of the Sea of Marmara to the Dardanelles. If steering for Constantinople, it was important to keep on the western, European side of this race; otherwise, it would sweep away the largest ship, which could only cross it from the Asiatic side with a strong south-easterly wind. But Duckworth unwittingly led his ships to the east of the current and, finding that he could not reach Constantinople, he anchored on the evening of the 20th February, eight miles from the city, to await the necessary wind.

Next day a light breeze enabled a frigate to move four miles nearer and to despatch by boat a letter from Duckworth addressed to the Sultan. This bluntly made the political demands, adding that he 'had it in his power to destroy the capital and all the Turkish vessels' and, to this end 'the British fleet will avail itself of the first favourable wind to proceed towards Constantinople', boasting that 'when orders have been given to British officers, no difficulties, no dangers, can retard their execution a single moment'. A reply was demanded half an hour after the letter's delivery to the Sultan.

However, the courier was forbidden to land from the boat
flying a white flag of truce and a second attempt, carrying an
even more hectoring letter, was also rebuffed. But it was clear
to the Turks what was afoot and General Sebastiani persuaded
the Sultan to prolong any such preliminaries as long as possible while the city's fortifications were strengthened and new
batteries mounted in the narrows of the Dardanelles to trap
the British in the Sea of Marmara. Twenty-four hours later,
Duckworth was writing, and hoping to deliver, another letter:
'As it has been discovered by our glasses, that the time granted
the Sublime Porte to take its decision is employed in warping
ships into places more susceptible of defence and in construct-
ing batteries along the coast, it is the duty of the Vice-Admiral
to lose no time.'[38]

At dawn on the 22nd, a south-easterly breeze was blowing
and the signal to prepare to weigh anchor was proudly run up
the halyards of Duckworth's flagship, the *Royal George*.

That afternoon, before the signal to weigh was made, the
wind dropped and the sea became a flat calm. 'The effect of
mortified pride was very serious upon the ambassador,' wrote
a contemporary, 'for he was taken sick that very afternoon and
became so very ill on the day following that the admiral, whose
frame was formed of tougher materials, had the whole burden
of diplomacy upon himself.'[39] When the fleet had been at
anchor for a week, Duckworth decided to consult Sir Sidney
Smith and sent him four written questions. He replied at
length, stressing that negotiations would always be more prof-
itable than threats; if that failed, he would advise against
risking ships of the line in the currents of the Bosphorous,
recommending a blockade and what amounted to psychological warfare, making out that the Sultan was, in effect, a prisoner
of the French and encouraging the Sultan against the pro-
French factions within the city. Meanwhile, the fleet, which was
victualled for at least three months, should remain in the Sea of
Marmara, where, even if they did not succeed in their aims,
their implied threats to Constantinople should ensure a guar-
antee of an unopposed retreat through the narrows. Finally,
Smith offered to go ashore himself and reason with his old
friend, the Sultan; the offer was refused.

But there was still no wind and reports reached Duckworth
of new batteries nearing completion to cut his retreat to the

Aegean. On the day he wrote to Smith, the Turks occupied a small island near his anchorage, marines were landed and, as skirmishing began, were recalled to their ships without it being realized that amongst the enemy was General Sebastiani, whose capture might have resolved Duckworth's problems; instead, it was remarked, 'Sir John might as well have sent a party of old women to drive away the Turks.'[40] The calm weather had been followed by a westerly wind and then, on 1st March, it shifted to the north-east, which was the wind necessary either for a slightly closer approach to Constantinople, or a return through the Dardanelles. So that morning Duckworth's fleet weighed anchor and stood towards the city in what the admiral later described as a challenge to the Turkish fleet to come out and fight. It was, however, no more than a gesture to salvage a little pride because he had realized that the mission was a failure, as he reported to Collingwood:

when the unavoidable sacrifice of the squadron committed to my charge (which must have arisen, had I waited for a wind to have enabled me to cannonade the town, unattended by the remotest chance of obtaining any advantage for His Majesty's service) must have been the consequence of pursuing that object, it at once became my positive duty, however wounded in pride and ambition, to relinquish it.[41]

Therefore, on the morning of 3rd March, he ordered his ships to put about and steer for the narrows of the Dardanelles, and the dangerous passage to safety beyond.

Watching the departing fleet with mingled surprise and triumph, General Sebastiani reflected on what he saw as having been, for the French cause, a close-run crisis. Later, when asked whether its outcome might have been different had Duckworth allowed Smith to go ashore to negotiate, his reply was recorded:

Sebastiani answered that if he had landed ... the game would probably have been up with him (Sebastiani): for that the Sultan had already sent for him as soon as he found the English fleet were proceeding towards the capital. In great alarm, he said to him that 'he thought it right to tell him, he valued his capital more than he did his connexion with the French nation' and this candid intimation was at once considered by the French ambassador as a hint so very significant as to induce him to get together the necessary papers of the embassy to be destroyed if necessary; so that he and his suite might hold themselves in readiness to embark and claim the protection of the English fleet.[42]

The anonymous acquaintance of Sebastiani's, who reported this, also added, 'The same jealous feeling which followed Sir Sidney everywhere all through his services appears to have been conspicuous on this occasion. Had he commanded this expedition, as ought to have been the case, the result would most certainly have been very different. His name alone would have acted as a charm with the Turks, by whom he was respected and beloved. The moral influence, which he possessed over them to such an extraordinary degree, was here thrown away by the councils of England ... The fleet ought not to have passed the Dardanelles until diplomatic measures had been brought to an end.'[43] For his part, Sultan Selim may have felt regret and apprehension, and with reason, because tensions increased within the court as the Janissaries – an elite military caste of Christian ancestry, like the Mamelukes, who had become a political force – plotted against him: in May, he was deposed and murdered by his cousin Mustapha, who replaced him as Sultan.*

But while Sebastiani and the Sultan sighed with relief, or regret, the British were fighting their way back through the Dardanelles. As Duckworth passed the forts guarding the northern entrance to the narrows, he hopefully fired a salute of thirteen guns, to which the Turks replied with round-shot. Further down, the Turks had sited new batteries of mortars able to throw huge stone cannon balls made of granite, or marble, said to have been made from the columns of Greek and Roman temples. As the ships slowly approached, the bare, brown hills disappeared in gunsmoke. One stone ball of 800 pounds cut through the mainmast of the *Windsor Castle* and another, 2 feet 6 inches in diameter, caused a fire and explosion in the *Standard*, killing 8 and wounding 47.

The *Pompée* escaped damage but many of the other ships were hit, often by the stone shot, Captain Moubray of the *Active*, looking over the side to see what damage had been done

---

* He, in turn, was murdered a year later and the courtiers of the last two sultans murdered and 260 of their harem women tied in sacks and thrown into the Bosphorus.

saw 2 of his sailors leaning together through the shot-hole. In all, British casualties on the run south were 29 killed and 138 wounded. When the battered fleet emerged into the Aegean, they found the Russian squadron at anchor waiting for their return, and were galled when the Russian admiral suggested that he return up the narrows with Duckworth for another attempt; the offer was declined.

Yet this humiliating defeat of the British was not seen as such in London. A positive gloss was put upon the gallantry of 'forcing the Dardanelles' for a show of strength against Constantinople. The great granite and marble cannon-balls leant an epic quality to the story – even, to those with a Classical education, an Homeric touch with echoes of the giant Cyclops flinging rocks at the Argonauts – and one of them was brought back to Portsmouth as a trophy. Even the gallant Captain Hoste, who was at Malta for repairs to his frigate after storm-damage when some of Duckworth's ships arrived, accepted that it had been 'one of the most daring attempts in our naval annals' and joked that 'Jack says it is strange work playing at marbles with the Turks'.[44]*

Smith himself made the most of the adventure, despite his disappointment, delighted by praise in Duckworth's despatch to Collingwood 'in bearing testimony to the zeal and distinguished ability of Sir Sidney Smith; the manner in which he executed the service entrusted to him was worthy of the reputation, which he has long since so justly and so generally established.'[45] Smith responded by writing a long poem, extravagantly evoking the classical and patriotic allusions of the ships' names and glorifying the failure:

> Canopus led the way, 'twixt 'neighbouring strands'
> Of Hellespontus, thronged with Turkish bands.
> Dreading Repulse, the Turks dared not assail;
> The British Standard turned the Crescent pale:
> On Caesar's allies, Pompée vengeance wreaks
> And, rushing in the midst, their line he breaks;
> While showers of deadly bolts the Thunderer hurled,
> The anchor goes, again the sails are furled ...
> The Pasha's fleet in fragments on the coast,

* Duckworth's reputation survived relatively untarnished and frigates were named after him and Louis – but not Smith – in the Second World War.

> Propontis now doth bear the British host;
> Its dread approach each Turkish heart appals,
> Lo! *Windsor Castle*'s at Byzantium's walls ...[46]

Such braggadocio would have rung even more hollow had it been realized that year that Napoleon was paying his first visit to Venice, which had been to him a mythological city below the southern horizon when his army had taken it in 1797. Imposing his will upon the fabric of its history – demolishing ancient buildings to make way for his own palace and batteries to keep out the British – he was again inspired by dreams of eastern conquest as the Venetians had been. There was again a chance of marching on India through Constantinople, which he could reach overland as the Royal Navy barred his way by sea.

Duckworth was now ordered to make for Aboukir Bay to support a small British expeditionary force of 5,000 troops, which had been landed there and at Alexandria to bring other pressure to bear on Turkey. The day before he arrived on 22nd March 1807, the city had fallen and Duckworth's arrival encouraged the army commander, General Fraser, to attack Rosetta, which was well defended, and he was driven off with heavy loss. Luckily for Duckworth, orders arrived from Collingwood instructing him to hand over command to Louis and return to England; otherwise, he would have been involved in another failure because the British were compelled to evacuate Egypt in September, having lost a fifth of their strength. Smith, too, was recalled, arriving early in June – a few days after the fall of Selim in Constantinople – and making straight for Bath to take the medicinal waters.

It was, however, the social life that appealed to him most for he was a gregarious man. A friend remembered:

> Sir Sidney had an extraordinary memory, always ready. He could repeat pages of poetry, English, Latin and French; when, where or how he learned them no one in his family pretended to know, but they were always ready and appropriate in company, when conversation turned that way. He was equally ready in enlivening a party of young ladies, by every variety of charades and conundrums, generally made on the spur of the moment; by cutting paper into curious figures; and by a display of clever tricks; for all of which his demand in payment was a kiss from each.[47]

He was, it was recalled:

like all British sailors, an ardent admirer of the fair sex and of elegance of form and beauty in particular. On one occasion, he had been rather lavish in his praise and admiration of a very pretty woman, whose figure had struck his attention as being remarkably elegant and he pronounced her to be the perfect model. 'Stop, admiral,' said a naval friend, 'her face is pretty, I concede, but as to her form, when I saw her last she had none unless it were that of being as thin as an inch deal board.' 'Well, well,' said Sir Sidney, 'I shall not argue the point with you but I shall take a closer observation next time I see her.' After his next meeting with the lady, Smith confessed, 'I felt very indignant at the manner in which my friend had libelled her, for more perfect symmetry I never beheld. But judge my surprise when in course of a very animated conversation, I observed her taking a *marlin-spike* [a hair-pin] out of her head and plunge it to the hilt in her bosom several times without once drawing blood. I never saw my friend again, so he did not enjoy his triumph; and the craft, which sailed under false colours, is now dead, or I should not have told the story.[48]

In July, while Smith was enjoying the pleasures of Bath, Napoleon and Tsar Alexander signed the Treaty of Tilsit under which Russia joined the Continental System to exclude Britain from Europe. There were two weak points in this blockade: Denmark and Portugal. The British tried and failed to persuade the Danes to join them against France and, as result, bombarded Copenhagen, Colonel Congreve's rockets at last proving what effective fire-raisers they could be. Napoleon now determined to slam the Portuguese door and, to this end, signed a treaty with Spain, on 27th October 1807, to divide Portugal between them and, to enforce this, an army, led by Marshal Junot, prepared to march through Spain to Lisbon. The fearful Prince Regent of Portugal, Prince John, immediately declared his compliance with the Continental System and ordered the arrest of all British subjects in the country. Response was to be a task for Sir Sidney Smith and, on 12th November, he hoisted his flag in the *Hibernia* and led a squadron of nine ships of the line towards Lisbon. His principal instructions – in addition to which he received secret orders about intelligence assignments from the War Office, rather than the Admiralty, which were so secret that not even the Foreign

Secretary, George Canning, knew about them – began by instructing him that, if he could not persuade the Regent to reverse his policy, he was to attempt the destruction of the Portuguese fleet and blockade Lisbon.

Five days later, the British ambassador to Portugal, the young, inexperienced but ambitious Lord Strangford, who had sailed from the Tagus, joined the flagship at sea and told Smith that Junot's army was already close to the capital. So the two of them decided to repeat an offer made by Canning to the Prince Regent that he and his government should board the Portuguese fleet and sail under British protection to Rio de Janeiro, the capital of their colony, Brazil. When this offer had first been made, some months earlier, it had been rejected; now it was accepted and, two days later, a fleet of thirty-six ships, including eight sail of the line, emerged from the Tagus with almost all the Portuguese leadership – plus the gold from the vaults of the treasury – on board, just as Junot's cavalry reached the outskirts of Lisbon. No sooner had they met their escort of British ships than a violent gale blew out of the Atlantic and by the end of November, the armada sailed through heavy seas for South America. It had been a repeat of Nelson's rescue of the Bourbons from Naples in 1798 on an oceanic scale.

Smith reported to the Admiralty on his success, and that French-occupied Lisbon was now under blockade, with his customary flourishes, remarking that 'the scene impressed every beholder, except the French army on the hills' and he ended, 'our Knight of the Sword is at it again!',[49] a reference to his much-mocked Swedish title. But in his enthusiasm he and Lord Strangford had, by accident or design, overlooked the need to keep other commanders in their theatre of war fully informed: neither Admiral Purvis, commanding the blockade of Cadiz, nor the Governor of Gibraltar had been told what had happened. More remarkably, Smith had not told Lieutenant-General Sir John Moore, who had just arrived at Gibraltar with 8,000 troops either to assist in the defence of Lisbon, or to help establish the Regent and his exiled government in the Portuguese islands of Madeira. 'This is most unaccountable conduct on their part,'[50] the general noted in his diary and it was never to be explained. Smith must have been aware of Moore's personal dislike but he was not a vindictive man and it was possible that he regarded the involvement of British troops as irrelevant once the evacuation had been completed, assuming that Moore would hear the news from Lisbon soon enough. In the event, he did and decided to return to England, but before he could reach London and complain to the War Office, the Admiralty had sent Smith fulsome congratulations beginning with their 'high approbation of your judicious and able conduct'.[51]

In the Atlantic, Smith mused on the transfer of the Portuguese government to Brazil and his ideas seemed to echo those that had inspired the expedition into Nicaragua in 1780, when Nelson had first come to public attention, the purpose which had been to take over the huge, ramshackle Spanish empire in the Americas. Now, Smith wondered, could this not be achieved through the Portuguese? Writing to Lord Keith, he speculated on the Regent being followed to South America by vast numbers of emigrants so that 'it is not improbable that the heterogeneous classes of which the population of South America is composed might gradually be brought under one government ... a consideration of no small account to Great Britain.'[52]

Smith himself did not arrive at Rio de Janeiro until 17th May 1808, where, as commander-in-chief of His Majesty's Naval Forces on the South American Station, he was showered with honours and flattery by the Regent and quickly became immersed in Portuguese politics. There were two principal factions, one led by the Prince Regent, the other by the Princess, who was said to be supported secretly by Admiral Smith. The aim of both was to take over Buenos Aires and the province of La Plata but each had a different scenario. The Prince wished the territory to be Portuguese and ruled by himself as Prince of the Brazils; his wife, who was of Spanish royal blood, wanted it annexed in the name of her brother, who, in March 1807, took the throne of Spain by *coup d'état* to become King Ferdinand VII, and was expected to oppose the French in Europe.

Smith's position was particularly delicate and, to him, stimulating because, the British had tried and failed to make a lodgement in South America when, in 1806, Commodore Sir Home Popham had led an unauthorized expedition to attack the Spanish in Buenos Aires. Although reinforced, the expedition had ended in total failure, heavy losses and finally, humiliating evacuation in the summer of 1807. So he became involved in contingency planning for another such operation, mounted from Rio de Janeiro with Portuguese help, on the pretext that the French might be planning a landing there. This was bedeviled by rivalries and contrary political views not only within the Portuguese government but between Smith and Strangford. The latter confrontation came to a head in May 1809, when another, more junior British flag officer, Rear-Admiral the Honourable Michael de Courcy arrived off Rio and the ambassador wrote to him, asking him to relieve Sir Sidney of his command. However, Smith had no intention of complying and Strangford wrote letters of complaint to the Foreign Secretary, George Canning. However, it had been the Admiralty's intention that de Courcy should relieve Smith but had not informed him of this. The two admirals remained on friendly terms, even when the true position became clear, and, before hauling down his flag, Smith wrote to his successor, 'I have not found His Majesty's Minister Plenipotentiary to act frankly and cordially with me, as the admiral on this station, and that my experience does not warrant my giving you any ground for expectation that he will do so with you.'[53] His spell in the South Atlantic had produced one little victory when one of his captains led Portuguese troops to capture from the French the island of Cayenne off Guiana. It also produced a curious historical footnote when a captain Folger of the American ship *Topaz* reported to him his discovery of an English castaway named Alexander Smith on the remote Pacific island of Pitcairn; so Sir Sidney forwarded to the Admiralty the first news of the fugitive mutineers who had taken the *Bounty* from Captain Bligh in 1789. With that, he sailed for home.

On arrival in London, Smith was summoned by Canning to be reprimanded yet again for having 'arrogated to himself in his transactions respecting South America an authority not derived from any instructions given him by H.M. Government'. But Smith was able to explain that his political intrigues were the result of his secret orders and Canning had to confess to him in a letter that his concerns had been 'completely removed by the secret despatch addressed to you from the War Department on the 5th August, 1808 ... of which ... I had no knowledge whatsoever'.[54]

Smith's return to London in August 1809, could not have

been better timed because the British were hungry for heroes. Nelson had been dead for four years and the shock of that first spasm of national grief had calmed, so Sir Sidney Smith could step on to an empty stage. There had been no great naval battles – hence, no heroes – since Trafalgar, yet there might have been one in the Basque roads off La Rochelle in April 1809; but Admiral Gambier had failed to take advantage of an attack by fireships by Captain Lord Cochrane – a dashing eccentric in the mould of Sidney Smith – who had been court-martialled for his failure, and acquitted. There were still French squadrons to fight but they chose to avoid action. Moore's failure to reinforce Capri had led to its recapture by the French, who had commandeered ladders from Neapolitan lamp-lighters to scale the cliffs. Moore himself had been sent to Spain to oppose the French but could do nothing but make a fighting retreat to the sea at Corunna, himself being killed just before his troops could be evacuated by the Navy. Lieutenant-General Sir Arthur Wellesley had taken command in Portugal and was holding his own, while, throughout the Iberian peninsula, Smith's views of the value of guerrillas fighting in cooperation with regular troops were being vindicated.

In London, Smith 'entered into society and enjoyed all its gaieties and amusements'[55] and received formal thanks from London merchants trading with South America. Then, like Nelson, he received the acclaim of the provinces, being given the Freedom of Edinburgh and Plymouth and civic receptions in Manchester and Liverpool. Nelson had been awarded an honorary degree in civil law by Oxford University, an honour that Smith was also accorded, which prompted the *Naval Chronicle* to quip, 'We hope he will not abandon the practice of the *cannon law*, in which he has hitherto been so eminent.'[56] At Oxford, he was told, 'Your country, sir, has long beheld with mingled emotions of shame, anger and indignation the affronting neglect with which the brilliant character of Sir Sidney Smith has been insulted ... it was in the theatre of Oxford, sir, that the splendid and living attestation of your merit burst upon us.'[57] The ceremony was marked by the reading of the poem 'Palestine, Relative to the Exploits of Bonaparte and Sir Sidney Smith' by the Reverend Reginald Heber of All Souls' College, which began:

When he, from tow'ry MALTA's yielding isle,
And the green waters of reluctant NILE
Th' Apostate Chief from Misraim's subject Shore
To ACRE's walls his trophied banner bore ...[58]

Soon afterwards, Cambridge University also honoured him. At the Senate House 'the public orator most happily introduced the only conqueror of the conqueror of Europe into his Latin harangue', and he was also awarded an honorary degree of Master of Arts 'by acclamation'.[59] More specific was another poem by a Dr Houlton, which was printed in full by the *Naval Chronicle* – the monthly journal edited by Nelson's biographers, James Clarke and John M'Arthur, who were also well disposed towards Smith – snatches of which provided publicity for the subject, 'Sir Sidney Smith, or The Gem of Renown':

Says Fame t'other day to the Genius of song,
A fav'rite of mine you've neglected too long;
He's a sound bit of oak, a son of the wave,
The scourge of dire France, Sir Sidney the brave ...

Madame Fame, cries the genius, no Bard in my Train,
Of Sir Sidney's desert can equal the strain,
Bonaparte alone can best sing his merit,
His laurels and glory, his valour and spirit ...

Neptune swore it was true, for so active was he,
That he never can rest, with Sir Sidney at sea ...
Master Neptune, said Mars, I claim, as my Son,
A share in the glory Sir Sidney has won ...

Since Fame and their Godships thus jointly agree,
Sir Sidney's a hero on Land, or on Sea ...[60]

On 31st July 1810, Smith was promoted to vice-admiral, the most senior rank reached by Nelson, and, although this was automatic, unless he committed some serious and acknowledged misdemeanour as he moved up the *Navy List* each year – it embellished a name that had been neglected in awards of honour by King and Government. That his future would not be cloudless was suggested by a remark made by Admiral Sir Roger Curtis, the Commander-in-Chief, Portsmouth, to the newly appointed Secretary to the Admiralty, John Croker; speaking of Smith, he said, 'My dear friend, beware of *Heroes* – the more you come to know them, the less you will think of them.'[61]

Smith's satisfaction was crowned by his courtship of a widow, four years his senior, Caroline, the widow of Sir George Rumbold, a diplomat who had also been involved in secret intelligence work. Sir George had been British ambassador to the Hanse towns in Germany and had been arrested by the French on suspicion of being involved in the same conspiracy as the Duc d'Enghien, Cadoudal, Captain Wright and the rest. Fouché had him brought to Paris in 1804 but diplomatic pressure had secured his repatriation; he had returned to Hamburg in 1806 but had died a year later. Smith had another link with his widow because one of her three daughters was married to Captain Septimus Arabin, whom he had known as a midshipman in the *Tigre*. In October 1810, they were married and his brother-officers wondered whether the gasconade would continue.

CHAPTER NINE

'A little crazy, perhaps'

ON 18TH JULY 1812, Vice-Admiral Sir Sidney Smith, newly appointed as second-in-command in the Mediterranean, hoisted his flag in a seventy-four-gun ship of the line, named with suitable flamboyance, *Tremendous*. He was to serve a new Commander-in-Chief, Vice-Admiral Sir Edward Pellew, seven years' Smith's senior, who had been chosen to succeed Vice-Admiral Sir Charles Cotton, the immediate successor to Lord Collingwood, who had died on board his flagship in 1810. Sir Edward's success had been due to a brilliant record as a fighting captain, particularly in command of frigates. He was, however, very different from Smith in looks as much as temperament and opinions: a bluff seaman, bulky and phlegmatic, lacking the flair for leadership displayed by Nelson, or, indeed, Smith; a deep-water sailor. Pellew had, when a Member of Parliament, supported St Vincent against putting resources into the inshore naval operations that Smith favoured, holding that maritime supremacy would be decided by fleets on the open sea. Smith had relieved Vice-Admiral Sir Richard Keats, who had been a close friend of Pellew's and, indeed, of Nelson's.

Naturally accepting his appointment as a mark of the Government's confidence, Smith did not know that he had been selected by a narrow margin and that the casting vote had been given by John Croker, an Irish politician and the shrewd but manipulative Secretary to the Admiralty, who had persuaded the First Lord to give him another chance:

'I myself knew Sir Sidney Smith,' he was to say, 'and though I thought him, as most people did, a little crazy – perhaps with vanity – I, though with some difficulty, prevailed with Lord Melville to employ him as second in the Mediterranean Fleet, which was, I thought, due to his former distinguished services and the noise he had made in the world, and I thought that, having been so long unemployed, he had a peculiar claim to be brought forward at that time. The seamen on the Board were rather averse; for certainly he was not what is called a sailor.'[1]

Smith was to meet Pellew off Toulon, which was again under blockade, but on the way he called at Cartagena on the east coast of Spain to support British troops fighting ashore. For the past three years, war had engulfed the Iberian peninsula. Smith could only see these campaigns as a vindication of his own ideas, for regular soldiers were collaborating with Spanish guerrillas to devastating effect. At Cartagena, more of his expertise was required, for the port was threatened by 70,000 French troops, so he adapted ideas used at Acre for its defence.

In his enthusiasm, Smith made more gaffes. On 21st September, he wrote a report, urging that British troops elsewhere on the Spanish coast should concentrate on the defence of Cartagena to make it their principal base for operations inland. But instead of sending this to Admiral Pellew for possible forwarding to the Admiralty for transmission to the War Office, Smith by-passed them all, sending it direct to the headquarters of the British Army at the Horse Guards in Whitehall, asking them to pass on to the Duke of Wellington in Spain his view that Cartagena was 'the only port by which the Navy can effectually supply the Army in the south of the Peninsula'.[2] Nine days later, on arrival off Toulon, where Pellew was lying, he wrote to London again, this time to the Admiralty, reporting his arrival off the French coast and claiming that he had left Cartagena in a better state of preparedness than he found it.

The reply from the Admiralty was sent to Smith via Admiral Pellew, ignoring Cartagena and stating tartly that, 'Their Lordships are greatly surprised at receiving these communications direct from him, which, if necessary to be communicated at all, should have been transmitted to his Commander-in-Chief, whom their Lordship cannot permit to be set aside and passed over by a flag-officer serving under his command.'[3] However, Pellew chose not to make an issue of this but was annoyed when Smith upheld the verdict of a court-martial, which cleared an officer, whom he had thought guilty.

Shifting his flag to the *Hibernia*, a big ship of 110 guns, Smith became involved in the tedium of blockading Toulon, where the French admiral was showing no inclination to come out and fight. Recognizing the dangers of boredom to morale, he tried to relieve it, setting up a library in his flagship for officers and petty officers with a cabin designated as a silent reading room, well stocked with reference books and magazines from London; he even had a printing press on board. More ambitiously he encouraged amateur theatricals, arranging for these to be performed ashore when a theatre was available in a friendly port. 'The mania of the day consisted of theatrical exhibitions ... and, as far as liberality of purse was concerned, mainly assisted by Sir Sidney,'[4] noted a contemporary. One of these was a deconsecrated church in Port Mahon – Minorca was a base for the blockade – and another was at Cagliari, the capital of Sardinia. There, there was diplomatic work to be done because, it was reported, the French were being favoured by the Sardinians, who had even fired on a British frigate, chasing a French privateer close inshore. The British ambassador was away in London so there was another sovereign – King Victor Emmanuel – to be cultivated and, on 4th June 1813, the birthday of King George III, he, his daughter and son-in-law, an Austrian archduke, were dined with full pomp on board the flagship. As result, Smith told Pellew, 'I have obtained the most distinct assurances of a ready cooperation against the common enemy.'[5] Smith, who understood the diplomatic and warlike flexibility of warships, gave credit to his ship's company for giving the *Hibernia* the 'fitness to bear the very minute inspection, which hath been bestowed upon her by his Sardinian Majesty and many thousands of his subjects, who thronged daily to see her as an object of stupendous and awful novelty to them.'[6] In response the Queen gave the ship five bullocks and three pipes of wine.

Smith thought he had achieved a diplomatic success but Pellew was not impressed, reporting to the Admiralty that 'it did not appear that any security had been obtained from the result of Sir Sidney's mission. No formal treaty or agreement had been executed and only royal assurances had been obtained.'[7] It had been expensive entertaining and Smith, knowing that he would not be reimbursed by the Admiralty, wrote to the Under-Secretary of State at the Foreign Office, William Hamilton:

When a crowned head with his royal family ... condescend to visit a public officer in his place, whose appointments and allowances are not calculated to meet such a contingency, it would require the power of working a miracle, like that of the loaves and fishes, to meet it without expense for, on such an occasion, a man of my rank in the world ... could not set a 'leg of mutton and turnips' before such guests ... The *Admiralty* may not choose to make a precedent of allowing table-money to a flag-officer, *second* in command, I therefore look to the Foreign Office, which may exercise a discretionary power in my *peculiar* case, under *peculiar* circumstances.[8]

He added that it had been worthwhile 'because peace and friendship is cheaper than hostility'.[9] Eventually, the Foreign Office did pay his bills.

The Mediterranean was quiet although there was intense activity in the Adriatic. There, Captain Hoste had followed his brilliant victory over a squadron of French and Venetian frigates off Lissa in 1811 with the capture, in the first six months of 1814, of both Cattaro [Kotor] and Ragusa [Dubrovnik] by dragging his ships guns to the summits of mountains over-looking the fortress-cities and subjecting their French garrisons to what amounted to aerial bombardment. This alone might have been enough to halt Napoleon's plans for an overland march on Constantinople and the East but at last it seemed the French were beginning to crumble. Following his disastrous invasion of Russia in 1812 and the loss of most of the *Grande Armée* in the winter retreat from Moscow, his armies had been defeated in Spain by Wellington, who had crossed the Pyrenees into France in October 1813, the same month that Napoleon had been defeated by the Russians, Prussians and Austrians at Leipzig. As time passed, Smith increasingly irritated Pellew, who expected his second-in-command to be more conventional in manners if not in ideas. So, early in 1814, when Smith tried to persuade him to take action against the French, or Italian coasts, he wrote dismissively to a friend that Smith was 'as gay and thoughtless as ever, wants to go with 5 sail to summon Genoa'.[10]

At the end of March, the allies entered Paris and the Napoleonic system collapsed, the Emperor himself abdicating unconditionally on 11th April. It was decided that 'the great, bad man', as he was to be called, should be exiled to the island

of Elba off the Italian coast and on 4th May, Napoleon boarded
the British frigate *Undaunted* off Provençal fishing port of
Fréjus. On board, he was introduced to a Midshipman William
Sidney Smith and told that he was the nephew of Admiral
Smith and, mishearing, he expressed surprise that Sir Sidney
Smith was now commander-in-chief in the Mediterranean; it
was almost the prophecy Smith had written on the shutter in
the Temple prison coming true. As Napoleon, who had
conquered Europe from the Atlantic to Moscow, and, but for
Nelson and Smith, might have conquered the East as well, tried
to come to terms with a future on an island eighteen miles by
twelve, Sir Sidney Smith, unaware of the event at Fréjus, was
cruising off the coast of Spain. His health had not been good
and he hankered after new and more active employment, so he
suggested a change, which Pellew was quick to approve. He
now sailed for home and, on 1st July, the *Hibernia* anchored off
Plymouth and he struck his flag.

That autumn, the statesmen of the victorious allies met the
representatives of defeated France in Vienna, who, with King
Louis XVIII on the throne, were now monarchist. More than
peace terms were to be discussed at the Congress of Vienna
because it was recognized that, after more than twenty years of
war, the future of Europe itself must be addressed. Not to be
left in the wings, Sir Sidney Smith took himself, his wife and his
three step-daughters on to what he saw as the stage of history,
and wrote himself a part. He needed a cause, for, otherwise,
there could be no reason for a vice-admiral – albeit a well-
known one – to join that dazzling array of politicians. While
wondering what rôle he could play, Smith was visited in
London by an old royalist émigré friend, Hyde de Neuville,
who had arrived from Paris as a diplomat for the restored
Bourbons. Remembering Smith's lively mind, he called to ask
his opinion of the current state of international relations and
possible contingencies for which they might prepare.

Smith began by shocking de Neuville with his view that they
had not seen the last of Napoleon, whom he expected to
attempt an escape from Elba and return to France, saying, 'Your
countrymen are under a great illusion if they believe that the
prestige that surrounds his name is destroyed by France's
recent defeats.'[11] He feared his return would rekindle the
passion for glory that he had awakened and nurtured in the

French. As it happened, he thought, the necessary precautions against such an escape could be combined with a great European cause, which could bring Smith back into the centre of the stage.

Apart from the crusade against Napoleon, the great focus of idealism had been on the abolition of slavery. The economies of the West Indies, the southern United States and other countries in the western hemisphere had long been based on the labour of African slaves and this had been accepted as normal practice. Now the moral issues had been raised, particularly by evangelical Christians and Methodists, and a forceful campaign had been led by William Wilberforce, himself an evangelical and a Member of Parliament, whom Smith had known in the House of Commons and as a friend of William Pitt. In 1807, he had, after a twenty-year campaign, finally persuaded Parliament to ban the slave trade in the British West Indies. But the new law was not retrospective and did not apply to those already enslaved, so that the plight of African slaves was still an issue preached with passion.

Most of Smith's service had been in the Mediterranean and there, too, slavery was a reality but not an issue, even though the slaves were likely to be Christians and Europeans, and occasionally British. In the Islamic countries, from Turkey, clockwise around the sea to Gibraltar, slavery was accepted as an economic tradition. Crews of European ships taken by corsairs from Morocco, Algiers and Tunis were enslaved and, as Smith remembered from his time in Constantinople, the Turks enslaved prisoners of war. Piracy continued in the Mediterranean but the intense naval activity by the British, French and Spanish over the past two decades had reduced it. Then there was still the danger of corsair raids on coastal villages, by which they carried off young women to the harems of North Africa, although this, too, had been inhibited by the European navies.

So Smith explained to Hyde de Neuville that the next crusade to unite Europe should be against the slavery of both Europeans and Africans in the Mediterranean countries. Catching his enthusiasm, de Neuville suggested they put this into writing and together they composed *A Memorial upon the Necessity and the Means to End the Piracies of the Barbary Powers* by concerted diplomatic and naval pressure. Smith saw this as the cause which could take him to Vienna to command the attention of the assembled statesmen but de Neuville reported privately and candidly to the new Bourbon government in Paris. 'Sir Sidney wishes to go to Vienna,' he wrote, 'but I doubt if he would be very useful there: he is a man of action, a true *chevalier sans peur et sans reproche*, but his head is not so good as his heart ...' De Neuville explained that, despite his sound qualities he had a reputation for imaginative airiness, which would inhibit his value among politicians. But he continued, 'He would be useful, however, in the enterprise against the corsairs; and also, with his well-merited reputation for bravery and energy, he would have the confidence of the Sovereigns and the important thing is to interest them in this great project.'[12]

An important ally would be Wilberforce himself. They met in London and Smith followed this with a letter to Wilberforce's home at Sandgate on the Kent coast. When a reply eventually came it rambled with apologies for the delay and about reading in the newspapers of Sir Sidney and Lady Smith as people of fashion. There was little about the anti-slavery campaign beyond complaints that the new French government was showing no enthusiasm for his own efforts and achievements and that, because Smith was going to Vienna, the problems of corresponding made it more convenient 'to delay, till after Christmas, any motion for doing tardy justice to Sir Sidney Smith'.[13] So Smith would, once again, have to rely on his own powers of persuasion.

There could be another cause, however, one that harked back to Smith's early experience of war in the Baltic. The son of his patron, the assassinated King Gustavus III of Sweden, was exiled in London having himself been deposed in 1809. Having come to the throne as Gustavus IV under the regency of his uncle, the Duke of Södermanland, and taken full royal powers four years later, he had stood firm against French blandishments and threats, remaining an ally of the British until overthrown in a *coup d'état* when Sweden too was absorbed in Napoleonic Europe. Now he was planning to plead the case for his restoration at the Congress of Vienna and he urged Smith, who had been knighted by his father, to come, too, and speak on his behalf.

So the Smith family set out in a spanking coach with Sir

Sidney's coat of arms emblazoned on the door panels. They arrived in Vienna in time to attend the great ball in the Spanish Riding School – draped with white satin and silver tassels and lit by 8,000 candles for the occasion – to celebrate the arrival of the Tsar of Russia and the King of Prussia. Smith's three attractive step-daughters were belles of the balls and he himself cut a dash, although his tendency to tell at length the story of the siege of Acre caused him to be nicknamed after a London street, 'Long Acre'.[14]

Loyally, he first promoted the cause of King Gustavus only to find his influential audiences sympathetic but unsupportive. While they recognized the justice of his claim there was an unseen obstacle. As a secret bribe to persuade Marshal Bernadotte, who had been, in effect, Napoleon's viceroy in Stockholm, from involving the Swedes in the invasion of Russia, he had secretly been offered the throne of Sweden. That was a lost cause and that of 'white slavery' seemed to arouse only polite interest before signs of boredom.

But Smith always had a flair for catching attention and he planned to do so with a lavish party. What he called a 'pic-nic dinner' was in fact to be a subscription dinner and ball. He would not be raising funds for any active campaign against the slave-states because that would be for the governments to prosecute. The contributions would fund the entertainment and then buy a colossal silver lamp to be hung in the Church of the Holy Sepulchre in Jerusalem to burn as a reminder of Christians suffering under slavery. It was the most lavish occasion most of the guests could remember. The huge Augarten hall was draped with the flags of the victorious nations, an orchestra played at each end and, each arriving monarch was heralded by a fanfare from trumpeters on horseback. At dinner, the wine flowed and Sir Sidney made a long and impassioned speech against slavery after which a collection of gold coins was taken from the guests. All agreed it had been a triumph but it remained to be seen whether any sovereigns or statesmen had been persuaded to take action against the beys and sultans of the Barbary Coast.

If others were tardy, Sir Sidney was not and he set about organizing the reluctant crusaders into what he called the Knights Liberators of the Slaves in Africa, of whom he would be president. As such, he relentlessly buttonholed the delegates in Vienna throughout that sociable winter. That was hardly over when news broke that surprised all but Sir Sidney Smith: on 1st March 1815, Napoleon Bonaparte had escaped from Elba and landed in France. At the Congress of Vienna, delegates declared Napoleon an outlaw and set about meeting him on the field of battle.

Napoleon entered Paris on the 20th, and, as Smith had forecast, the French rallied to his standard; within weeks, a new *Grande Armée* of 120,000 men was on the march. Other armies were marching, too, from Russia, Prussia, the Netherlands and Austria, while the British sent another expeditionary force, commanded by the Duke of Wellington. While the armies slowly closed, Smith and his family travelled homeward across the Continent and, when they arrived in Brussels, heard that Napoleon had fought the Prussians at Ligny and the British and Dutch at Quatre Bras, and was now advancing on the city. Wellington had been there and was expected to meet the French some miles to the south.

As might have been expected, Smith left his family in Brussels and rode towards the sound of the guns. By its volume, he knew that the great battle had begun and soon the roads were crowded with wounded men stumbling towards the city, French prisoners under guard and deserters. Seeing a wounded British officer riding back, wounded, and recognizing him as Sir George Berkeley, he decided, as he wrote later, that 'thinking his sword a better one to meet my old antagonist *on horseback*, I borrowed it'. Smith was in civilian dress but his air of command was such that, as he put it, 'I stemmed the torrent of the disabled and *givers-in* the best way I could; I was now and then jammed among broken wagons of disarmed Napoleonist janissaries and finally reached the Duke of Wellington's person', and shook him by the hand. It never occurred to him now that a visitor might not be any more welcome than he had been initially at Toulon twenty-two years before. The great battle had been won and the victorious armies had surged forward in pursuit, so Smith rode from the battlefield at the Duke's side to the village of Waterloo. 'Though I was not allowed to have any of the fun,' he later recalled, 'I had the heartfelt gratification of being the first Englishman, that was not in the battle, who shook hands with him before he got off his horse and of drinking his health at his table.'[15] He did not, of course, then know that the last French division to abandon the battlefield had been commanded by General Jacques-Jean de Tromelin, once called John Bromley, who would not fight for a revolution but would fight for an Emperor.

On the ride to Waterloo, he had seen through the drifting smoke, that the slopes up which the French had attacked the British squares was littered with dead and wounded men and horses and he knew that the survivors would be too exhausted to care for them. So he now made it his business to find a wagoner and commissioned him to take his carts out on to the battlefield and bring in as many wounded as possible. The wagoner, whose name was Kierulff, made repeated journeys, bringing 134 wounded soldiers – 68 of them French, only 4 British, the remainder German, Dutch or Belgian – to a Jesuit hospital in Brussels, or to surgeons at dressing-stations on the edge of the battlefield.* In his written report to Smith, Kierulff said that he had told the Brussels authorities that more than 3,000 dead men and horses still lay, awaiting burial, on the battlefield and that 280 more wagons would be needed to bring the wounded into the city. 'It is impossible for me to convey to you the gratitude of the soldiers for your humanity,'[16] he concluded.

As his command of French would be useful, Wellington asked Smith first to arrange for the surrender of the garrisons of Arras and Amiens and then to inspect the route that King Louis XVIII would take on his return to Paris and to try to ensure there were unlikely to be hostile demonstrations. On 6th July, he reported to Wellington's headquarters at Neuilly, where he met the surrendered General de Tromelin, and was then commissioned to be liaison officer with the Duke of Otranto – formerly Josef Fouché, the Directory's Minister for Police – to arrange a peaceful entry into Paris for the allied armies.

If Smith had hoped that his prophecy would be wholly fulfilled and that Napoleon would be imprisoned in his own cell in the Temple, he had been forestalled. It was said that Napoleon, on his precipitate arrival in Paris, hearing that

---

* As result of this experience, Smith was to design an ambulance, a six-wheeled, strongly sprung wagon for carrying wounded across rough country as smoothly as possible, noting, 'A Palanquin, Hammock, Char-a-banc, or indeed a Carriage body of any form required can be suspended from the springs.'

Smith's prophecy was still read as a reprinted leaflet, ordered that the prison should be demolished immediately so that it could not be fulfilled. On 15th July, Napoleon had reached the coast at Rochefort and there, once again, the Royal Navy was present and he surrendered to the captain of one of the familiar 'seventy-fours', the *Bellerophon*.

The year ended with a banquet at the Elysée Palace in Paris at which the Duke of Wellington presided, taking the opportunity to invest Sir Sidney Smith with the insignia of a Knight Commander of the Order of the Bath, so that at last he was a British, as well as a Swedish knight. After they had dined and toasts had been drunk to the King and the Prince Regent, the Duke proposed another to Smith and then, invited him to propose a toast himself. This was, he said, the first anniversary of another toast he had proposed in Vienna and he asked them to raise their glasses to, 'The health and deliverance of the White Slaves in the Barbary States.' Smith was gratified by the occasion but aware that as a Knight Commander of the Bath, he was in the second rank of the Order, having been awarded an honour 'bestowed on officers for good but ordinary services'.[17]

Yet he was happy to add the new knighthood to his list of titles in a bold letter to a Turkish bey asking whether the Ottoman government, which had already freed some European slaves, might extend their mercy to Africans; this was Smith at his most optimistic, bearing in mind the purpose of his last visit to the approaches to Constantinople. He addressed this as from, 'Vice-Admiral Sir W. Sidney Smith, Knight Grand Cross of the Tower and the Sword, Knight Commander of the Bath, Companion of the Imperial Ottoman Order of the Crescent, President of the Knights Liberators of the Slaves in Africa, to His Highness the High and Puissant Prince Bey.' He began:

High and Mighty Sir, the fame of your exalted virtues has reached us. The many instances of your justice, benevolence and hospitality are known to us. We therefore address you in confidence and offer you the opportunity of becoming a member of our illustrious society of Knights Liberators of the Slaves in Africa. This illustrious and highly noble association being composed of the persons of the most exalted rank and highest endowments in the world at large, you will no doubt be desirous to enrol yourself a member thereof ... [18]

In Vienna, Brussels and Paris, Smith had been at his most expansive but had been living far beyond his means. There was, he considered, a great deal of money owed him by the British Government for his expenses as a diplomat in Constantinople, the financing of the Calabrian partisans, for entertaining royalty in Palermo, Rio de Janeiro and Cagliari and for supporting his French royalist friends. Hearing of this, Lord Castlereagh belatedly arranged for him to be paid for his diplomatic services in Constantinople but most of the rest remained unpaid. In London, he had lived in smart, rented houses, and had belonged to several fashionable clubs, where unpaid bills awaited him. Knowing the harshness of British law towards debtors and that failure to meet such obligations could lead to the King's Bench Prison, he decided to live abroad for the time being and, in the year of Waterloo, set up house in Paris at 6 Rue d'Anjou, close to the Rue St Honoré, where he had once dined when on parole from the Temple prison.

His return to the scene of his imprisonment brought back memories, particularly of Captain John Wright, who had died so violently in the Temple a week after Trafalgar. He determined to solve the mystery but there were difficulties: the prison itself had been demolished and many police files had been destroyed. Even the Duke of Wellington, to whom all doors seemed to be open, could not help; he had tired of Smith's relentless lobbying and, in any case, preferred expatriate English gentlemen to be urbane and laconic. He confided in the Secretary to the Admiralty, John Croker:

> Of all the men, whom I ever knew who have any reputation, the man who least deserves it is Sir Sidney Smith. During my embassy at Paris (where he was living to avoid his creditors in England) I saw a good deal of him and had eternal projects from him as long as I would listen to them. At first, out of deference to his name and reputation, I attended to him but soon I found he was a mere vapouriser. I cannot believe that a man so silly in all other affairs can be a good naval officer.[19]

But Smith had influential French friends. There was General de Tromelin, who had been forgiven by the Bourbons as he had been by Napoleon, and his wife, both of whom had been involved in his escape from Paris; Napoleon's *savants*, many now even more distinguished academics, were grateful to him for help he had given them during the collapse of French military rule in Egypt; then there were many retired French army officers, who had fought against him at Acre and admired his courage and chivalry. Through such as these he sought to discover the truth about Captain Wright.

Such friends helped with the enquiries, finding witnesses to talk about nocturnal comings and goings in the Temple on the night of 27th October 1805. Nothing could be proved except that it seemed certain that Wright had not committed suicide. He had been found lying on his bed with his throat deeply slashed from right to left but the closed razor was in his right hand, which lay by his side; also there was far less blood than would have been expected from such a wound. Some accused Napoleon of having ordered his murder; others, Fouché. Smith himself said publicly that it must have been 'an act of private vengeance',[20] which offended none of his French friends. But Smith did erect an elaborate memorial to Wright at his own expense in the cemetery of Père Lachaise, where he had been buried: something between an obelisk and a pyramid, surmounted by an urn and weeping cherubs, flanked by mourning caryatids holding inverted torches. It was inscribed with a long epitaph in Latin, proclaiming Wright's virtues and that he had been 'confined in the prison, called the Temple, infamous for midnight murders' and that, while 'his fortitude of mind and fidelity to his country remain unshaken ... he was found ... with his throat cut and dead in his bed'.[21] When all possible evidence was collated it was published in a long series of articles in several successive issues of the *Naval Chronicle*, which had always been friendly to Smith and with which he had links through his brother, Spencer. Copies finally reached as far afield as St Helena, where an Irish doctor, Barry O'Meara, showed them to his patient, Napoleon, who had been exiled to the remote island in the South Atlantic.

The death of Wright worried the former Emperor, who felt that he was being accused of his murder, and he spoke of it several times to O'Meara:

They accuse me of the death of a poor little post-captain[22] ... If Wright was put to death, it must have been by my authority. If he was put to death in prison, I ordered it. Fouché, even if so inclined, never would have dared to do it ... But the fact is, Wright killed himself and I do not believe that he was personally ill-treated in prison ... Sidney Smith has acted in a manner unworthy of himself ... in the epitaph which he wrote upon Wright ... Sidney Smith, above all men, knew from having been so long in the Temple that it is as impossible to have assassinated a prisoner without the knowledge of such a number of persons as would have made concealment impossible.[23]

Wright, Napoleon said, had killed himself to avoid implicating others in the plot to assassinate himself, and he added:

If I had known that Wright had been one of Sidney Smith's officers and that he had fought against me at Acre, I would have sent for and questioned him about the siege and released him. I recollect perfectly well seeing an officer wounded and carried off at Acre, whose bravery I admired at the time. I think that I should have released him, if I had found him to be that officer.[24]

Yet Smith was determined not to live in the past, although the war was over. Nobody seemed to think that there was any chance of Napoleon escaping, like a recurrent nightmare, from St Helena, as he had from Elba. However, that belief might possibly have been mistaken because there was a plot to rescue him, a plot that even eclipsed Smith's escape from the Temple in its ingenuity. Oddly, it threw echoes from his own past, although he did not, of course, know of it. Captain Tom Johnson, the smuggler and Channel pilot, who was to have guided the rocket and torpedo attack on Boulogne, had also been involved with Robert Fulton and had continued with the research and development of the submarine. He had, in fact, been commissioned by the Government to build a prototype in the upper reaches of the Thames but the patronage had ended with the war. In an effort to recover his costs, Johnson had been open to offers for his services and was said to have accepted one from Bonapartists plotting to rescue the exiled Emperor. He had been offered £40,000 with more to follow if the attempt succeeded, after the submarine had been towed to St Helena by a sailing ship and ferried the fugitive from shore. The craft was apparently brought down the Thames for the attempt in 1820 when, as the Chelsea waterman and artist Walter Greaves recorded:

My father said there was a mysterious boat that was intended to go under water ... for the purpose of getting Napoleon off the island of St. Helena. So on one dark night in November, she proceeded down the river (not being able to sink as the water was not deep enough). Anyhow, she managed to get below London Bridge. The officers boarding her, Capt. Johnson in the meantime threatening to shoot them. But they paid no attention to his threats, seized her and, taking her to Blackwall, destroyed her.[25]

Six months later, Napoleon was dead and a scheme worthy of Sidney Smith was forgotten.

The future could still hold promise, Smith believed. While campaigning for the liberation of European slaves, he sought active employment at sea, writing repeatedly to the Admiralty whenever he heard that a command, even as port admiral at Portsmouth, or Plymouth, was becoming vacant. Then he heard with mingled delight and dismay that his appeals for action over North African slavery were to be acted upon. An international naval force was to be assembled to present an ultimatum to each of the Barbary States and take action if necessary. However, the fleet was, he heard, to be commanded by Lord Exmouth, his former superior Admiral Pellew, who had been raised to the peerage in 1814. He himself, he knew, was the only officer suited to such delicate diplomacy, with the mailed fish in the most elegantly embroidered glove. Then news arrived that Exmouth's mission had already started successfully by persuading the beys of Tunis and Tripoli to release hundreds of European slaves and to undertake to enslave no more in return for financial compensation. At Algiers, the core of the problem, the admiral had quickly run into difficulties: trying to negotiate with the Dey himself, he had lost his temper and in the violent quarrel that ensued was lucky to escape with his life; so he had sailed away with his squadron to Gibraltar to await further orders. But Algerian piracy and enslavement had continued and, in May, an attempt to arrest coral fishermen, who held British fishing licences, had led to the massacre of 200 of them. The time for decisive action had come.

Now was the moment for Smith to propose himself for the next move against Algiers; indeed, there were many officers in the Royal Navy who agreed with him that he should be called upon; but he needed an influential ally to convince the British Government of this. He had always been more successful in influencing royalty than politicians and the closest to hand was, of course, the elderly King Louis XVIII of France, so he sought an audience and, in August 1816, this was finally granted.

Smith told the King that he had doubtless learned of the planned action against Algiers and continued, as the Duke of Wellington was to tell John Croker at the Admiralty:

> His business was to acquaint the King that the expedition must fail; that the force was insufficient and bad of its kind; but that, above all, the commander was ill-selected; that he knew [Admiral Pellew] well, having served with him, and that whatever qualities he might have as a mere sailor, he was the most unfit man in all other respects to command such an enterprise; that he himself was, from a variety of considerations, the only person who ought to have been selected; and finally, by this omission, an affair so vitally important to the civlised world must, to an absolute and demonstrative certainty, fail.
>
> The old King was sly and had a quiet kind of humour; he listened to Smith without interruption; and when he had concluded a very long speech, he told Sir Sidney that he was very much obliged to him for the information that he was so good as to give him … but, he added, 'I am sure it will give you additional pleasure, as it has done to me since I have heard your opinion, to learn that we have this morning heard, through Marseilles, that what you fear as impracticable has been accomplished with the most complete success!'[26]

It had been a battle that, had he been in command, would have crowned his career as Nelson's had been by Trafalgar. Exmouth had returned to Algiers in August with a fleet of 35 ships, including 6 sail of the line, 4 frigates and 5 Dutch frigates. He had taken them close inshore within point-blank range of the shore batteries – some 450 guns mounted behind stone embrasures of casemates – and when the Algerians fired on his ships, as he knew they would, he opened his broadsides. What followed was a contest 'between wooden walls and stone walls' and the horrific scenes were hidden in gunsmoke that hung in the windless air like 'twenty Vauxhalls at the end of fireworks on a cloudy night'.[27] The fighting lasted from early afternoon on 27th August until the early hours of the following morning. The shore batteries had been wrecked, the Algerian warships within the harbour burnt and the docks battered; but the British and Dutch had suffered heavily, too, losing 141 killed and 742 wounded. However, it had been a success because the Dey had complied with the ultimatum, more than 1,000 slaves were freed, ransom money was repaid and a promise made to enslave no more Christians. Exmouth reported triumphantly to the British Government that 'my rascally oponent, the Dey' had been tamed, 'his chastisement has humbled him to the Dust and he would receive me, if I chose it, on the Wharf on his knees.'[28]

Despite his disappointment, Smith wrote a generous letter to Exmouth, whom he had already enrolled as a Knight Liberator of the Slaves in Africa, praising the 'heroic devotion you manifested in the execution of the – to many – hopeless enterprise'.[29] He had read his despatch to the Anti-Piratical Society, of which he was also president, and they were to strike a commemorative medal in his honour. But it was galling that the balladeers praised others:

> Wilberforce's goodly tongue
> Afric from bondage clears
> And Exmouth has redress'd each wrong
> Of Christians at Algiers.[30]

It was widely recognized – though seldom in print – that Exmouth's success had sprung directly from Smith's campaign, so it was gratifying when the latter received a fulsome letter from the Duke of Gloucester giving him some credit for Exmouth's success: 'I have now to congratulate you upon the success of the attack upon Algiers.'[31]

Although the enslavement of Christians had been ended, piracy began again, not only by Algerians but along the length of the Barbary Coast. Also, the defences of Algiers were massively strengthened. After further warnings were ignored, the British sent another squadron to Algiers in 1824 – Sir Sidney Smith again being passed over – under Vice-Admiral Sir Harry Neale, Commander-in-Chief in the Mediterranean. He, too, anchored his ships off the city and the Dey agreed to all British demands except that the British flag should be allowed to fly over the British consul's residence and this, said the Dey, was against Algerian law. The admiral repeated his demand and another bloody battle was expected. But there was a sympathy among British naval officers for the Algerians that echoed the understanding that Smith might have shown. The first lieutenant of the *Revenge*, Lieutenant Robert James, wrote:

There was not the least hope whatever of terminating this unpleasant business. Although we had commenced hostilities, it had not the least appearance of a war, but we were provoking it, more and more everyday. The *Naiad* burnt a fine [Algerian] man-of-war brig at Bona. Yet, throughout the whole business there appeared a dignified forbearance on the part of the Algerians, while on ours, we carried it with such a high hand that seemed as we only expected a force that would blow them all to the devil. But the feeling that prevailed in the whole squadron was pity and respect for this nation. Pity, because war was declared against them for a very frivolous cause. That it could never justify the shedding of so much human blood as was very naturally expected and the expenditure of so much public money, that England could not well afford. Respect because the Algerians are a brave and fine race of men and, since Christian slavery has been done away with, they are greatly improved. They have the highest opinion of England and I think them the only true friends we have in the whole Mediterranean and we shall want them one day. Better keep them as friends than cause them to be our eternal enemies. In the case of politics, or in the case of war, we should find the Barbary States of the highest importance.

It might have been Sir Sidney Smith talking.

Another bombardment seemed inevitable and Lieutenant James described the long wait for action:

During a fortnight, the *Revenge* showed a most beautiful battery. Everything was clear fore and aft, not a cabin nor a screen to be seen. At dinner each of us had, instead of a table, a shot box with a cheese of wads [a roll of wadding rammed down gun barrels between powder and shot] on it and a clear napkin spread overall, and another shot box for a seat. It was fine fun to see the long faces at tearing up love letters; and the humorous puns serving out by all hands on the occasion. Others were making wills and leaving legacies. In fact, we all expected hard knocks and some to lose the number of their mess, so it was nothing but bitter waiting ... and the hopes of promotion seemed to predominate over every feeling.

Finally on 24th July:

the whole squadron bore up for the grand attack. It was light winds, therefore the steam boat took the *Revenge* in tow ... As soon as the squadron was anchored, the green standard of the Prophet was hoisted on the Dey's palace and a gun fired by way of a signal. In a moment after, the whole line of fortifications opened on us, both with shot and shell, about seven hundred pieces of very heavy cannon and mortars were blazing away like fury. But not a shot or a shell fell among the squadron, they all fell short ...[32]

Before the British could reply, a white flag was hoisted ashore, negotiations began again and the Dey complied with the British demands. Tranquillity did not last and finally, in 1830, European dominance was assured when the French occupied Algiers and absorbed it into a new French empire. Smith and his friends were sure that he could have achieved more at less cost at Algiers and again in 1827, when, in Navarino Bay on the coast of Greece, Vice-Admiral Sir Edward Codrington chose action rather than diplomacy in a dispute with Turkey over Greek independence, and destroyed the Turkish fleet at anchor.

Overcoming his disappointment, Smith immersed himself in the social life of Paris, to which he introduced his wife, daughters and his sons-in-law, Captain Arabin, who had now been joined by Baron de Delmar, a Prussian, and a Colonel St Clair. His brother Spencer, who had married Baroness Constance Herbert, the daughter of the Austrian ambassador to Constantinople, had settled in Normandy with their two sons.* Sir Sidney was now past fifty and still intensely active, enjoying boating parties on the Seine; once, noted one of his companions, 'when we got to the wharf and all the old watermen came, they were evidently his delight and equally it appeared that he was theirs; he desired me to go to the opposite tavern and give them a treat; bread and brandy was the fare and was distributed to a crowd in the street'.[33] He enjoyed the company of the young, particularly when female and he could take them to a fair outside the city, where he could, as it was said:

> deliver himself up to its humours and fun with all the abandon of a boy of fifteen. On such occasions he never forgot a fairing [fairground gift] for each of his fair young friends, reminding them, when presenting a gilt brooch, a plated thimble, a pincushion, ring, hair-comb, many other *vingt-cinq-sous* article (for his present seldom exceeded that sum) that he would not offer so trifling a proof of his regard were he not sensible of the value they so kindly set upon the donor.[34]

* He died at Caen in 1845.

He was compulsively generous for 'like a true sailor, he scarcely knew the value of money', and gave generously to charity, and was to be seen setting out 'with the seats of his carriage literally piled up with plates of well confectioned viands for the poor and unfortunate inhabitants of garrets or hovels, many of whom had seen better days and were too proud to beg'.[35]

He was as generous and careless with larger sums as with little fairground gifts and plates of food for the old. Demands arrived for the unpaid subscriptions to his London clubs – including the fashionable Thatched House Club in St James's – and he borrowed money from his son-in-law, who pompously lectured him about the need to live within his means. In answer to one such pleading, he wrote one of his long letters, complaining that:

> some *substantial reward* is due to a successful and indefatigable labourer in the service of the state; considering that *others, who have not* filled the situations I have of Minister Plenipotentiary and of *Commander-in-Chief* have been rewarded not only with greater pecuniary advantages but with rank and honorary distinctions beyond the *second* class of the Order of the Bath, which I have in common with lieutenant-colonels of the Army, who were subalterns at the time that the thanks of Parliament were conveyed to me in such flattering terms for a service of great *national* importance.[36]

There was substance in his complaints because most naval officers of his rank with less achievements to their credit would be spending their retirement in the comfort of country houses within a spread of parkland, or, perhaps, in one of the tall terraces of houses in the new London suburb between Oxford Street and the Regent's Park. So he took another title, assuming that, having been presented, in Cyprus, with the cross worn by King Richard I, he had been appointed Grand Prior of the Order of the Knights Templar in England. So he declared himself a Knight Templar, read the history of the Order and hung its white cloak with a red cross on the breast in his bedroom.

In Paris, he became a familiar, rather eccentric figure, often wearing his uniform, blazing with decorations. Once when attending a late party in the Rue du Faubourg St Honoré, he was leaving to walk home to the Rue d'Anjou when his host insisted on escorting him; there had been an outbreak of garrotting in the streets, gangs lassoing those walking home from upstairs windows and strangling them with the cord before robbing them. 'His host offered to accompany him ... thinking that the many glittering stars upon his breast might offer considerable temptation to the lawless people' and Smith accepted. But, on arriving at his door, he refused to let his host walk home alone and he 'seeing how utterly useless it would be to contend with the admiral, took his arm and walked back again ... probably the whole night would have been passed in going and returning' had not they agreed to part at the Boulevard de la Madeleine half way between their houses, Smith insisting that his host need not fear for his safety 'as what he lacked in strength he could supply in science'.[37]

He was known for his little witticisms; for example, telling one hostess who was showing him the 'dumb-waiter' serving-table in her dining-room, 'a dumb-waiter, madam, is a misnomer and would offer little advantage to us as servants are not in the habit of talking at their master's table; you mean a deaf-waiter ... or its *deafness* is the most useful trait in the construction of our wooden friend'.[38] Another of his jokes was, when politics were under discussion, to remark how odd it was that 'England was ruled by *two houses*, France by *two chambers*, Austria by a *cabinet* and Rome by a *seat*'.[39]

Finally, the British Government refunded more of the money he had spent on their behalf: in 1817, the £4,500 spent on helping the Calabrian partisans in 1806 and, in 1818, he was told that the rest should be covered by an additional annual pension of £1,000. Further comfort came with the news that, as he had been increasing his seniority in the *Navy List*, he had now been promoted – albeit, automatically – to full admiral and could therefore be seen to have reached a higher rank than Nelson.

His socially agreeable but professionally frustrating life in Paris was broken in 1826, when, on 16th May, his wife Caroline died and was buried in the cemetery of Père Lachaise close to the grave of Captain Wright. But, even then, Smith did not consider himself retired, although past sixty, and continued to write to British ministers asking for active employment either as a naval officer or as a diplomat. When the Duke of Wellington became Prime Minister in 1828 he wrote to him, unaware of his hostility, asking that his past services should be recognized and rewarded. The Duke replied at length, saying that it would have been for his predecessors in government to take such action:

> The question which naturally occurs is why did not Mr. Pitt, Lord Melville, Mr. Percival, Lord Liverpool or Mr. Canning, under whom these services were performed, and who had a knowledge of all the circumstances of the cases respectively, reward these services? The answer is they have rewarded them but inadequately ... I really have no means at my disposal of rewarding such services, I feel great objection to recur back to transactions, however honourable and meritorious, which occurred many years ago ...

He maintained that he had nothing to do with naval appointments and wrote bluntly that, as to Smith becoming a diplomat again, he could 'not do otherwise than decline to recommend to Lord Aberdeen that you be employed'.[40] As late as 1832, he asked to be appointed commander-in-chief in the Mediterranean and the First Lord of the Admiralty, Sir James Graham, replied that another officer had been chosen and that, 'I am quite aware of your unabated zeal for the service of His Majesty ... but at the present moment it is not necessary to demand your exertions.'[41]

However, further reward was, after all, forthcoming, and, on 4th July 1838, he received a letter from Lord Minto announcing that the young Queen Victoria, who had come to the throne the year before, had conferred on him the Grand Cross of the Order of the Bath, adding that: 'The Navy generally will, I am sure, rejoice to see one of its most illustrious chiefs thus invested with the highest honours of professional distinction.'[42] One of the first letters to reach him was from Lieutenant-General Sir Charles Doyle, who had fought in the Egyptian campaign of 1801, congratulating him on 'Tardy justice has at last overtaken thee! ... However, better late than never.'[43]

There was a new consolation and, ironically, it came from an unlikely quarter. On 5th May 1821, Napoleon Bonaparte died of stomach cancer at the age of fifty-one on the island of St Helena. A year later, his doctor, Barry O'Meara, published an account of their conversations in *Napoleon in Exile, or A Voice from St. Helena*. This had, of course, reached Paris and was a principal topic of conversation. There was only one reference to

Nelson – 'He spoke in very high terms of Lord Nelson' – and blamed his one 'stigma to his memory' in the suppression of the liberal revolt in Naples as due to the influence of Queen Maria Carolina – 'that wicked woman'[44] – and Lady Hamilton. But he spoke of Sidney Smith and John Wright on a number of occasions; there were five references in the index to Smith, six to Wright and one to Nelson.

The mystery of Captain Wright's death haunted Napoleon. When a British naval surgeon, William Warden, told him, 'There are many in England who imagine your jealousy and hatred of Sir Sidney Smith influenced your conduct towards Captain Wright', he 'smiled with astonishment', and replied, 'Ridiculous! Nonsense!'[45]

He had admitted that Smith had thwarted him in the Levant:

the chief case of the failure there was that he took all my battering train, which was on board of several small vessels. Had it not been for that, I would have taken Acre in spite of him … He dispersed proclamations among my troops, which certainly shook some of them, and I, in consequence, published an order stating that he was *mad* …

Speaking of the campaign in Egypt, he continued, 'Sidney Smith is a brave officer. He displayed considerable ability in the treaty for the evacuation of Egypt by the French … He is active, intelligent, intriguing and indefatigable; but I believe he is *mezzo passo* [half mad].[46] Returning to the campaign in Egypt, he said:

Sidney Smith displayed great honour in informing Kléber of the refusal of Lord Keith to consent to the Convention of El Arish. Had he delayed it for twenty-four hours longer, Kléber would have evacuated the forts to the Turks and would have been obliged to surrender to the English. He treated the French prisoners of war very well … Notwithstanding that Sidney Smith has ill-treated me, I should still have a pleasure in seeing him. I should like to receive *ce gaillard là*. He has certain good qualities and, as an old enemy, I should like to see him.[47]

Other memoirs of St Helena by the exiled Emperor's staff and visitors were published and the pattern was repeated. General Gourgaud wrote that Napoleon had told him, 'I should have done better to remain in Egypt; by now, I would have been Emperor of all the East.'[48] He had told the Comte de Las Cases,

'If St. Jean d'Acre had yielded to the French, a great revolution would have taken place in the East. I would have founded an empire there and the destinies of France would have been left to assume other forms',[49] and he added, 'I am sorry I spoke ill of Smith. They tell me he is a good fellow. His government does not appreciate his services in Egypt and Syria.'[50] In one reference to his return from Egypt and France, Napoleon had said, 'The fury of the English was turned against Sir Sidney Smith and Nelson, who commanded the British naval force in the Mediterranean.'[51] It would not have been lost on Sir Sidney that his name had been mentioned first. Finally, there was the ultimate tribute, 'That man made me miss my destiny.'[52] Nelson might be the martyred hero of his country but, it seemed, Smith had made the deeper imprint on the mind of their enemy.

Once, on St Helena, Napoleon was in a conversation with the French-speaking Captain Beatty of the Royal Marines, who, he was then told, had fought at Acre. Thereupon, according to an eyewitness, he:

> with great good humour seizing the Captain by the ear, exclaiming, 'Ah, you rogue! You were there?' He then asked what had become of Sir Sidney Smith and, when he was told that the gallant Knight ... had submitted a proposal to the Congress of Vienna to destroy the Corsairs on the Coast of Barbary, an instant reply was given, that it was, as it had long been, most disgraceful of the European powers to permit the existence of such a nest of miscreants.[53]

As a widower in his sixties and seventies, Smith became an increasingly eccentric but lovable Parisian character. Now that the campaign for the abolition of slavery was largely won, he concentrated on the misty romanticism of the Knights Templars, worrying that if he became their 'Regent' – presumably a self-appointment in an extinct order of chivalry – he might offend Queen Victoria. Early in May 1840, the chaplain at the British Embassy, Bishop Michael Luscombe of the Scottish Episcopal Church, visited Smith at his house and found that he had suffered a stroke. He immediately called Captain Arabin, who recorded:

> finding him in a state not to be left with strangers, I caused him to be removed to my house [now 9 Rue Aguesseau, another street off the Rue St. Honoré]. In fact, he had received a stroke of

apoplexy, which was followed by paralysis; and the second or third day after he had been with us, he became totally paralysed, and, on the 26th of May he departed this life in the seventy-sixth year of his age.[54]

Sir Sidney's funeral in his former enemy's capital was magnificent. His nephew, Captain William Smith, had made the arrangements because, a year after Lady Smith's death, he had visited his uncle, who:

asked me to take a drive with him, without having said a word about his recent loss. We stopped at the gate of Père Lachaise, which we entered on foot, and walked among the tombs. At length he stopped to contemplate a respectable-looking tomb, before which he stood silent. I observed the tears rolling down his cheeks. I began to suspect the cause and perceived, by glancing over the inscription, that he had brought me to see my aunt's tomb. In the course of our return he said, 'Perhaps it will become your duty to bury me; and, if so, I trust you will bury me in the same grave with my departed wife. I have taken care to arrange it for two and have bought the ground in perpetuity.[55]

Now he fulfilled that duty and recorded, 'the car, ornamented with black plumes and silver, displayed the coffin, black and gilt, partially concealed by the cocked-hat, sword and British Union Jack'.[56] The pallbearers included Admiral Sir Charles Rowley, who had once fought under Smith's command in the Mediterranean, and the French Admiral Bergeret, who had been offered – but refused – in exchange for the captive Captain Smith in the Temple. The eight mourning coaches by nearly a hundred private carriages joined the procession to the cemetery of Père Lachaise, followed by, wrote Captain Smith, 'more than one hundred respectable tradesmen of the quarter wherein he had dwelt ... Several old servants came many leagues from the country, one of whom was observed to kneel by the coffin, to utter a prayer and then take a sorrowing departure.'[57] Beside the grave of his wife, where he was to be buried, and close to that of John Wright, addresses were delivered. One was on behalf of the Knights Templars, to whom he had left the cross of King Richard Lionheart, which the Greek bishop had given in Cyprus and which he had worn next to his heart ever since.

News of his death was published in *The Times* on 29th May

and all trace of past controversy was forgotten. The obituarist described him as 'gallant and illustrious', 'beloved and respected by all', 'chivalrous and lofty' and 'deeply impressed with Christian principles'; one quality that old friends would wryly recognize was 'his unbounded fund of anecdote'. The notice concluded with what proved to be a vain hope that 'we have no doubt a grateful nation will raise a monument, where repose the mortal remains of the illustrious dead, in one of the great receptacles of its heroes – St. Paul's or Westminster Abbey'.

The monument set up over the grave was handsome and ornamented with a marble relief of Sir Sidney in profile after a portrait by Jacques-Louis David. Epitaphs in verse commemorated them both, his running:

> Here rests the hero, who undaunted stood
> When Acre's street were red with Turkish blood;
> In warlike France, where great Napoleon rose,
> The man who check's his conquests finds repose.
> Britain, who claims his triumphs as her own
> has raised for him her monumental stone;
> This tomb, which marks his grave, is now supplied
> By friends with whom he lived, midst whom he died;
> A tribute to his memory – Here beneath
> Lies the bold heart of England's Sidney Smith.

When Sir Sidney died, a memorial to Lord Nelson, once his commanding officer and latterly his friend, was being erected in the centre of London. Already the great fluted column that would raise his statue 185 feet above the capital was visible, dominating the view up Whitehall from Westminster. But Smith's own step-daughters and their families showed little interest in commemorating him by preserving the medals, orders and presentation swords that had meant so much to him, and these were included, with his other belongings, for sale by public auction in Paris. An Englishman who was present later said that among these were:

> several swords, but one in particular was singled out and declared by the auctioneer as being the sword Sir Sidney wore at the siege of Acre. Thus announced, a strong sensation was produced in the company and a very general competition took place for this instrument of death or glory. It was observed in the

eagerness of bidding, the French party generally went beyond the English, and among the rest an old French general was remarked to watch each bidder with intense anxiety and to head every bidding, until at length, finding that the price was getting beyond his means, he thus pathetically appealed to the assembly: 'Gentlemen, long had I the honour of Sir Sidney's friendship; as he was a lion in war, so was he a lamb in peace. I have fought against him and, I am not ashamed to own, that the very sword now put up to public sale, has been the instrument that conquered me; I am but a poor man but the hero's sword shall be mine if it cost me the last *franc* I have in the world.' The appeal and the noble sentiment that accompanied it, produced general applause; and, it is almost needless to say, was irresistible and that the sword was immediately knocked down without further contest to the gallant French officer.[58]

Epilogue

SIDNEY SMITH AND Horatio Nelson shared the credit for stopping and reversing Napoleon Bonaparte's ambition to follow the march of Alexander the Great. But for those two men, he might well have founded a French empire throughout the Middle East on the ruins of the Ottoman Empire, marched on India and, perhaps, established French dominance of southern Asia and the Far East.

Nelson, of course, fought the climactic sea battle off Cape Trafalgar, which finally removed the danger of invasion from the British Isles. Smith achieved no such triumph at sea, although, if his advice had been heeded, the course of the war in the Mediterranean and Middle East might have run more swiftly and successfully for the British with many thousands of lives and much money saved. So Nelson became the national hero with towns and mountains and children named after him; the toast of Trafalgar Night dinners to this day. Smith was almost forgotten, his only visible memorial, a marble statue of him, sword in hand, on the walls of Acre, outside the National Maritime Museum at Greenwich.

Nelson was killed in the grand finale of the great age of sail and British maritime power. Smith, however, lived on into the modern world. He was born, in 1764, in the heyday of the eighteenth century; in the lifetimes of Dr Johnson, Clive of India, Gibbon, Gainsborough and Mozart. He died a Victorian and, had he lived a few more years, he would doubtless have been photographed as a Parisian celebrity. A measure of his lifespan is that, when he was born, Australia was virtually unknown; it was seen to be an unexplored continent by Captain Cook in the 1770s, and Smith would have known men who sailed with him. In November 1786, when, as a young captain, he was taking his brother Spencer to sea and they were at Deptford on the Thames, the latter noted in his diary, 'See fitting H.M. Ships *Sirius* and *Supply* destined to convoy a fleet of transports with convicts to colonise the coast of New South Wales under the Government of Capt. Arthur Phillip, the Commodore, the *Supply*, a little brig, commanded by Lieut. H.L. Ball, apparently much too small and uncomfortable for such a voyage.' In the following April, he wrote at Spithead off Portsmouth, 'At the Motherbank, the fleet bound to New Holland consisting of 11 sail'[1]: this was, of course, 'The First Fleet'. When Sidney Smith died in 1840, the Australian coast had been charted, the coastal hinterland mapped and the cities of Sydney, Melbourne, Brisbane, Adelaide and Perth founded. The outlines, at least, of the world could be seen as complete.

As Nelson's reputation was fostered and his commemoration continued, Smith was either overlooked, or belittled. Historians took their cues from his contemporary critics, among them: J.W. Fortescue, who described him as 'a brilliant imposter, who chose his time cunningly for approaching Ministers and came to them stuffed with facts, figures and pledges, one and all of them fallacious'.[2] Much later, C. Northcote Parkinson wrote that Smith had 'aroused the hatred of all right-minded naval officers'.[3] Piers Mackesy, who made a study of the Mediterranean campaigns, wrote with some reason, that 'the defence of Acre had left him with ... an unbridled thirst for glory'.[4]

Yet, one of Smith's most perceptive but hostile contemporary critics had been Nelson – and he had changed his mind. Both men were driven by the thirst for personal and national glory. Both were intensely patriotic with an inherent reverence for royalty at home and abroad. Both were intelligent, imaginative, brave and natural leaders of men. Nelson had instinctive tactical and strategic judgement but Smith was more of a diplomat and was a brilliant linguist, which Nelson was not. Perhaps a principal difference between the two was in their backgrounds – Nelson from a parson's family; Smith from a rake's – the effect of each can only be a matter for conjecture. Both were generous in their dealings with other men but while Nelson was usually tactful, Smith's enthusiasms could sweep him over the heads of those whom he should have consulted, or informed, to deal directly with the sovereigns, or statesmen whom he could sometimes dazzle. Both were eloquent but, whereas Nelson could edit words into a memorable essence, Smith gave vent to a hot stream of opinion, complaint, flattery, anecdote and ideas, which could overwhelm and, finally, bore those to whom it was addressed.

Both were Englishmen but Sidney Smith did not appear so; he was excitable and boastful in the Mediterranean manner, which matched his looks. In the Turkish robes he liked to wear – like Lawrence of Arabia – he could, indeed, have passed for a fine-boned Arab; he could also appear French with his perfect command of the language, his swagger and his fashionably high collars. His originality and fertility of imagination were not matched by a willingness to reconsider and he was too sophisticated for the run of his naval contemporaries. He lived at a time when the mould of the gentleman, as calm as he was intrepid and wise as he was modest, was being cast by such as the Duke of Wellington and Sir John Moore.

At the end of the twentieth century, the name of Sidney Smith is usually confused with that of his contemporary, Sydney Smith, the witty cleric. His monument still stands in the cemetery of Père Lachaise in Paris but the relief portrait of him in marble has been stolen. Captain John Wright, who was said to lie nearby, is still elusive – the monument Smith set up for him is nowhere to be seen and there is no record of his burial in the cemetery's archives – but that, perhaps, is as it should be.

Occasionally, Smith's name and face come into view: perhaps in a tattered engraving in an auctioneer's folio, his dash springing from the foxed paper; or, on a collector's tray of commemorative medallions, the fine, hawkish profile distinct on the tarnished silver; on the back, is the alternative to the epithet Napoleon gave him, 'mezzo passo' (half mad), the one in fact that he gave himself, but with which none would have disagreed: 'Coeur de Lion'.

Reference Notes

PROLOGUE

1. Elgood, P.G. *Bonaparte's Adventure in Egypt*, p.47.
2. Herold, Christopher. *Bonaparte in Egypt*, p.20.
3. Yorke, H.R. *Paris et le France Sous le Consulat.*
4. Goethe, J.W. *Italian Journey.*
5. Guerrini, Domenico. *La Spedizione Francese in Egitto*, p.52
6. Howard, J.E. (ed.) *Letters and Documents of Napoleon*, Vol. 1., p.201. Bonaparte to Talleyrand, 13.9. 1797.
7. Elgood, p.49.
8. Chair, Somerset de, (ed.) *Napoleon on Napoleon*, p.107.
9. Elgood, p.48.
10. *Correspondence de Napoléon le*, Vol. XXIX, p.429.
11. *Correspondence* Vol. III, p.235.
12 Elgood, p.52.
13. Nicholas, Sir Harris (ed.). *The Dispatches and Letters of Lord Nelson* 11, p.435. Nelson to Jervis, 16.8.97.

CHAPTER ONE

1. Howard, E.G.G. *Memoirs of Admiral Sir Sidney Smith*, p.14.
2. Ibid., p.13.
3. Ibid., pp.14–15.
4. Rodney
5. Barrow, John. *Memoirs of Admiral Sir Sidney Smith*, Vol. 1, p.8.
6. Ibid., Vol. 1, pp.10–11.
7. Smith, John Spencer. *Manuscript Diary*, p.13. 14th May 1781.
8. Ibid., p.24. 29th January 1782.
9. Ibid., p.27. 18th May 1782.
10. Ibid., p.28. 17th June 1782.
11. John Munday Archive.
12. Will of Pinkney Wilkinson.
13. Barrow, Vol. 1, p.17.

14. Ibid., Vol. 1, pp.21–23. Sidney Smith to Charles Smith, Caen, June, 1785.
15. Ibid., Vol. 1, pp.29–30.
16. Smith, John Spencer. *Diary*, p.159–67. 4th November 1787.
17. Barrow, Vol. 1, p.32–4. Smith to Admiralty, Tuy, 30th April 1788.
18. Howard, Vol. 1, p.22.
19. Barrow, Vol. 1, p.38. King Gustavus III to Smith, Haga, 17th January 1790.
20. Ibid., Vol. 1, p.40. Duke of Sodermanland to Smith, 18th January 1790.
21. Ibid., Vol. 1, p.41.
22. Ibid., Vol. 1, p.44. Smith to Liston, Karlskrona, 9th May 1790.
23. Ibid. , Vol. 1, p.48. Ibid., Svenskasund, 21st May 1790.
24. Russell, Lord of Liverpool. *Knight of the Sword*, p.28.
25. Barrow, Vol. 1, p.64. Smith to Liston, Viborg, 7th June 1790.
26. Ibid., Vol. 1, p.66. Gustavus to Smith, 9th June 1790.
27. Ibid., Vol. 1, p.64. Smith to Liston, 7th June 1790.
28. Ibid., Vol. 1, pp.68–9.
29. Ibid., Vol. 1, p.53.
30. Ibid., Vol. 1, p.73.
31. Ibid., Vol. 1, p.71.
32. Ibid., Vol. 1, p.99.
33. Ibid., Vol. 1, p.101.

CHAPTER TWO

1. Howard, p.41.
2. Nicolas, Sir Nicholas Harris. *The Dispatches and Letters of Lord Viscount Nelson*, Vol. 1, p.320.
3. Chair, de, (ed.), p.75.
4. Barrow, Vol. 1, p.155.
5. Ibid., p.127.
6. Nicolas, Vol. 1, p.338. Nelson to Locker, Tunis, 1st December 1793.
7. Russell, p.37.
8. Barrow, Vol. 1, p.156. Smith to Sir William Hamilton, H.M.S. *Victory*, Hyeres Bay, 24th December 1793.
9. Ibid., Vol. 1, p.157. Hood to Smith, 18th December 1793.
10. Ibid., Vol. 1, pp.129–134.
11. Chair, de., p.80.
12. Barrow, Vol 1, pp.134–5.
13. Ibid., Vol 1, p.155.
14. Nicolas, Vol. 1, p.342. Nelson to William Nelson, Leghorn, 27th December 1793.
15. Howard, Vol. 1, p.68.
16. Ibid., Vol. 1, p.69.
17. Barrow, Vol. 1, pp.155–6.
18. Ibid., Vol. 1, p.149. Hood to Admiralty, 20th December 1793.
19. Russell, p.39.
20. Nicolas, Vol. 2, p.46. Nelson to the Rev. Dixon Hoste, H.M.S. *Agamemnon*, 22nd June, 1795.

21. Chair, de., pp.81–2.
22. Barrow, Vol. 1, p.158.
23. James, William. *The Naval History of Great Britain*, (1873), Vol. 1, p.89.
24. Howard, Vol. 1, p.100.
25. *Windham Papers*, Vol. 1, pp.221–2. Earl Spencer to William Windham, 12th August, 1794.
26. Ibid., Vol. 1, pp.223–7. Smith to Windham, H.M.S. *Diamond*, at Plymouth, 13th August 1794.
27. Barrow, Vol. 1, p.165.
28. Ibid., Vol. 1, pp.166–8. Smith to Admiralty, H.M.S. *Diamond*, at sea, 4th January.
29. Ibid., Vol. 1, pp.163–4. Smith to Admiralty, H.M.S. *Diamond*, at sea, 4th September, 1795.
30. Ibid., Vol. 1, p.173. Smith to Admiralty, H.M.S. *Diamond*, off St Marcou, 5th July 1795.
31. Wetton, Thomas. Manuscript journal, H.M.S. *Robust*, 26th June 1795.
32. Barrow, Vol. 1, p.186.
33. Ibid., Vol. 1, pp.195–6. Smith to his father, Paris, 30th April 1796.

CHAPTER THREE

1. Barrow, Vol. 1, p.191.
2. Ibid., Vol. 1, p.190.
3. Russell, pp.59–60.
4. Barrow, Vol. 1, pp.194–5.
5. Ibid., Vol. 1, pp.195–6.
6. Shankland, Peter. *Beware of Heroes*, p.13.
7. Russell, p.56.
8. *The Windham Papers*, Vol. 2, p.213. (BM Add MSS. 37852 fo.61).
9. Ibid., Vol. 2, p.26. (BM Add MSS. 37852 fo.66).
10. Ibid., Vol. 2, pp.30–1. (BM Add MSS. 37852 fo.68.)
11. Shankland, p.15.
12. Howard, Vol. 1, pp.114–5.
13. Ibid., Vol. 1, p.116.
14. Ibid., Vol. 1, p.122.
15. Ibid., Vol. 1, pp.123–4.
16. Ibid., Vol. 1, pp.125–6.
17. Shankland, p.15.
18. Ibid., p.15.
19. Barrow, Vol. 1, pp.216–7.
20. Shankland, p.19.
21. Elgood, p.52.
22. Shankland, p.20.
23. Ibid., pp.20–1.
24. Ibid., p.20.
25. Ibid., pp.20–1. (Barrow, Vol. 1, p.220.)
26. Shankland, p.21.

27. Barrow, Vol. 1, p.223.
28. Ibid., Vol. 1, p.224.
29. Shankland, p.23.
30. Barrow, Vol. 1, p.209.
31. Ibid., Vol. 1, pp.207–8.

CHAPTER FOUR

1. Russell, p.64.
2. Nicolas, Vol. 2, p.346.
3. Naish, George (ed.). *Nelson's Letters to His Wife*, 1958, p.381.
4. Richard, W.H. (ed.). *Spencer Papers*, Vol. 2, p.437.
5. Warner, Oliver. *A Portrait of Lord Nelson*, p.140.
6. Nicolas, Vol. 3, p.23. Nelson to Howe, Palermo, 8th January 1799.
7. The Dropmore Papers, Vol. 4, p.193.
8. Belliard, A.D. *Histoire Scientifique et Militaire de l'Expédition Francais en Egypte*, Vol. 3, pp.43–4.
9. Howard, Vol. 1, p.137.
10. Naish, p.399. Nelson to Lady Nelson, 11th August 1798.
11. Russell, p.64.
12. Shankland, p.45.
13. Russell, p.65.
14. Ibid., pp.65–6.
15. Howard, Vol. 1, p.145.
16. Shankland, pp.152–3.
17. Ibid., p.47.
18. Ibid., p.48.
19. Pocock, Tom, *Horatio Nelson*, p.181.
20. Nicolas, Vol. 3, p.215. Nelson to St Vincent, Palermo, 31st December 1798.
21. Ibid., Vol. 3, pp.216–7. Nelson to Smith, Palermo, 31st December 1798.
22. Ibid., Vol. 3, pp.217–8. Nelson to Spencer, Palmero, 1st January 1798.
23. Barrow, Vol. 1, p.238. St. Vincent to Nelson, 28th April 1799.
24. Ibid., p.240.
25. Ibid., p.240.
26. Ibid., p.241.
27. Ibid., p.241.
28. Shankland, p.53.
29. Barrow, Vol. 1, p.263.
30. *Correspondence*, Vol. 29, p.450.
31. Shankland, p.56.
32. Ibid., pp.56–7.
33. *Correspondence*, Vol. 30, p.27.
34. Bourrienne, L.-A., *Mémoires*, Chapt. 15.
35. Howard, J.E. *Letters and Documents of Napoleon*, Vol. 1, p.285. Bonaparte to Berthier, Jaffa, 9th March 1799.
36. Barrow, Vol. 1, pp.262–3.
37. Herold, p.277.

38. La Jonquiere, C. de. *L'Expédition en Egypte*, Vol. 4, pp.271–2.
39. Shankland, p.64.
40. Howard (ed.). Vol. 1, p.286.
41. *Correspondence de Napoléon*, Vol. 5, p.353. Napoleon to Marmont, 9th March 1799.
42. Barrow, Vol. 1, p.262.

CHAPTER FIVE

1. Howard, Vol. 1, p.163.
2. Barrow, Vol. 1, pp.266–9.
3. La Jonquiere, Vol. 4, p.336.
4. Shankland, p.71.
5. La Jonquiere, Vol. 4, p.343.
6. *Naval Chronicle* (1803, Vol. 10, pp.186–8 and Howard, Vol. 1, pp.200–1.
7. Berthier, Gen. A. *The French Expedition into Syria, 1799*, p.478.
8. Howard, Vol. 1, p.157.
9. La Jonquiere, Vol. 4, p.453.
10. Shankland, p.76.
11. Parsons, G.S. *Nelsonian Reminiscences*, p.220.
12. Barrow, Vol. 1, p.282.
13. Ibid., pp.284–91.
14. Shankland, p.82.
15. Herold, p.300.
16. Barrow, Vol. 1, p.291.
17. Ibid., p.298.
18. Ibid., p.302.
19. Ibid., pp.306–7.
20. Ibid., pp.292–4.
21. Shankland, p.85.
22. Barrow, Vol. 1, pp.307–14. Smith to Nelson, *Tigre*, off Jaffa, 30th May 1799.
23. Nicolas, Vol. 3, p.281. Nelson to St Vincent, Palermo, 6th March 1799.
24. Ibid., p.344., 30th April 1799.
25. Ibid., p.373. Nelson to Spencer Smith, Palermo, 5th May 1799.
26. Shankland, p.95.
27. Nicolas, Vol. 3, pp.416–8. Nelson to Smith, Palermo, 20th August 1799.
28. Barrow, Vol. 2, p.470.
29. Nicolas, Vol. 3, pp.455–6. Ibid., Palermo, 20th August 1799.
30. Barrow, Vol. 1, p.321.
31. Ibid., pp.322–3.
32. Ibid., p.324.
33. Ibid., p.336.
34. *The Naval Magazine*, August 1800, p.415.
35. Thiers, L.A. L'Expedition de Bonaparte en Egypte, p.59.

CHAPTER SIX

1. *Correspondence*, Vol. 5, pp.429–430.
2. Ibid., p.428.
3. Bourrienne, Vol. 2, Chapt. 16.
4. Barrow, Vol. 1, pp.311–2.
5. Parsons, pp.239–240.
6. Shankland, p.94.
7. La Jonquiere, Vol. 4, p.625.
8. Ibid., Vol. 4, pp.625–6.
9. Barrow, Vol. 1, p.260.
10. Howard, J.E. (ed.). *Letters and Documents of Napoleon*, Vol. 1, p.304.
11. Shankland, pp.100–1.
12. Dane, Clemence. *The Nelson Touch*, p.109. Nelson to Spencer, *Foudroyant*, 19th July 1799.
13. *Correspondence*, Vol. 5, p.577.
14. Rousseau, Francois. *Kléber en Egypte depuis le Départ de Bonaparte*, p.80.
15. Ibid., p.104.
16. Barrow, Vol. 1, pp.379–80.
17. Shankland, p.107.
18. Ibid., p.108.
19. Ibid., p.110.
20. Barrow, Vol. 1, p.381.
21. Shankland, pp.109–10.
22. Ibid., p.110.
23. *The Naval Chronicle*, Vol. 4, (1801), p.336.
24. Shankland, p.111.
25. Rousseau, pp.238–9.
26. Barrow, Vol. 1, pp.384–9.
27. Ibid., Vol. 2, p.22.
28. Ibid., p.51.
29. Shankland, p.116.
30. Ibid., pp.116–7.
31. Russell, p.90.
32. Turc, Nicolas, *Chronique d'Egypte, 1798–1804*, 1950, p.97.
33. Herold, p.356.
34. Shankland, p.121.
35. Russell, p.92.
36. Barrow, Vol. 2, pp.36–7.
37. Shankland, p.126.
38. Bunbury, Sir Henry. *Narratives of Some Passages of the Great War with France, 1799–1810*, p.26.
39. Russell, p.94.
40. Shankland, p.131.
41. Hutchinson, Christopher. MS journal, Donoughmore.
42. Shankland, p.131.
43. Ibid., p.137.
44. Brodie, Col. George. MS journal, Brodie Castle.

45. Mackesy, p.71.
46. Wilson, Lt Col. Sir Robert. *History of the British Expedition to Egypt*, Vol. 1, p.75.
47. Ibid., p.52.
48. MacDonald, Sir John. *Blackwood's Magazine*, December 1915, p.845.
49. Wilson, Vol. 1, p.75.
50. Ibid., p.77.
51. Shankland, p.136.
52. Ibid., p.136.
53. Ibid., p.143.
54. Wilson, Vol. 1, pp.102–3.

CHAPTER SEVEN

1. Parsons, p.209.
2. Barrow, Vol. 1, p.441.
3. Parsons, pp.211–7.
4. Ibid., p.221.
5. Ibid., p.221.
6. Ibid., pp.216–225.
7. Russell, p.99.
8. *The Times*, 10th November 1801.
9. Russell, p.100.
10. Ibid., p.101.
11. Ibid., p.102.
12. Pocock, Tom. *Horatio Nelson*, p.267.
13. Ibid.
14. Nicolas, Vol. 4, p.520. Nelson to Captain Sutton, Merton, 31st October 1801.
15. Inscription on drawing of Nelson, Christie's Boardroom, London.
16. *Naval Chronicle*, Vol. 7, pp.516–8.
17. Fairbairn, J. *An Inquiry, or The Delicate Investigation*, p.76.
18. Ibid., p.76.
19. Ibid., pp.49–91.
20. Ibid.
21. Bunbury, p.232. Mino MSS. 11054.
22. Fairbairn, p.106.
23. Fraser, Flora. *The Unruly Queen*, p.138.
24. Fairbairn, App. B, pp.86–9.
25. Ibid., pp.86–7.
26. *The Parliamentary History of England*, Vol. 36, column 1040.
27. Ibid.
28. Barrow, Vol. 2, p.127.
20. Ibid., p.134.
30. Wheeler, H.F.B. and A.M. Broadley, *Napoleon and the Invasion of England*, Vol. 2, p.117.
31. *Naval Chronicle*, Vol. 34, p.441.

32. Ibid., p.443.
33. Ibid., pp.444–5.
34. Ibid., p.445.
35. Ibid., p.445.
36. Ibid., p.446.
37. Ibid., p.448.
38. Ibid., p.449.
39. Barrow, Vol. 2, pp.152–3.
40. Popham, p.120.
41. Ibid., p.112.
42. Robert Fulton MSS, New York Public Library.
43. Ibid.
44. Bourrienne, Vol. 2, p.43.
45. Desbriere, Edouard. *Projets et Tentatives de Débarquement aux Iles Britanniques*, Vol. 3, p.312.
46. Hutcheon, Wallace, S., Jr. *Robert Fulton*, p.84.
47. Castlereagh, Vol. 5, p.120.
48. *American State Papers: Naval Affairs*, Vol. 1, p.213.
49. Castlereagh, Vol. 5, p.113. Keith to Barham, 3rd October 1805.
50. Ibid., Vol. 2, pp.130–1.
51. Ibid., Vol. 5, p.115. Barham to Castlereagh, 5th October 1805.
52. Shankland, p.170.
53. *The Windham Papers*, Vol. 2, p.291.
54. Castlereagh, Vol. 5, p.100.
55. Ibid., pp.101–2.
56. Ibid., p.109, Castlereagh to Smith, October 1805.
57. Ibid., p.97.
58. Ibid., p.111.
59. Ibid., pp.124–5.
60. Ibid., p.126.
61. Shankland, p.168.
62. *Naval Chronicle*, Vol. 34, p.450.
63. O'Meara, Barry. *Napoleon in Exile*, Vol. 2, p.182.

CHAPTER EIGHT

1. Windham, Vol. 2, pp.290–4.
2. Pocock, Tom. *Remember Nelson*, p.118. Hoste Papers, National Maritime Museum microfilm.
3. Collingwood, G.L. Newnham (ed.). *Correspondence and Memoirs of Lord Collingwood*, pp.205–6. Collingwood to Grey, *Queen*, off Cadiz, 1st April 1806.
4. Shankland, pp.172–3.
5. Knowles, Sir Lees. *The British in Capri*, 1806–8, p.60.
6. Cerio, Edwin. *The Masque of Capri*, p.49.
7. Oman, Carola. *Sir John Moore*, p.393.
8. Bunbury Papers, BL Add. MSS. 37053.
9. Boothby, Charles. *Under England's Flag*, pp.65–6.

10. Shankland, p.176.
11. Bunbury, pp.244–5.
12. Ibid., pp.248–9.
13. Ibid., p.250.
14. Ibid., p.250.
15. Shankland, p.178.
16. Bunbury, p.259.
17. Ibid., pp.267–8.
18. Maurice, Major-Gen. Sir J.F. (ed.). *The Diary of Sir John Moore* (2 vols.), p.126.
19. Ibid., Vol. 2, p.131.
20. Ibid., p.135.
21. Ibid., p.138.
22. Nicolas, Vol. 3, p.138. Nelson to St Vincent, Naples, 30th September 1798.
23. Bunbury, pp.272–3.
24. Maurice, *Moore*, Vol. 2, p.132.
25. Collingwood, pp.241–2. Collingwood to Mrs. Collingwood, *Queen*, off Cadiz, 13th September 1806.
26. Ibid., pp.246–7. Collingwood to Smith, *Queen*, off Cadiz, 7th October 1806.
27. Shankland, p.180.
28. Boothby, pp.35–67.
29. Public Record Office – War Office 1/305, p.551.
30. Maurice, *Moore*, Vol. 2, p.146.
31. Windham, Vol. 2, pp.315–6. Grenville to Windham, 9th September 1806.
32. Maurice, Moore, Vol. 2, p.139.
33. Ibid., Vol. 2, p.148.
34. Shankland, p.185.
35. James, William. *The Naval History of Great Britain* (1878 ed.), Vol. 4, p.230.
36. Barrow, Vol. 2, p.219.
37. *Naval Chronicle*, Vol. 26, pp.367–8.
38. James, Vol. 4, p.223.
39. Ibid., p.224.
40. Ibid., p.226.
41. Barrow, Vol. 2, pp.238–9.
42. Ibid., p.241.
43. Ibid., p.242.
44. Pocock, Tom. *Remember Nelson*, p.132. Hoste Papers.
45. Barrow, Vol.2, p.229.
46. Ibid., p.244.
47. Ibid., pp.471–2.
48. Ibid., p.459.
49. Shankland, pp.167–8.
50. Maurice, *Moore*, Vol. 2, p.200.
51. Russell, p.171.
52. Ibid., pp.172–3.
53. Ibid., p.181.
54. Barrow, Vol. 2, pp.317–8.
55. Ibid., p.351.

56. *Naval Chronicle*, Vol. 24, p.29.
57. Howard, Vol. 2, pp.168–9.
58. Ibid., Vol. 11, p.390.
59. *Naval Chronicle*, Vol. 26, p.42.
60. Ibid., p.331.
61. Croker, J.W. *The Croker Papers*, Vol. 1, p.350.

CHAPTER NINE

1. Croker, Vol. 1, p.349.
2. Barrow, Vol. 2, p.352.
3. Ibid., Vol. 2, p.355.
4. Howard, Vol. 2, p.185.
5. Barrow, Vol. 2, p.357.
6. Ibid., Vol. 2, p.358.
7. Russell, p.190.
8. Barrow, Vol. 2, pp.360–4.
9. Shankland, p.194.
10. Parkinson, C. Northcote. *Edward Pellew*, p.406.
11. Neuville, Hyde de. *Mémoires*.
12. Ibid.
13. Barrow, Vol. 2, p.273.
14. Shankland, p.196.
15. Barrow, pp.394–5.
16. Ibid., p.390.
17. Ibid., p.406.
18. Ibid., pp.283–4.
19. Croker, Vol. 1, pp.348–9.
20. Hoard, Vol. 2, p.301.
21. *Naval Chronicle*, Vol. 34, p.121.
22. Warden, William. *Letters Written in H.M.S. Northumberland and St. Helena*, p.141.
23. O'Meara. *Napoleon in Exile, or A Voice from St. Helena*, Vol. 2, p.182.
24. Ibid., pp.217–8.
25. Pocock, Tom. *Sailor King*, pp.202–3. Walter Greaves MSS.
26. O'Meara, Vol. 2, p.349.
27. Parkinson, p.458.
28. Ibid., pp.465–6. Exmouth to Sidmouth, *Queen Charlotte*, Algiers Bay, 29th August 1816.
29. Barrow, Vol. 2, p.374.
30. Parkinson, p.469.
31. Barrow, Vol. 2, p.382.
32. Lt. Robert James's *Memoirs*, MSS.
33. Barrow, Vol. 2, p.436.
34. Ibid., pp.462–3.
35. Ibid., p.460.
36. Smith Papers, National Maritime Museum, *Guide to MSS*, 260.

37. Barrow, Vol. 2, pp.461–2.
38. Ibid., p.476.
39. Ibid., p.466.
40. Ibid., pp.441–2.
41. Ibid., p.443.
42. Ibid., p.449.
43. Ibid., p.450.
44. O'Meara, Vol. 1, p.308.
45. Warden, p.155.
46. Ibid., Vol. 1, pp.208–10.
47. Ibid., Vol. 2, pp.183–4.
48. Gourgaud, Gen. Baron Gaspard. *Journal*, Vol. 1, p.166.
49. Las Cases, Comte de. *Mémoires*, p.88.
50. Ibid., p.107.
51. Chair, de, p.139.
52. Russell, p.87.
53. Warden, pp.49–50.
54. Barrow, Vol. 2, p.484.
55. Ibid., p.490.
56. Ibid., p.485.
57. Ibid., p.486.
58. Ibid., pp.480–1.

EPILOGUE

1. Spencer Smith journal, MSS.
2. Fortescue, J.W. *British Statesmen of the Great War, 1793–1814*.
3. Parkinson, p.399.
4. Mackesy, Piers. *The War in the Mediterranean, 1803–10*, p.121

MANUSCRIPT SOURCES

A small archive of Admiral Sir Sidney Smith's papers is in the National Maritime Museum. Other manuscripts relating to Smith are in the Admiralty, War Office and Foreign Office Collections, and in the logs of ships' captains, at the Public Record Office and in the Nelson, Collingwood and Bunbury papers at the British Library. The journal (1779–90) of John Spencer Smith and the memoirs (1803–26) of Lieutenant Robert James are in the collections of Mr John Munday and Mr Alexander Wills respectively.

Bibliography

Anderson, R.C. *Naval Wars in the Baltic*. (London, 1910)

Barrow, John. *The Life and Correspondence of Admiral Sir William Sidney Smith*, (2 vols.) (London, 1848)

Berthier, Gen. Alexandre. *The French Expedition into Syria*. (London, 1799)

Boothby, Charles. *Under England's Flag: 1804–09*. (London, 1900)

Clowes, W.L. *The Royal Navy: A History*, (7 vols.) (London, 1900)

de Chair, Somerset, (ed.). *Napoleon on Napoleon: An Autobiography of the Emperor*. (London, 1992)

Elgood, P.G. *Bonaparte's Adventure in Egypt*. (London, 1931)

Fraser, Flora. *The Unruly Queen: The Life of Queen Caroline*. (London, 1996)

Gourgaud, Gen. Baron Gaspard. *Journal, 1815–18*. (Paris, 1932)

Howard, The Hon. E.G.G. *The Memoirs of Sir Sidney Smith*. (London, 1839)

Herold, J. Christopher. *Bonaparte in Egypt*. (London, 1963)

Hutcheon, Wallace, S., Jr. *Robert Fulton Pioneer of Undersea Warfare*. (Annapolis, USA., 1981)

James, William. *The Naval History of Great Britain*, (5 vols.) (London, 1822–24)

Jennings, Louis, J., ed. *The Croker Papers* (3 vols.) (London, 1884)

Knowles, Sir Lees. *The British in Capri, 1806–1808*. (London, 1918)

Lloyd, Christopher. *The Nile Campaign: Nelson and Napoleon in Egypt*. (London, 1973)

Londonderry, Marquess of (ed.) *Correspondence and Despatches of Viscount Castlereagh*, (5 vols.) (London, 1851)

Mackesy, Piers. *The War in the Mediterranean, 1803–10*. (London, 1957)

Mackesy, Piers. *British Victory in Egypt, 1801*. (London, 1995)

Nicolay, Fernand. *Napoleon at the Boulogne Camp*. (London, 1907)

O'Meara, Barry. *Napoleon in Exile, or A Voice from St. Helena* (2 vols.) (London, 1822)

Parkinson, C. Northcote. *Edward Pellew, Viscount Exmouth*. (London, 1934)

Parsons, G.S. *Nelsonian Reminiscences*. (London, 1905)

Pocock, Tom. *Remember Nelson: The Life of Captain Sir William Hoste*. (London, 1977)

Pocock, Tom. *Horatio Nelson*. (London, 1987)

Pocock, Tom. *Sailor King*. (London, 1991)

Popham, Hugh. *A Damned Cunning Fellow: The Life of Rear-Admiral Sir Home*

Popham. (Cornwall, 1991)

Puryear, Vernon J. *Napoleon and the Dardanelles*. (Los Angeles, 1951)

Russell, Lord. *Knight of the Sword: The Life and Letters of Admiral Sir Sidney William Smith*. (London, 1964)

Shankland, Peter. *Beware of Heroes: Admiral Sir Sidney Smith's War Against Napoleon*. (London, 1975)

Tolstoy, Nikolai. *The Half-Mad Lord: The Life of Lord Camelford*. (London, 1978)

Warden, William. *Letters Written in H.M.S. Northumberland and St. Helena*. (London, 1817)

Wilson, Lt. Col. Sir Robert. *The History of the British Expedition to Egypt*. (London, 1803)

Woodward, David. *The Russians at Sea*. (London, 1965)

Index